To Bill

F

lots to highlight,

Bob Sheldon

The Long Ascent

The Long Ascent

Genesis 1–11 in Science & Myth, Volume 1

Robert Sheldon

FOREWORD BY
David Mackie

RESOURCE *Publications* • Eugene, Oregon

THE LONG ASCENT
Genesis 1–11 in Science & Myth, Volume 1

Resource Publications
An Imprint of Wipf and Stock Publishers
199 W. 8th Ave., Suite 3
Eugene, OR 97401

www.wipfandstock.com

PAPERBACK ISBN: 978-1-5326-1214-5
HARDCOVER ISBN: 978-1-5326-1216-9
EBOOK ISBN: 978-1-5326-1215-2

Manufactured in the U.S.A.

In memory of my father, Rev. Benjamin E. Sheldon (1928–2012)

Contents

Figures

Tables

Foreword

January, 2017

My first week of physics graduate school, 32 years ago, I was excited to notice one of my office-mates had a Bible on his desk. I also noticed there was a strange guy who walked around with a rear-view mirror attached to his glasses. To my (short-lived) dismay, both were the same: Robert Sheldon. (Fortunately he had a semi-reasonable excuse for the mirror—he was a cyclist. Even more fortunately, his fiancée made him stop wearing it when not cycling.) This was my introduction to my unconventional colleague, and we quickly became great friends. I soon discovered that Rob could converse about almost anything, and usually at a deeper level than me. We started a Physics Bible Study together, at Rob's urging. We both got married and had children while still in graduate school, although Rob also earned a master of arts in religion degree and had twice the children.

I graduated and settled into a conventional career as a government scientist. Rob remained as unconventional as ever, continually challenging the boundaries as a scientist and theologian wherever he went. We've kept in touch for three decades now, and I've been blessed to observe Rob's trust in our Savior, his tenderness toward his wife and children, his devotion to Scripture and science, and his fierce defense of truth. I cannot help but think that my old friend has been providentially prepared for this role at this moment, because a revolution in our understanding is long overdue.

How did we come to this? Reconciling science and the Bible—especially the early chapters of Genesis—has a long and honorable history in both theology and science, to their mutual profit. Sadly, over the last century, that lively back-and-forth has degenerated into senseless war, with both sides entrenched in positions dictated by ideologues. The brave souls who ventured into no-man's-land, whether to explore or to conduct peace negotiations, were likely to have their careers annihilated by verbal artillery from both camps. Accumulating evidence that both sides were wrong has not budged the resolve of the generals, who allowed the data to pile up and rot rather than risk ceding ground to the enemy. But the troops can smell the stench, and they badly want a new paradigm for a new century. In this book, Dr. Robert Sheldon offers hope to earnest Bible-believers and honest scientists alike—if they are prepared to leave their fortifications and follow the evidence where it leads. I doubt there is anyone better qualified to overthrow everything you thought was true about the beginnings of the universe, of life on Earth, and of humanity.

Dr. David Mackie,

Research Electronics Engineer
BioTechnology Branch
Army Research Laboratory
US Army Research, Development, and Engineering Command
Adelphi, MD

[The views expressed above are entirely mine, and not to be taken as an official endorsement by any government agency.]

Preface

THIS BOOK WOULD HAVE never begun if it were not for my father Benjamin E. Sheldon, a graduate of Maryville College and Princeton Theological Seminary, a Presbyterian missionary to Korea, and a preacher all his life. When he had a stroke and could no longer preach, I made the trip to see him. Not only was it difficult for him to talk, it was impossible for him to read. I found myself monologuing about my seminary research, and what I wanted to tell the world about Science and the Bible. I told him I would write it in a book, and started the first chapter. But then his condition deteriorated, and despite racing to his bedside, he died before I had a chance to read it to him. For another year I grieved, and could write nothing. But the following summer three near-death experiences befell me.

I had taken the family to the Gulf of Mexico, where a storm caused such riptides that five people drowned, and I came close to being the sixth, but my son was able to reach me in the surf, seconds before I went unconscious. A few weeks later I was taking my daughter to get her driver's license, and while giving her experience driving on the Interstate, she lost control of the Camry at 70mph, skidded over the median, struck and rolled an oncoming Suburban onto the shoulder. A few weeks later, we were pulling our pop-up trailer over Independence Pass in the Colorado Rockies approaching a switchback when the brakes overheated, faded away, and smoke poured out of the wheel wells. The next week, in a reflective mood, I asked my wife, "Do you think God is trying to tell me something?" She gave an exasperated look and replied, "What do you want to do before you die?"

My interest in Science and Religion began when my father encouraged me to pursue science, asking me to explain how science could be reconciled with the Bible. When I was in high school, he listened to a seminar by Henry

Morris, and bought me his book The Genesis Flood.[1] I read it cover to cover, and it taught me a lot of geology, but it appeared to me then, and even now when I review the book, that it was more of a theology book than a science book. And like most theology books, it was deductive and not inductive, always sure of the answer before presenting the evidence. I put the book away, wishing there were a better way to reconcile the Bible with Science.

I went off to college at a leading Christian evangelical liberal arts institution that strove to be "scientific." We were taught that "all truth is God's truth," and that in the final analysis, there could be no conflict between Science and the Bible. Our biology courses were taught from a theistic evolutionary perspective, and we were encouraged to read and present articles from the Journal of the American Scientific Affiliation, an organization of Protestant scientists. A small brouhaha occurred when the two geology professors were forced into early retirement, perhaps for being too open to Henry Morris' sentiments. But whenever a "conflict" between science and the Bible arose, I always knew what the answer would be before the evidence was presented. When I graduated and went off to graduate school, I put my degree behind me, thinking there must be a better way to reconcile science with the Bible.

Physics graduate school was not kind to liberal arts graduates, and after three semesters, I was burnt out from successive all-nighters and comprehensive exams. My father encouraged me to consider seminary. So, taking a leave-of-absence, I applied to Princeton and two others. The only one that accepted me for January term was Westminster Theological Seminary, and to my surprise I found Greek and Hebrew exegesis far more exciting than I had expected. But the most unexpected discovery was the classmate who became my wife. Upon our graduation, I had to make the difficult decision whether to pursue academic theology, or finish the physics degree.

I chose physics, and with my new bride's encouragement completed my PhD five years later. My father was proud of my degrees, though he always regretted that I had chosen physics over theology. My career was rising fast, and soon I had appointments at the University of Bern, Boston University and then the University of Alabama in Huntsville (UAH), where I worked very hard on NASA programs involving space plasma experiments. But then it seemed to leak out that I was a "creationist," and soon my colleagues were distancing themselves from me, and I was disinvited to team meetings. When I taught an honors course entitled "Physics, Philosophy and Fundamentalism," it was the straw that broke the camel's back. Using

1. Whitcomb and Morris. *The Genesis Flood*:

many pretexts, the president sent me my pink slip. At the same time, a tenure-track position opened at my *alma mater*, and I saw this as providential.

Alas, the environment had changed in the 22 years since I had graduated, and now even JASA was too conservative. A new course entitled "Origins" was team-taught by a biologist, a physicist, and a theologian. The biologist taught Evolution, the physicist taught the inflationary Big Bang, and the theologian taught that Genesis was a Mesopotamian temple dedication ritual. I found myself in complete disagreement with all the viewpoints being taught in the course. Around that time, World Magazine carried a spread on the movement spearheaded by Phillip Johnson, William Dembski, and Michael Behe.[2] These men were saying all the things I had discovered while teaching the honors course—that evolutionary mechanisms are too weak to achieve the effects claimed. For the second time, I left the faculty of the college thinking there must be a better way to integrate "Faith and Learning."

After a few years of consulting for NASA and blogging about "Bible and Science," my wife was concerned that my theological training was fading—I was certainly very rusty in Greek and Hebrew. So I applied to Westminster's graduate school, and eventually was accepted into the New Testament program, with a requirement of two semesters of study. It was 850 miles away, but my wife insisted I go. So with fear and trepidation, I immersed myself in Hebrew and exegesis, writing several papers on Genesis and Mark that became the core of this book. My thesis and my interest in Science and the Bible, however, were not received well. So for the second time, I left the seminary thinking that there must be a better way to express the universal truths of Science and Scripture.

I went back to consulting for NASA, working on nuclear rockets for a manned Mars mission. The work was exciting and took me back into the world of science. Then came that fateful summer and my wife's question about my bucket list. I thought a minute and said, "Finish the book I was going to give my Dad." She said, "Great. I'll send you to Westminster library to do the research," and she did exactly that. And what could I say, I didn't want to die.

It took a week or two to work through the Genesis flood material, and then on Micah's hunch, I looked up Norse mythology flood stories. What I found nearly knocked my socks off. For I had been trying so hard to bring Science and Scripture to the altar, and all along Myth was holding the wedding band. I began to realize that I was not the first person to attempt this marriage, but rather Genesis stands in a long line of stories about origins,

2. Perry "Courtly Combatant".

stories about floods, stories about man's elevation above the animals. And now as I brought the tools of archeology, paleontology, and geochronology to bear, I was finding the story told by Science had been told before, had been told often, and had been told more accurately. Science reported little about the climate in Eden, but Genesis and Gilgamesh told me about the weather; Greek taught me the agriculture, Norse described the irrigation system, and Egyptian whispered about the roads. And last, as someone exiled to a foreign land, Sanskrit sang of its haunting beauties.

This trilogy is my attempt to convey all these voices. We do not need to fear Science or Myth, as if they are competing stories to Genesis, rather they are complementary harmonies, telling us the important things we need to know—where we came from, why we do not now live in paradise, and ultimately, how we can return.

R. B. Sheldon

Feb 18, 2016

Acknowledgments

My earliest supporter and the one to whom this book is dedicated, was my father. He encouraged me to pursue both physics and theology, asking his scientist son to explain how Science and the Bible could be reconciled.

My greatest supporter has been my wife, Sunmi. She not only made graduate school worth enduring, but unflaggingly supported me in the face of much opposition, to the extent that she worked, homeschooled, and raised nine children through my long absences at seminary. When my job ended prematurely at the University of Bern, her response was typical, "Don't feel bad, they didn't give Einstein a job either, you know."

Then there is a long list of people who contributed to this book directly and indirectly. My children were a constant audience for the ideas, and it was often their suggestions that became the breakthroughs I needed. Micah suggested that Genesis 1:2 referred to comets, and was instrumental in getting me to read the Norse Eddas. Leah saw the rainbow bridge as adjacent to a waterfall. Rebekah read the manuscript multiple times with a virtual yellow highlighter, and Hannah provided great help with the Hebrew. Sarah walked me through some hairy philosophical positions, Elijah dragged me from the surf, Keziah declared astrophysics "cool," Malkah prayed the storm be stilled, and Tirzah begged me to write more fictional stories. While the ideas here may seem radical for my generation, I realized they were never too radical for the next.

I want to thank my advisor, Vern Poythress, for enabling me to get those refresher courses at seminary, as well as incorporating Science in his lectures and books. Even from my earliest studies 30 years ago, Vern modeled what a scientific exegete should aspire to become. I want to thank Leslie Altena, the director of the writing center, who patiently taught me to write in a thesis genre. Thanks go to Kirk Lowery, who taught me linguistics and the joy of parsing Hebrew syntax and to Fred Putnam who could make even

Hebrew poetic. And to the many classmates who endured my rambling papers and offered constructive criticism.

I especially want to thank Denyse O'Leary, who has made this book a better one in every way. I could not have found a more qualified editor. Getting her time was an act of divine providence.

Then there are the many friends who read parts or drafts of the whole book offering helpful comments: Noel Rude, Peter Sidebotham, Thaddeus McClatchey, David Falconer, Vincent Torley, Jonathan Bartlett, Jesse Crikelair, Louis Klauder Jr., Glee Violette, and Doug Walker. My thanks go out to those who have gone on to glory—to Al Groves who began the Hebrew coding program, and later admitted me as a graduate student to WTS; to my father-in-law, Wesley Hansoon Im, who opened his house to board me many times while I attended seminary; to Lloyd Hillman, who begged me not to teach the honors course; to Larry Smalley who supported me despite my wild ideas; to Jim Horowitz who couldn't. All these people made this book possible by opening some doors and shutting others.

For when I stood in the surf, far from the shore with the waves breaking over my head, the current dragging me out to sea, and my heart bursting with exertion, I realized that I only thought I was the master of my fate, the captain of my soul. The vast ocean rolls on like the years and centuries since Noah, unmindful of my petty quarrels and my unfinished plans, but there is one whom the seas obey, and it was to that one my daughter cried out from the shore, asking for a break in the relentless surf, which He did when three rollers failed to materialize, my son reached my side, put my arm over his neck, and dragged me to safety. That same ruler of the millennia chose this beach, this time to reveal the mystery of Genesis, and it is to Him I owe my greatest gratitude.

Soli Deo Gloria

R. B. Sheldon

Abbreviations

ACTG	Adenine, Cytosine, Guanine, Thymine: Nucleobases encoding information in DNA.
ANE	Ancient Near East: 3000 BC to 100 AD.
ASA	American Scientific Affiliation: Society of Protestant scientists.
BB	Big Bang: A model of early universe.
BDB	Brown Driver Briggs: A Biblical Hebrew to English lexicon.
C-14	Carbon-14: An isotope of carbon.
CDM	Cold Dark Matter: Hypothesized massive material made in the BB.
CMBR	Cosmic Microwave Background Radiation: Fossil light from the BB.
CO2	Carbon dioxide: An atmospheric gas providing carbon.
CPR	Cardio Pulmonary Resuscitation: A technique to breathe for a non-breathing patient.
DNA	Deoxyribonucleic Acid: The molecule making up genes.
ENCODE	ENCyclopedia Of DNA Elements: Consortium that is mapping active DNA.
ESV	English Standard Version: A revision of the RSV Bible.
GISP2	Greenland Ice Sheet Project 2: Ice cores from Greenland's ice cap.

Gya	Gigayears ago: Number of 1,000,000,000 years before the present.
HALOT	Hebrew-Aramaic Lexicon of the Old Testament: Update of BDB.
JPS	Jewish Publication Society: English translation of the MT.
ka	Kilo years ago: Number of millenia before present.
KJV	King James Version: 1611 English translation of the Bible.
kyBC	Kilo years before Christ. 1000's of years before 0 AD.
LXX	Septuagint: Greek translation of Hebrew circa 200 BC.
MACHO	MAssive Compact Halo Objects: Small black holes thought to be dark matter.
Med bed	Bed of the Mediterranean: A dried out Mediterranean sea.
MT	Masoretic Text: Transcribed version of the Hebrew old testament circa 100 AD.
My	Megayear: A millenia of millenia of time.
Mya	Megayears ago: Number of millenia of millenia before present.
MyBC	Megayears before Christ: Number of millenia of millenia before 0 AD.
N2	Molecular nitrogen: A diatomic gas of nitrogen.
NAS	New American Standard Bible: English translation of the Bible.
NASA	National Aeronautic and Space Administration: Agency involved in satellites.
NR	Neolithic Revolution: Northward spread of farming, ~8-6 kyBC.
OC	Medieval Occasionalism: View that God acts directly without secondary causes.
PC	Progressive Creation. View that creation continues over long stretch of time.
PIE	Proto-Indo-European: Language carried by NR settlers.
PNAS	Proceeding of the National Academy of Science. A journal.
PPNA/B	Pre-Pottery Neolithic A/B: Transition between Paleolithic and Neolithic.

RNA	Ribonucleic Acid: Molecule communicating between DNA and ribosomes.
Roy G Biv	Red Orange Yellow Green Blue Indigo Violet: Rainbow mnemonic.
SPIE	Society of Photonics Engineers. Scientific conference with proceedings.
TE	Theistic Evolution: Syncretic theory that God directed Evolution.
TWOT	Theological Wordbook of the Old Testament: Glossary of important words.
UV	Ultra Violet: Light just beyond the violet in the spectrum.
WIMP	Weakly Interacting Massive Particles: Invisible particles proposed for dark matter.
WTJ	Westminster Theological Journal. A publication of WTS.
WTS	Westminster Theological Seminary: Presbyterian seminary in Philadelphia.
yBC	Years before Christ: Number of years before 0 AD.
YD/PB	Younger Dryas/Pre-Boreal: Transition from European glaciation to warm Holocene.

PART 1

When we come to relate that part to the whole, the divined glimmer to the fire we suppose to be its source, we see why Hermes is the patron of so many other trades besides interpretation. There has to be trickery. And we interpret always as transients—of whom he is also patron—both in the book and in the world which resembles the book. For the world is our beloved codex. We may not see it, as Dante did, in perfect order, gathered by love into one volume; but we do, living as reading, like to think of it as a place where we can travel back and forth at will, divining congruences, conjunctions, opposites; extracting secrets from its secrecy, making understood relations, an appropriate algebra. This is the way we satisfy ourselves with explanations of the unfollowable world—as if it were a structured narrative, of which more might always be said by trained readers of it, by insiders. World and book, it may be, are hopelessly plural, endlessly disappointing; we stand alone before them, aware of their arbitrariness and impenetrability, knowing that they may be narratives only because of our impudent intervention, and susceptible of interpretation only by our hermetic tricks.

Frank Kermode, *The Genesis of Secrecy*

Hence one must say that there is a right and wrong in the interpretation of Rom 7, and a right and wrong in a theological system. However, it is not necessarily easy for human beings to arrive at what is right. Larger frameworks or disciplinary matrices have an influence. In part, the influence is a good one. An effective, fruitful disciplinary matrix regularly steers researchers towards fruitful ways of looking at a passage and fruitful ways of analyzing and solving theological difficulties. But any disciplinary matrix, by suggesting solutions primarily in one direction, can make people almost blind to the possibility of solutions in another direction. Such, surely, is one of the lessons to draw from the history of interpretation of Rom 7.

Vern Poythress, *Science and Hermeneutics*

Figure 1.0: Hermes/Mercury after Greco-Roman sculpture. (Albino Magno)

CHAPTER 1

Hermes

1.1 The Garden of Children

MY DADDY HAD A new job, and so did we. We used to live in Korea, where he was a missionary, but now he was going to be pastor of the Sixth Presbyterian Church of Washington DC. It was very important, and we were going to help him; we were going to Sunday School, me, my three brothers, and my sister. In McLean, Virginia where we used to live on furlough, I didn't go to school, because I was in kindergarten, and they didn't have kindergarten. So I played school with my little brother. He was four, and sometimes he didn't like school. But now we'd moved to Washington. I was going to first grade Sunday School and was going to learn about God from the Bible.

Sixth was a big stone church with tall stone columns on the inside. It had a tower and behind a locked door, a secret metal ladder that went all the way up to the top. There were lots of pigeons living in it, so you had to be careful where you stepped. On top of the tower was the bell room with tall narrow windows, just like a castle. I was glad my Daddy worked there. Lots of grownups said they were glad too. They laughed when I asked if it had been a castle. "No," they said, "it isn't even a hundred years old. It's just copied from an older church."

Mrs. Merrill was my Sunday School teacher and Paul was my best friend. Paul knew lots about the Bible because Mrs. Merrill was his mother. She taught us the 23rd Psalm and I memorized it just as fast as Paul. She said Jesus was our shepherd and we were his sheep. I didn't know what sheep were, but she showed us pictures—sort of fuzzy dogs. Mommy wouldn't let us have a dog, she said she had enough pets to take care of. Mrs. Merrill said sheep were very cute and dumb, they needed a shepherd to take care of them, lead them out and bring them home. I wasn't going to be a sheep, when I got to first grade next month, I was going to walk home from Lafayette Elementary school all by myself. "No," said Mrs. Merrill, "we are all like sheep, even I am his sheep because the Lord is my shepherd."

She also told us about Adam and Eve and Noah's ark. She said Adam and Eve didn't wear anything because God didn't make clothes for them yet. That seemed dumb, but Paul showed me his comic book Bible, where they had pictures of everything. I couldn't tell if they wore clothes or not, they were always standing in a bush, but Paul said they weren't. Noah had clothes, but it was a dress. Paul said that everybody wore dresses back then. They all had beards too, so people would know they weren't girls.

We turned the page. Noah was building a boat in his back yard. We were going to have an amazing tree fort in our front yard. My older brothers had already climbed the big oak tree, with a first branch so high they needed a ladder, but once you got up on it you could climb higher than the roof of the manse. You could see the whole neighborhood! We were going to build a fort big enough to sleep in. Noah was going to sleep in his boat too. But it didn't have very many windows. "Are you sure that's what an ark looks like?" I asked Paul, "It doesn't look like the one they have in the nursery with a giraffe sticking out. I don't think the giraffe would fit without a window."

"All the animals fit in the ark," Paul said.

"Even a blue whale?"

Paul laughed, "A whale isn't an animal, it lives in the ocean. Noah only put in the animals that couldn't swim."

I looked at the picture again. It was much taller than Noah, even if it didn't have many windows. Maybe the whole Zoo could fit in it. Daddy said he would take us to the Zoo someday. They had an elephant house, a monkey house, a lion house, even Smokey the Bear. "If lions or bears or, or elephants fought each other, who would win?"

"No," said Paul, "they each have their own room, like the Zoo." I didn't have my own room. I always shared it with my little brother. Noah's ark was bigger than my house, but just for animals.

Sunday School was fun. I learned a lot about the Bible. But I didn't want to be a sheep, even if Mrs. Merrill wanted to. Mrs. Merrill said we needed to obey the Bible if we wanted to be a member of Sixth. I wanted to help Daddy, but I wasn't going to be a sissy and wear a dress. "No," said Mrs. Merrill, "you just have to learn it, you don't have to copy it, because people back then didn't live like we do today."

I'm glad I'm big enough to go to Sunday School and learn about people back then, but you shouldn't just copy them.

1.2 The Garden of Eden

In this chapter I want to discuss the importance of language and the core problem of interpretation—the hermeneutical circle. Without realizing it, that was the problem I was struggling with as a child. After exploring the concept and the importance of the hermeneutical circle, I hope to suggest a way forward.

In our early lives, there is a point when we are suddenly aware of the wide, wide world that holds our small vulnerable self and we ask "What is the meaning of it all?" Psychologists were astounded to find that even small babies who have not yet learned to talk expect causes or reasons for every event. For example, in one study babies were astonished when the stuffed animal disappeared from behind the screen.[1] Teleology is hard-wired into our brains; just as we are born curious, so also we are born for purpose. Aristotle famously categorized the four kinds of causes that might explain the stuffed animal: the material cause explains what it is made of (pink fur); the formal cause explains what it looks like (a baby bear); the efficient cause explains how it arrives (the funny man pulled it from a box); and the final cause explains why it is there (Daddy wanted me to have it). The final cause is so unlike the other three, that the twentieth century sages refused to permit the question even to be asked, on the grounds that "If it isn't material, it isn't science!" Many attributed the rise of Western technology to the abandonment of the final cause with its stifling dogma. One of the many ways that final causes differ from the others, is that they cannot be answered without a messenger. That is, we might be able to determine how the toy animal is stuffed without dialogue or determine its form in a picture book without seeing one in the room or even find out how it got here from a video. But we cannot determine its purpose, the ultimate reason why it is here, without asking questions that take us into philosophical territory.

And we cannot ask questions without a language. And we cannot learn a language without a tutor. And a tutor implies a body of words, a community of speakers, a heritage of traditions. Therefore, the question "Why?" is fundamentally a religious question, a question about purpose, about origins; it is a mother's bane and a priest's livelihood; it is the death of self and the birth of community; it is one of the first things a child learns and the last thing he forgets; its instruction marks the beginning and its absence marks the end of culture. This book is about language, where it came from, what it meant at the time, and how its meaning is extracted today. One of the purposes of this book is to inspire a new way of looking at language,

1. Leslie. "The Perception of Causality," 173–186.

a new method of hermeneutics based on explanatory power rather than etymology and usage. Language, for all of its mundane taken-for-granted existence, can and should still surprise us with its unexpected richness, power, and personality.

Whence came the birth of language, the beginning of religion, the self-awareness of humanity? Was it with the beginning of history 6000 years ago? Or perhaps the distant mists of pre-history, the world of giants and gods? Or did it predate even those mythological beginnings stretching back to the invention of fire and the ocher hand prints found in the deep recesses of natural caves?

Unfortunately oral language leaves few artifacts, so the paleontologists cannot tell us. But what the paleontologists could not find despite intensive search, the biologists have repeatedly stumbled over, dismissed, and even hidden again. For what biologists have found in the past fifty years is a language far older than the Neolithic, far older even than the Paleolithic, more ancient than the mountains, written before the continents. It is not a language made of cryptic pictographs or hieroglyphics, but one containing just four letters and twenty words. It is not a language found in a distant desert excavation, nor preserved only in fragmentary form, but a language so well attested that its recorded messages would stretch from here to the nearest star. It is not a representative language like a monkey's with words that stand for objects, nor even a symbolic language like a theologian's where the words can be manipulated in the place of objects, rather it is a living language like a magician's incantation, by which the words control the objects. It is a language whose words were translated fifty years ago, whose dictionary cost a billion dollars ten years ago, yet whose message remains obscure even to the present.

This book reflects on that truly ancient language and what it tells us of our origins, our purpose, perhaps even of our life. It is closely connected to another ancient language, another book we have known for 3500 years, whose familiarity has perhaps made many think its message stale, out-of-date, sterile. So it may be with great surprise that we find the second language describing the first, the first language explaining the second, and both telling us about our origin, our purpose, and our end. With this new biology and the understanding from our picture book, we can translate the Rosetta Stone of culture, the meaning of myth, the meaning of all myths, because just as language has one origin, so all myths have a single origin.

This may change your view of mankind. Not because it will discuss aliens but because it could open your eyes to a world you had always seen but dimly understood; a world you had previously felt only in your gut; a world that you were told had died with the Olympian thrones, the gilded halls of Valhalla, and the demi-gods in the mists of pre-history. But the Story (and there can really be only one story) was not forgotten nor erased, rather it was written in indelible ink, in compressed form, in the most indestructible of places, in the most protected spot in the cosmos; it was written and remains written in our genes.

Surely, ours and every culture has a story about origins: who were our ancestors, whence came our language, and why we are a special race in a world of many. These stories likely include an account of human origins and of how humans separated from the animals who preceded them. Books have been written, anthologies collected, academic chairs endowed to study these stories. Because whether we admit it or not, origins are big part of our mental furniture, determining how we view the environment, the manifold races, and even the differences between the sexes. That is why Darwin's 1859 account, *On the Origin of Species*,[2] is just the latest in a six-millennial effort to retell the story of where we all come from and where we are all headed.

The difference is that in the last few decades, the language of the genes, the ACTG that make up the alphabet of our DNA, has finally been transcribed. What had previously been an oral tradition of origins, what had previously been guarded as jealously as a cultural treasure committed to heart, has now been read from meticulous slabs of molecular memory duplicated error-free a hundred trillion times in every human being. A message copied over the millennia some ten billion times, copied and annotated every time a baby cries its first squall. And despite what you may have heard in biology class, the modern story of the genome does not match Darwin's guesses very well. Others have built the persuasive case that recent efforts to fit the genome into Darwin's tree of life are plagued with inconsistencies, but this book addresses a different myth, that progress is inexorable and cumulative, that we have all ascended from brute beasts, that this generation knows more than any previous, in short, the myth that we no longer have need for myths.

For despite Lucretius's (55 BC) complaint in *De Rerum Natura*[3] that the sages rejected the Olympian gods because of their inconsistent, petty, and irrational outbursts, it was rather because of and precisely for their trite and petty consistencies that monotheism triumphed over polytheism. For one did not come to a priest for logical proofs but for healing, for consolation, for restitution, for the all-important repair of body and soul.[4] It was not for lack of knowledge that the ancients chose the heart and not the brain

2. Darwin. *On the Origin.*

3. Lucretius. *De Rerum Natura.*

4. Benzmüller and Woltzenlogel-Paleo. "Formalization."

as the seat of the soul. So, if I were to stoop to tell this story as a collection of chance events that through material means progressively generated the greatest civilization the world has ever seen, I would deeply misrepresent the history—the story of glorious beginnings and ignominious declines, spectacular design and pernicious decay, men gaining immortality and gods becoming mortal. And that is why I return to the pre-modern way of telling the history of human origins as a story full of mystery and significance, as a story spoken softly in rooms full of smoking incense, to wide-eyed novitiates in the holy temple of knowledge.

In the fall of 2013, when I began this book in earnest, I had no inkling of the mysteries I would uncover. While at seminary in 2008, my preliminary research had shown that modern genetic discoveries were highly relevant to the first two chapters of Genesis. I wanted to expand that research to cover the first eleven chapters of Genesis, beginning with Noah's Flood, which I believe has left an indirect signature in the Greenland Ice Cores.[5] The first of many surprises that had me racing through the halls to find someone to tell, was finding the Flood in Norse mythology, hidden in personal names with Semitic etymology. Then it was accurate terrain descriptions that matched digital bathymetry maps of the Aegean, which led me into Ancient Near East (ANE) mythology, from whose dark burial chambers I emerged into the light of Plato's dialogues.[6] At each step, the discoveries created their own compelling logic that forced me into fields I knew little about, until in a crashing finale, my journey led me back home, to the Hebrew language, to Moses's peculiar behavior on a very fateful night in Egypt. If this book (the first in a series) seems haphazardly organized, be advised that it is a chronological account of my *annus mirabilis*, of the odyssey that took me from theology to science to mythology and back again. As Bilbo warned, "It's a dangerous business, Frodo, going out of your door; you step into the Road, and if you don't keep your feet, there is no telling where you might be swept off to."[7] For Frodo's road took him down the Anduin, that ancient river of paradise, into Middle Earth, which the Romans called Mediterra, the Norse called Ymer and Muspelheim, the Egyptians called Seth and Horus, and the Rig Veda called Agnis and Danu.

I had never expected that all these stories were about the same places, the same landmarks, and the same events. What began as a series of evocative coincidences with Genesis turned into a line-by-line comparison that filled a hundred dense pages. Not only was Genesis telling us about Norse,

5. NOAA. "GISP."

6. Plato. *Timaeus-Critias.*

7. Tolkien. *The Fellowship of the Ring*, 102.

but Norse was telling us about Greek, and Greek about Sumerian, and Sumerian about Egyptian, and Egyptian about the Sanskrit Vedas. I have chosen to put that interleaved comparison in Volume 2 and write this one simply on the relationship between science and Hebrew, between NASA and Moses. Yet once I had heard the music of the Norse saga, once I had seen the alien grandeur of the Egyptian Duat, once I had tasted the sweat of Sumer and felt the longing of the Vedas, I knew that this book could not properly convey the awe and majesty of Eden without story, without song. It seemed fitting then to open each chapter with a narrative, a first-hand account as it were, of the events in the chapter.

1.2.1 The Hermeneutical Circle

The story of Noah's flood is a decision point for many devout people. They are given a stark choice between "taking the Bible literally" despite misgivings or implicitly accusing the Biblical writers of gross exaggeration and deception.[8] It is difficult for any scholar to talk of a "local flood" without also denying the inerrancy of the Bible.[9] Many thoughtful believers have simply abandoned the first eleven chapters of Genesis, holding them to be myth, written in a genre never intended to be taken literally, much less as science.[10] In all seriousness, they present their discovery that the first eleven chapters of Genesis were lifted from a dodgy Elamite disaster movie or a bad Sumerian romance novel.[11] Some argue that Judaism and Christianity lose little if we do away with the first eleven chapters because only in the Law of Moses do we find the first substantial contribution to modern society. I claim otherwise: If we lose the first eleven chapters, we lose the story of origins. And if we lose origins, we lose purpose; and if we lose purpose, we will never find our way to the end of the Book.

8. Whitcomb and Morris. *The Genesis Flood.*
9. Poythress. *Redeeming Science.*
10. Gledhill. "Catholic Church."
11. Walton. *The Lost World.*

Figure 1.1: The Garden of Eden by Thomas Cole (1828) with tropical mountains. (Wiki Commons)

Now it simply does not do to solve this conundrum, as many well-meaning scholars have advised, by believing "six impossible things before breakfast,"[12] or as Pudd'nhead Wilson said, "Faith is believin' what you know ain't so."[13] This is because of the two strange properties of belief. First, belief does something more than rescue our brain from damnation. It creates. As Donald Evans reminds us,[14] observations are tied to beliefs, actions are tied to observations, and more beliefs are tied to actions. Before you know it, an entire universe is concocted in our brains by both conscious and unconscious beliefs.

Therefore belief is a creative process, a maker of worlds and a creator of cosmos. But that brings up the second property: beliefs about beliefs are a recursive, self-referential, positive-feedback sort of creation. Just as everyone knows that holding a microphone in front of a loudspeaker creates a very bad noise unrelated to our voice, so beliefs about beliefs create a world completely unrelated to the one in which we live with others. Beliefs about beliefs take on a life of their own and no longer tolerate the life of others;

12. Carroll. *Through the Looking Glass*, 38.
13. Twain. *Following the Equator*, chapt 16.
14. Evans. *Logic of Self Involvement*.

they become selfish, exclusive, denying, or what Chesterton, in his discussion of materialism, called "maniacal."[15]

Of course there are always some topics that we are maniacal about, so what makes a maniacal story about Noah so controversial?

Noah's story is not just another religious education topic, it is about our origins. And if we make up stuff about our origins, then we are likely to make up stuff about purpose or intent and lose our way again. I said likely, but I do not mean a 10 percent or even a 50 percent likely. It is a 99.9 percent likely. Think back to that microphone: Is it possible to get it close to the loudspeaker without setting off the horrible screech? No, because the slightest whisper, the slightest pin drop anywhere in the room will be amplified, picked up, and amplified still further.[16] The noise is unstoppable because it is out of our control. In the same way, paradoxically, belief about belief is sold as a mechanism to give us control, but instead becomes the master that controls us. And now we come again to the dilemma of all parables—if we ignore Noah we drown, but if we believe Noah we perish.

What can rescue us from this deadly story, this vicious circle?

For many years I had no answer. And while I have seen many solutions, starting with the day my first-grade buddy showed me the David C. Cook comic book Bible,[17] none of them really delivered me from the horns of the dilemma. In seminary this dilemma was called "the hermeneutical circle," which gave it a name, but did not remove the tension.[18] Much later, two realizations rescued me: First, that it was not my brain but my heart that needed salvation. I did not need to believe in belief, rather I needed to believe in a person. And second, that belief should never be circular. That is, belief must always be based on logical, factual, or personal foundations. These are not exclusive categories, for if we are to believe persons, they should be both factual and logical. Likewise, the logical must also be factual and personal, which is to say, logical for a computer is not the same as logical for a human. So, if we are to believe Noah, we must not excuse his narrative by saying "believe or else," rather we must look for the logical and factual witness that confirms it.

Can we really do this? At bottom, are not all historical claims simply appeals to authority without support from either logic or fact? After all, if

15. Chesterton. *Orthodoxy.* Chapter 1.

16. Berg and Stork. *The Physics of Sound.*

17. Hoth. *The Picture Bible.* Chapter 1.

18. Hirsch. *Validity in Interpretation*; Fish. *Is There a Text*; Hoy. *The Critical Circle.*

Noah exaggerates, who can prove it, or if Noah tells it as it is, who can disprove it?[19]

Neither history nor science boils down to simple appeals to authority. For there is someone who does know, someone who does see, someone who can communicate, and that someone is God. To claim that everything is a matter of arbitrary authority is to ignore the God who communicates with us here and now, confirming or denying our theories about the past. And the method of His communication can be factual through our observation, it can be logical using our reason, or it can be personal speaking to our heart. More than likely, it will be all three.[20] What delivers us from a post-modern debate on the relativity of history is a personal relationship with the Maker of history.[21]

In practice, this means that we must test Noah's story as we would test any other person's story—by comparing it to facts and reason. This is what the "local flood" people attempt to do when they rationally scale down a global flood to a manageable size. But there is a second way we can test a person's story—we question them. Now it may seem odd to question a man who is dead these many millennia but really that is what the United States Supreme Court does when it invokes the "intent of the founders."[22] We read the texts, we compare the texts, and we attempt to recreate the thoughts of a Madison or a Hamilton so as to predict how they would respond to our new situation. This is what the "Biblical literalists" do when they insist that Noah's account requires universal destruction. Neither method is without pitfall, so we must try them all.

1.2.2 This book

That is why this book divides each chapter into thirds. The first third is given in the form of a pre-modern saga, that is, a traditional story. It introduces the facts as a rational whole, as a continuous narrative. The middle third addresses the text, the words, and the intent of the person who wrote the Bible story, examining how it is told in order to determine the best interpretation of the text. The final third addresses the science, the logic of the narrative, and the probable causes of the facts that we have collected from all sources. In one sense, we have attempted closure of logic, facts, and person, but in another sense there can never be complete closure, any more than the

19. Ham. *The Global Flood.*
20. Hodge. *Systematic Theology*, introduction.
21. Poythress. *In the beginning.*
22. Bork. *A Time to Speak.*

history of the Civil War can become an algebra book. For I do not claim to have found The Answer, or even told The Truth for all time. Rather I hope to have opened up a dialogue with Noah, a dialogue that will rescue us from drowning, that will find our origin, that will recover our purpose.

For the goal of this book is not to nail the "real meaning" of Genesis, but to let Genesis nail the "real meaning" of us. It is less important that I get the facts right than that the right facts get me. If I fail in this goal, then this book will be a forgettable exercise in speculative interpretation. But if I succeed, then I trust you will forgive my liberties with the text, my ignorance of history and Hebrew, and my limited literary skills. For if I succeed, I expect you to be writing the sequel yourself.

1.3 The Garden of Genetics

We escape the hermeneutical circle by reaching outside it, outside the text, outside the interpretation, to something which does not change and is not under our control. This is the picture book of science, a promise to provide us objective knowledge of an external reality independent of our dictionaries and uncontaminated by our desires. In this section, I discuss how scientific discoveries can provide an interpretive key that unlocks the text.

My goal is to appreciate the way in which the scientific advances of the past two decades— paleoclimatology, paleoanthropology and genetics—provide a new interpretation of the text of Noah's flood, satisfying both the purpose and the method God used to cleanse evil from the Earth. In doing so, I am telling the story backwards, working from the cleansing Flood back to the poisonous fruit, but that is how I discovered it, and it may also be the more inductive way. But it does mean that questions about causes must be postponed as I deal with the consequences before the actions. In later chapters of this book, I will indeed address the causes and conclusions, but let us first begin with several observations of changes that seem to have been results of the Flood.

First, Noah was the last man to have clocked more than 900 years (Gen 9:29). If, as modern science argues, long life is genetic, it would appear that something happened to longevity genes during the Flood. If, as the text indicates, only a small number of persons survived the Flood, then a genetic bottleneck would fundamentally transform the inherited nature of the entire human race. Whatever evil precipitated this disastrous cure must have included a genetic component. In 2001 we transcribed the complete genome of man,[23] and subsequently that of monkeys,[24] apes, and more recently Neanderthals.[25] So, we are finally in a position to list some of the evils that a genetic bottleneck might cure.

Second, it has often been suggested that rainbows were introduced after the Flood, which led to suggestions that either rain or sunshine was lacking before the Flood. While others have focused on sunshine, I will focus on rain, or more precisely, rain in the vicinity of man. The rainbow as a new feature suggests that the climate of human habitation prior to the Flood lacked rain, which is also suggested in Gen 2:5. If so, then crops must have been raised without rainfall, which suggests irrigation. It is a well-known coincidence that the three oldest civilizations known to archaeologists were all situated in sunny, dry, irrigated valleys—the Nile, the Euphrates and the Indus—suggesting that before the Flood, they farmed in a region that was irrigated and arid.[26]

Third, the connection between the first and second observations is farming. To be more rewarding than the hunting/gathering that preceded it, farming must balance the problems of year-to-year planting, watering and harvesting with the improvement of crops and livestock via decades of careful breeding. Historically, farming only began when wheat was cultivated and sheep domesticated sometime near the beginning of the Neolithic (New Stone) Age. This transition from the hunting-gathering Mesolithic into the farming Neolithic was so sudden and drastic that it has been called the Neolithic Revolution (NR). It is dated to about 10,000 years ago, intriguingly in the Middle East,[27] and was connected to three things: the spread of specific human genes (Sardinian),[28] genetic technology (breeding, domestication), and a particular language that we now call Indo-European. The NR began in the Middle East and traveled northward like a melting glacier for twenty-five centuries at the snail's pace of thirty centimeters per hour leaving a trail of artifacts in its wake. While we are not given much information about Noah's vocation before the Flood, we are told that he began to cultivate grapes afterward (Gen 9:20), which suggests that he was a farmer and took part in this important transition.

23. Lander et al. "Initial sequencing" 860–921; Collins. "The Human Genome Project" 286–290.

24. Waterston et al. "Initial sequence" 69-87.

25. Prufer et al. "The complete genome" 43–49; Green et al. "A draft sequence" 710–722.

26. Hancock. *Underworld.*

27. Bar-Yosef and Valla. "The Natufian Culture."

28. Haak et al. "Ancient DNA" 1016–1018; Ammerman and Cavalli-Sforza. *The Neolithic Transition.*

These three observations from the text, combined with what we now know of the NR, complement and reinforce each other in a novel way that is highly compelling. It is not that this example is the most compelling data we have, nor is the NR the most precise dating of the Flood, nor even the best exegesis of the Hebrew, but it serves as a good example of how science and Genesis interpret each other and simultaneously raise new questions. For if the Flood was associated with the NR, then there must be a relationship between technology and language, between genetics and Genesis, between migration and Eden that reinterprets both. It becomes significant that Adam was a farmer, that the animals God brought to him were domesticated, that animal husbandry was more favored than breeding wheat. We are being told reasons for obscure Hebrew words and for Neolithic migrations, as well as explanations for the genetic histories of nations. The story that emerges is greater than the sum of its parts because we could not fully understand the parts without the whole, any more than an ear makes sense without an eardrum.

And the story that emerges, like a butterfly from the chrysalis of the text, is a radically new interpretation of the Flood's purpose, its extent, and its connection with the present. The Flood is far more than a litmus test of our "literalist hermeneutics"; it becomes the Rosetta stone that explains both Greek myth and modern apostasy. For, like the Rosetta stone, it has been translated into nearly every language and inhabits every cultural tradition. It remains a stark warning about the dangers of presumption based on genetic knowledge and its pandemic judgment on mankind. For not only did American Indians, Norse, Greeks, Sumerians, Egyptians and Vedic authors repeat this warning, but even Jesus, Peter, and Paul remind us that the Flood is a signpost of danger, almost a definition of Apocalypse. Therefore, this story offers more than mere historical interest or homiletical value; it is highly relevant to the world we live in now and foretells what the future holds.

As great as my joy has been in discovering the translation of this "Rosetta Stone" of our history and destiny, equally great has been my dismay in reading it. Like John of the Apocalypse (Rev 10:10), I found it sweet to my mouth but bitter to my stomach. I once set this book aside for fourteen months as I pondered what it meant.

Why did the generations between Adam and Noah take but 1300 years, but from Noah to Abraham a full 7500 years? What disobedience was so deadly that even after total devastation it required another seventy-five long centuries of forgetting?

Just recently the United States and Europe have decided to allow genetic editing of human embryos.[29] It became clear why the chrysalis has split now and the text taken wing, for it tells us what the future will bring, what evils lurk in Pandora's box, what uncleanness dwells in Zechariah's basket. And since our ethicists have failed to report its advance, even cheered its return, Genesis must be the watchman on the wall (Ezek 33:1).

So gather round, and listen to a story of where we came from, why we are here, and what we were meant for. It began a long, long time ago in a beautiful land, where the wide sky was always blue, the lush grass was always green, the unfailing rivers ran like milk, the mist of the mile-high waterfalls rose like shining pillars, and the snow-capped mountains watched majestically on every side; it began in a country called Eden.

29. Liang et al. "CRISPR" 363–372; CRISPR. *GEN*; Petersen. "California stem cell."

PART 2

For the end of the world was long ago,
And all we dwell today
As children of some second birth,
Like a strange people left on earth
After a judgment day.
For the end of the world was long ago,
When the ends of the world waxed free,
When Rome was sunk in a waste of slaves,
And the sun drowned in the sea.

Gilbert Keith Chesterton,
Ballad of the White Horse

Figure 2.0: ***Jupiter verospi*** (Zeus) sculpture in Vatican. (Courtesy David Macchi)

CHAPTER 2

Zeru

2.1 Zeru's Ascent

THE SLATE CRUMBLED FROM under Zeru's feet as he climbed the last slope, the tumbling rocks making a dull splash as they landed in the water. The black water was only slightly darker than the sky, and stretched along the horizon. The slope terminated in a low mound just a few meters above the water. A shudder went through the earth, casting more stones into the water, which made Zeru scramble even faster.

"El" he panted as he dug his feet into the gravel to get more traction, "You won. You destroyed everything. Everything but," he gasped in the thin air, "me."

From his vantage point on the mound of rock he scanned the sky for any sign of a break in the bands of low clouds that had been pouring rain violently for the past forty days. "Fresh water," he said grimly, remembering the long, thirsty flight from Tandor across plains flooded with seawater. It was the rains that had saved him from Thera's fate, madly slaking her thirst from the in-rushing Atlantic.

But it was the rains that turned the highlands to mud. The rains that washed out the roads and destroyed the evacuation plans, that turned every creek into a river, every gully into a waterfall. Any who delayed or burdened themselves with books and food were forced toward higher ground, and then trapped into ridge lines and impassible peaks, only to be swallowed up by the rising sea and the howling wind.

Zeru had expected the rain, but not the wind, and not like this. The wind had come out of the east, and drove the rain into his face as fiercely as needles pierce the flesh. He didn't mind the discomfort so much as what the wind signified that chilled his soul. There just wasn't enough heat in the

Valley to cause this much rain from the infilling sea. Every centimeter of rain that dropped from the sky needed ten times as much hot rock to rise from the sea, and yet more than three meters of rain had fallen already. El was playing his cards boldly. Zeru studied the sky again. The parallel bands of cloud were loosening up, and the blackness that had stood like a wall to the south seemed lighter, letting more light from the distant sun filter through the washboard sky. It was clearly a cyclonic storm, and from the curvature of the clouds, at least 1500 kilometers across.

"Twice the size of the Caribbean storms," he spoke softly as if to himself, "twice the wind, four times the rain, and," he computed quickly while surveying his mound of rock, "about three times the storm surge."

Two centuries or so ago, he had surveyed this storage site himself, overseeing the laying of the huge slabs of stone that protected the food supplies from animals and the elements. He had been careful to keep it above sea level, and even for good measure, added ten meters of flood insurance. Of course, that was, what, sea level three and a half centuries ago and five meters lower. It took a long time to get the cragmen to finish a storehouse. The standing stones took a month per slab, lintels about three months, and each one of the trefoil chambers with hermetically sealed interior took no less than year. Every finished rock and bucket of plaster had to be hauled up the mountain from town 500 meters below. The work had to be done in spurts of construction between the grain harvests. When he heard from Herklu that the sea might rise due to global warming, he had started the construction of the two replacements at fifty and one hundred meters above sea level and the snowline. They were going smoothly enough, but they wouldn't be finished for another three decades.

"Which might as well be never."

There. He had spoken aloud what he had been avoiding thinking for the past fortnight. The words hung in the air like the eye of the storm, at the same time too close to ignore and too far to change. Like the baleful eye of El himself, damning his Garden, smashing his Gates, destroying the most beautiful spot on Earth. It would never come back, it would never return: the grassy plains, the forested hills, the deep blue skies, the snowy peaks, the filigreed cities, the living libraries, the angelic music, the creation songs, Thera's voice. Never. He shook his head and forced himself back into the present.

He had hoped that with the stored food and equipment he could weather the flood, build a boat out of the roof timbers and rejoin the Cretan cohort that had gone East. It had been a well-thought out plan at the time: a nearby fortification, supplies, weapons, a post-disaster transport contingency. He had warned the others that evacuation would be difficult, and that travel of more than 48 hours would be highly dangerous. How dangerous it had been still surprised to him. But of course, they had pointed out the difficulties of keeping multiple rescue storehouses in good repair and well stocked. Or rather, they had some sort of philosophical objection to Zeru's implementation. "El will not deal gently with you," they had warned him, "for misappropriating his name." But it was they who had vanished while racing the floods, they who had gone east toward the Cretan Cliffs, forcing their way into the teeth of the wind.

Zeru had only to convince the cragmen here in the Maltese Highlands to replenish the food every year and keep the roof in good repair, which amounted to keeping the ribs of an upside-down boat watertight. Once every five or ten years, he would make a tour of the different mountain villages and make sure that their temple store duties were not neglected. It was shamefully easy to cow the villagers into obedience, requiring only a refresher every few years.

Another shudder sent a few more stones ratting into the water. Zeru had anticipated the quakes caused by the shifting weight of three kilometers of water, and his storehouses had been built to handle both the rain and the shaking. As far as he could tell, these storehouses had been in unusually good condition for the first week of the flood, that is, before the 250-kilometer-per-hour winds had torn off the roof-boat, the ten-meter waves had pounded the walls, and the storm surge had floated out the remaining stores.

He had been almost mad with rage when at last he came upon the site. The cragmen had been no help at all, fleeing westward with the first howling of the wind and quaking of the mountains. There was no point in trying to find them huddled in their grimy caves; they would be completely beside themselves with terror. For all he knew, they held him personally responsible for this devastation, and then he would have had to resort to violence. No, it was best to let them run like the beasts they had become; there would be no refuge with them, even supposing they could survive the swim to Italy. They certainly couldn't survive here.

The snowfields that had prevented him from building higher were gone now, washed away with the rains, exposing the naked shingles of native limestone, bare of any tree or shrub or animal burrow. That was why he had returned to the bay where the storehouse had been, and why for the past three hours he had been diving into the ice-cold water searching for stores. Five meters down he had come upon the remains of the roof timbers. Judging by the splinters, they had endured the force of the waves as well as the wind. And not surprisingly, not a barrel of nectar, not a smoked ham remained of what should have been three months of comfortable rations.

Now that the wind was dying down, the waves and the storm surge subsiding, Zeru hoped for a better chance at finding some of his stored tools and weapons. "With a decent saw and adze," he had prayed, "I can make a raft in a few hours."

Now that he had a plan in mind and could learn little more from the desolate landscape, Zeru finally allowed himself the luxury of an hour's sleep, the first he had permitted himself in the last two weeks. It wasn't so much that he needed the rest or hoped it would help him survive as that the sleep would let him reprocess the rapid series of events that led to his stranding on a shrinking island. And from long experience, Zeru knew his best plans came in his sleep. As he settled in on the shore, he called his mind back to the events a half-year ago that started the unraveling of his world.

"Come look at this," Thera called, waking him from his slumber on the couch. He followed her into the courtyard and then up the spiral steps of the west tower. The fog lay upon the fields, as it always did in Eden, dropping its heavy dew on the thirsty plants. But it obscured the night sky for most of the evening so if one wanted to see the morning sky, one had to get above the fog bank. As Thera led him up to the roof by the spiral steps that encircled the fired-clay tower, Zeru looked out over his fields and orchards. Under the mist, the orange blossoms glimmered white in the moonlight, releasing perfume that wafted over the quiet fields. The wheat looked especially good; the hybrids were growing stronger than ever. Judging from the level carpet of gray-green shoots, they were thriving on the irrigation schedule he had devised last year. Another good year for the crops, he thought, would perhaps be a good year to spend on mathematics and astronomy. It troubled him that some astronomical observations didn't seem to follow the normal pattern; it would be good to fit them in.

"Look," said Thera as she stepped out on the parapet, and that was all she needed to say. For up in the sky, suspended against the milky background of the galaxy, was a fuzzy patch of light with a distinctive tail. Either it had grown brighter very quickly or had moved into a darker patch of sky. No one from the observatory had reported the comet in the last few weeks, even though the seeing was far better up on the Giza plateau.

"What do you think it means?" Thera asked.

Zeru was silent. It was, after all, El's creation, and El used to explain everything, at least to Adam. But Adam had been dead these past seven centuries, killed by that strange germ no one had ever seen before. He called it "The Curse," and refused to be treated with the stem-cell restoration elixir. And now El was silent, and his purposes mysterious. Perhaps he was planning something spectacular, or perhaps it was just an astronomical wonder to adorn the galaxy. Some argued that El had abandoned Eden, that he had lost interest in it after he had put the guard at the Garden. Others thought he had wanted to start all over again, and was planning a great recreation. But even among those who hoped for a recreation, some thought it would be destructive and not creative. And did this fiery messenger portend sorrow or joy? No one could tell.

And then there was Noeku. Noeku insisted that destruction must come first. It was tiresome to hear him talk about immorality, about El's disfavor, and the rights of cragmen. It was even more tiresome to hear him go on about his own rescue project. You would have thought that cows were divine to hear him rant about farming and the need to save breeding stock from the coming disaster. Surely it was possible to re-domesticate the wild oxen, why did Noeku think nothing had been learned in the two millennia since the Garden was planted?

"Is it the end?" Thera asked again.

"No, not the end." Zeru answered. "But we will have to watch it closely."

Over the next few weeks, Zeru went to the tower nightly. The comet grew brighter every night, noticeably brighter. Even more troubling, the tail grew longer and longer until it stretched nearly fifty degrees across the sky. No one had seen anything like it. Nothing else was talked about in the lanes and courtyards. Few, if any, were getting much sleep.

Then the day came when Atnu ran breathlessly into Eden. He had traveled the 1000 kilometers from the Giza Mountain observatory in less than a week, saying only that "it was downhill all the way." He called a meeting immediately and messengers went out to gather the Council. When Zeru pressed him for information, he brushed him off, saying only "Come to the Council, I will explain everything."

The council room was as full as could be expected on two days notice. Almost everyone came except for those, like Herklu, who had posts far from Eden. Atnu motioned for silence, and came to the point immediately.

"You all have seen the comet in the sky. We have been tracking it for over a month, and we now know that it will come very close and possibly even collide with the Earth in 107 days. Granted, comets are hard to predict because of their erratic motion, but this one has shown no active jets, no signature of breakup, in fact, a disturbing uniformity of motion. It looks and behaves like a messenger of El."

Everyone began speaking at once, and again Atnu motioned for silence.

"The best outcome is that it will come only inside the Moon's orbit, but worst is that it will hit the Earth. We know roughly the hour of the possible collision. The good news is that if it does hit the Earth, it will be over the Atlantic. If so, it is likely that the breakup in the atmosphere could form a chain of fragments that stretches 500 kilometers. But even if none of these fragments strike the Gates, the tidal waves will endanger them and our Valley will be affected. We must secure the Gates."

His words hung in the air as his audience took it all in. Noeku was the first to break the silence.

"The Gates are doomed. El has decreed it. We must prepare for a flood. We must save the breeds. I have prepared a boat that we can . . ."

He was drowned out by the clamor of many voices, and finally when order was restored, Zeru held the floor.

"While we all should take precautions against a disastrous flood, it would be prudent to pursue parallel courses of action. Surely we can engineer the Gates to survive all but a direct hit. And even if they are breached, could we not repair them? Why must we abandon our fertile Valley as Noeku keeps insisting, as long as there is life and hope? Even if the Valley is lost (may El forbid it!), can we not provide escape routes and safe houses? The flood will surely not rise more than a meter per hour, which is faster than a man can walk only on the flattest plains. So, if we are wise enough to evacuate the salt flats around the Garden, there will be time to prepare our journey toward the African, Cretan, or Italian mountains. But Noeku's boat would be both slower and more crowded, assuming it were even seaworthy."

Noeku objected, as expected, but it became obvious that his boat would be both cramped and smelly from his insistence that breeding pairs be brought aboard to preserve the lineages El had given Adam. Even the coolest heads lost patience with him when he had to estimate the outlay for food and provisions for both people and animals. In the end, the council made two decisions: A contingent would be sent to the Gates to fortify and prepare for an estimated 50 meter tidal wave, and runners would be sent to call for a second council meeting in 60 days, to plan the evacuation routes, should the Gates not hold.

"And that was why," Zeru repeated to himself as he awoke from his brief sleep, "everyone was in Eden when the dark comet fragment arrived earlier than expected, why the direct hit on the Gates destroyed Herklu, the Edenites, the cragmen work teams, and all our best defense works. That was why the flood was faster than expected, why the cyclonic storm was seeded, why our evacuation plans proved deadly. That was why the earthquakes finished what the comet began, which was why" he paused.

"Why Noeku was right. El *had* planned it all along."

Black water gently lapped at the stones, and suddenly Zeru stared at it. An hour ago the stones had been many centimeters above the spreading sea, and now the invading sea was rising again. Zeru scanned the horizon, looking for landmarks, staring at the creeping water.

"Fifty meters above sea level," he muttered, "yet with the surge subsiding, it should be dropping."

Once again he scanned the sky, looking for any sign of the eye of the storm that had vanished to the south.

"Impossible" he told himself quietly.

Surely any rise above sea level would flow back through the Gates unless, unless Herklu's tsunami wall had become clogged by the jetsam of the Valley. What was the plan, 50-meter defenses? If they were clogged that would mean 50 meters more flooding, but there had to be some other source of water. Dropping quickly to his hands and knees he scooped up a handful of water and tasted it.

"Sweet" he said, raising his head to look at the sky again.

The rain was certainly fading, no more than a centimeter or so per hour at the most.

No, it couldn't be the rain alone. Such an influx could only happen if a large body of fresh water had suddenly been dumped into the Valley, or rather, Sea. But where would this second flood come from?

The answer came even as he asked. The Black Sea was 3000 meters above the Valley floor and its water was carefully tapped for irrigation. The 30-kilometer irrigation channel through the Dardanelles had undoubtedly eroded on account of the rains, just as all the other evacuation routes had been destroyed. What if earthquakes had displaced the abutments on the Black sluice gates? Then the flood water from the Black could easily cause this rise in water level.

He did a quick calculation. "If the Gates are clogged, it will be a race between the emptying of the Black and the draining at the Gates. But regardless who wins," he said to himself, "there will be no tool-finding or raft-building here."

Standing on the highest point, he stretched his three-meter frame up to study the horizon. To the south and several hundred kilometers away lay the African coast, hidden by the curve of the Sea. To the north and only 80 kilometers away lay the mountains of Sicily, their snowy peaks undoubtedly denuded like Malta's. But there were the protected valleys above sea level, a favored resort for Edenites during the hot summers. Surely he could find refuge and perhaps even cragman refugees there. And while he was pretty sure that the Trans-Valley mountains were now below water, there was a good chance that the Sicilian Mountains still had a land bridge to the Italian Range. He just needed to get there.

It would be a long swim, a really long swim, and in fresh water, unlike the leisurely dips in the salty Serpent Lakes of his youth. Perhaps a board or tree could provide some flotation if needed. By now he could see a current flowing westward, carrying debris still floating toward the blockage at the Gates. Any wood he found would likely be trapped somewhere. It looked as if he would be diving back into the bay once again.

Then something caught his eye and he turned. To the north, in the strait separating Malta from Sicily something was moving, moving eastward, against the current. It was dark and traveling fast. It grew larger and then smaller and then larger again, a black triangle against the dark water and gray clouds. He lifted up his hands to cup his mouth and then froze, arms outstretched, transfixed upon the shingle. For the black triangle been joined by another, and yet another. Then the triangle lifted out of the water to reveal a black boat, and the boat rolled to expose a white keel, and the keel contained a black eye, and the eye viewed him pitilessly, like the eye of El.

"Orcas" he whispered aloud.

2.2 The Hebrew Flood

In this chapter I look at the word that has perhaps created the most contention among translators of the Noah story, the word for "earth" or "world." I want to focus on how translators in all places and at all times have operated when they try to understand meaning. We discover that dictionaries are only useful when there is no controversy, and surprisingly, that we now have the tools to improve on them. Using these available exegetical tools, I propose to show how the murky reason for the Flood can now be understood as a genetic curse, and how this genetic cleansing changes the goals the Flood must accomplish. Combining the work on the dictionary entry with the genetic exegesis shows how a historical Flood could achieve the tasks demanded by the text.

2.2.1 The Good Earth *ʾerets*, Genesis 6:11–13

Gen 6:11-13 *Now the earth was corrupt in God's sight, and the earth was filled with violence. And God saw the earth, and behold, it was corrupt, for all flesh had corrupted their way on the earth. And God said to Noah, "I have determined to make an end of all flesh, for the earth is filled with violence through them. Behold, I will destroy them with the earth. Make yourself an ark of gopher wood."*

'erets	land	earth	country	ground	world	way	common	field	nations	wilderness
2504	1543	712	140	98	4	3	1	1	1	1
100%	62%	28%	6%	4%	.15%	.12%	.04%	.04%	.04%	.04%

Table 2.1: KJV translation of אֶרֶץ (*'erets*).

The Flood story begins with the perspective of God. One might argue that Noah's self-description was exaggerated, but it would be hard to argue that God exaggerates. If we are to take an inerrant view of Scripture, this passage must be taken at face value. Unfortunately, that does not eliminate all the ambiguity. We know that God will occasionally use puns, and sometimes His promises get fulfilled in several stages, where successive stages are more complete than previous ones. His most famous staged promise was the surprise that the Messiah would come twice. So we must keep this possible ambiguity in mind as we read the passage.

The first controversial word we run into is *'erets*, "earth."

Does it mean "Earth" as in the third rock from the Sun or does it mean "land" or "dirt," as in Pearl Buck's *The Good Earth*?[1]

The English word can mean either, and that is the main bone of contention between the "global" and the "local" Flood proponents. The former interpret the Flood story "literally" as a global flood, including a miraculous arrival and departure of water, while the latter see the Flood "poetically" as a local flood which required no obvious miracle. But of course, the story is written in Hebrew, not English, so it does not use the word "earth."

What then does the Hebrew say?

We need to get out our kit of Hebrew tools and look. A pre-computer-era tool for the non-Hebrew reader is Strong's concordance, where every unique Hebrew word in the Old Testament (or Masoretic Text, MT) is given a number.[2] Then statistics and word searches can be accomplished without translation or transliteration obscuring the result. It has been an invaluable tool to theologians and scholars since 1890, and most preachers have a copy on their shelf. Professionals may scorn such archaic resources, but I make no apologies for my extensive use, greatly enhanced by other freely available tools at the *blueletterbible.com* website.

The MT for "earth" is *'erets*, and Strong's concordance lists both English meanings above as possibilities. Using the search engine on the King James Version (KJV), we can find all the occurrences where it is translated in Table 2.1. The translation as the global "world" is so rare, that we conservatively

1. Buck. *The Good Earth*.
2. Strong. *The Exhaustive Concordance*.

add in the more ambiguous "earth" to the sum of "global" meanings to find that at a minimum, 72 percent of the time *'erets* refers to a local rather than a global region, as for example, Gen 10:11 "out of that land (*'erets*) went Asshur." So it can have either meaning in English, but it more probably means "local."

Is this because modern English translations paraphrase the Hebrew, putting in the translators' opinion?

To find out, I also compiled statistics with the explicitly literal and more recent New American Standard (NAS) concordance, where *'erets* appears 2499x, with sums that differed little from the KJV. In fact, when the NAS, the KJV, the Jewish Publication Society (JPS), and the English Standard Version (ESV) translations are compared, I find myself siding with the KJV more often than not, perhaps because the translators in 1611 were very restrained about paraphrasing obscure Hebrew.

That is why simply looking up the word in a Hebrew-English dictionary or a concordance is not very helpful. In fact, there are very few times when a dictionary helps, in part because there are only 8000 words in a Hebrew dictionary. Fully 1500 of them appear in the Bible only once (*hapax legomena*), and of those, 400 are without related grammatical derivatives.[3] Because there is no other source of ancient Hebrew except the Bible, we depend on parallel constructions, early translations, or cognate languages like Ugaritic for the meaning of many of the words. Fortunately for us, *'erets* is very common and its multiple meanings are usually very clear.

Can we rely on grammar to resolve the ambiguity? For example, does not the Hebrew "construct state" of *'erets* mean "local" and the "absolute state" (*ha'arets*) mean "global"?

The English "word cloud" of the Hebrew *'erets* includes a global sense "Earth" and a local sense "land." When nouns are used as modifiers, Hebrew forms "construct chains," (much the way English lumps nouns together in descriptions such as "bus station coffee shop") where *'erets* is usually translated "land," as in "the land of Egypt" (*'erets mitsrayim*). Conversely, when it appears as an unmodified subject not in a construct chain (the "absolute state"), it is often translated "the Earth" as KJV/NAS/JPS does throughout Noah's flood account. However, the absolute state is not always translated this way because there are multiple accounts in Genesis, especially those of Abraham's journeys, where the KJV/JPS translates the absolute as "land." Here are two examples from the KJV:

> Gen 12:10 *And there was a famine in the land (*ba'arets*):and Abram went down into Egypt to sojourn there; for the famine was*

3. Jewish-Encyclopedia. "Hapax Legomena."

> *grievous in the land* (ba'arets). Gen 13:6–7 *And the land* (ha'arets) *was not able to bear them, that they might dwell together: for their substance was great, so that they could not dwell together. And there was a strife between the herdsmen of Abram's cattle and the herdsmen of Lot's cattle: and the Canaanite and the Perizzite dwelled then in the land* (ba'arets).

So I argue that, by analogy, if a local region was simply called "the Land" in Genesis, with no qualifying construct chain, then the account of Noah could also refer to the first land, Eden and its surroundings, where Adam's descendants lived.

But does not this translation go against two thousand years of grammatical tradition?

If we lived in an ideal world we might rely on grammatical authorities. But if a word is already the subject of some controversy, the human authors of dictionaries and grammars have often been forced to take sides even when the data are ambiguous. In Volume 3, I blame the ~200 BC Greek Septuagint (LXX) translation of the MT for many of these poor grammatical decisions that have become ironclad traditions. But truth be told, the computer tools we have today are superior to the best tools available to experts even fifty years ago, so we can do the statistics of nuance ourselves. One of the goals of this book is to demonstrate how a computer can make the original languages accessible to everyone.

Verse	Hebrew	Nouns	Verbs
6:11	*'erets*	Violence*,corrupt*,God*,sight	filled
6:12	upon *'erets*	all flesh*, his way	Looked*
6:13	*'erets*	Noah,end,them*	destroy

Table 2.2: Words associated with אֶרֶץ (*'erets*) in Gen 6:11–13.

Language is not always a jumble of imprecise statistics. Rather, it can be very precise because nearby words narrow the focus. Language is redundant, repeating itself to such an extent that even in a noisy crowd one can follow a conversation without hearing every word. As a result, it is rare to find an ambiguity that is not resolved simply by looking at the wider context. Unless, of course, the author is attempting to be ambiguous, which at first glance does not appear to be true of this passage.

Does the context tell us whether *'erets* is global?

In English, if "Earth" refers to the planet globally, there might also be nearby words associated with environment, global warming, planets, or the moon and the sun. On the other hand, if "earth" refers to a local concept, there might be mention of concepts like dirt, nation, boundaries, or farming. One way to determine which MT usage is meant would be to compile a list such as Table 2.2 where nearby words are listed, repeated words are flagged with asterisks.

No words in this table demand a global meaning. The verbs are not spatially universal. "End" is temporally absolute, but "Noah" and "them" are clearly particular. The only word that suggests a universal extent is "all flesh," but even that is ambiguous if it means "all blood relatives." Recall that Gen 6:2 has introduced two unrelated people groups—sons of God and daughters of men—so when Gen 6:3 says "*man . . . he also is flesh*," it would seem to exclude the first people group. If they are excluded, then it is possible the "all flesh" extinction in Gen 6:13 would not necessarily be universal. Now this may or may not be relevant to Gen 6:12, but it shows that if we are going to argue logically for a global Flood, then the context of this passage is ambiguous enough to evade conviction.

What about expanding the context to include the rest of the Noah story and even the whole MT usage of *'erets*?

Because tabulating all 2504 occurrences of *'erets* is a bit overwhelming, I narrow the context by searching for word pairs that appeared in Gen 6:11–13. I use the corresponding Strong's concordance numbers to avoid translation ambiguities as shown in Table 2.3. In the last column, I record the percentage of time that *'erets* is translated as "local land," excluding the Noah story from the statistics. This is what I need to determine the meaning.

#	H776 *'erets*+( )	in Noah	Elsewhere	%local
1	H7843 (corrupt)	5/35	global=0/35, local=30/35	100
2	H4390 (filled)	5/48	global=10/48, (Nu 14:21;Is 11:9; Ps 33:5;48:10;72:19;104:24;119:64 Je 23:24;Hab 2:14;3:3), local=33/48	69
3	H2555(violence)	2/13	global=0/13, 11/13=local	100
4	H3605+1320(all flesh)	8/13	global=0/13, Je 35:21 not, local=5/13	100
5	English "world"	28/28	(So not "earth." local=741)	0
6	Engl. "upon the earth"	10/14	global=1/14 Gen 2:5, local=3/14	75

Table 2.3: Word pairs involving אֶרֶץ (*'erets*).

I draw three conclusions. First, the word *ʾerets* appears to be translated differently in the Noah story than in the rest of the MT, as in word pairs (1),(3), and (4). Second, the English word pairs in (5) and (6) are almost all global, and the Noah story fits in with them. Thus it is not the Hebrew but the English that defines Noah's *ʾerets* to be global, which is to say it is the translator's choice which is most decisive. Third, the one Hebrew word pair that seems to span both local and global is (2), where it accounts for many of the global references outside the Noah account simply as variations on the phrase, "the earth is filled with the glory of God as the waters fill the sea." We take this phrase, however, as a deliberate echo of or literary reference to the Noah account. That is, if *ʾerets* means "local," the phrase would translate more accurately as: "the land is filled with God's glory as the waters fill the sea." This translation is arguably more literary, because the sea is contrasted appropriately with the land and not with the world. Just as the sea does not cover the whole earth, so also God's glory only covers the habitable land, with an inference that glory is not an impersonal and material substance but a person-related property. If we accept that argument, then 100 percent of word pair (2) is also local.

The overall impression is that Hebrew word pairs do not help resolve the dispute because there is no clear separation of contexts based on dictionary definitions. Conversely, the Noah story stands out as a unique unit, without connection to other dictionary usage. When I did get a clear separation in meaning between world and land, it was all from the English translation, which is to say, the translator's opinion.

But what does the translator base his opinion on, if not the dictionary entry?

He bases it on the meaning of the sentence or paragraph as a whole. Like the translator, we too can keep expanding our context outward until either the ambiguity disappears, or we conclude that it was intentional. And if we look at the sense of the sentence and paragraph, there is a certain logic to the argument that the Flood has to be global to achieve the purposes God set for it. We have phrases like "all flesh," which are clearly discussing the human race. But because humans are supposed to have "*filled the earth*" (Gen 1:26), a local flood would hardly suffice; rather a global flood seems necessary. Likewise, we have the instructions to build a rather large boat to save the animals. That hardly seems necessary for a local flood, because the animals could simply escape to later repopulate uninhabited regions.

The logic for a global *ʾerets* appears impeccable, yet the argument for translating it "world" remains circular. It is an attempt to fit the word to a logical outcome and not the other way around. If a global flood logically necessitates bringing birds into the Ark, so that we put a "global" definition in the *'erets* entry of the dictionary, we cannot then turn around and use this definition to prove that the Flood must be global. For in the attempt to achieve logical consistency, we have coerced the dictionary entry for *'erets* to mean "world" irrespective of the fact *'erets* was never used this way elsewhere in the MT, as our brief word study showed. Then we have elevated Reason above Revelation, the one thing the literalist litmus test was intended to prevent!

But what else could *'erets* mean?

If we do not force the word to fit our logic, there may be another explanation for its use, which will be the topic of the next chapter. Here I want to emphasize that Hebrew dictionaries are of limited use for some of the knottier problems in translation. They are based on logical inferences, useful but fallible. Therefore, we cannot baptize the fallible dictionary as inerrant, lest we miss important meanings of the text.

The process of building a dictionary is as much an exercise in hypothesis testing as is the process of building a scientific theory. They both require a certain amount of humility, of uncertainty, of rational sleuthing, and data discovery. Ultimately, the best judge of a translation is its explanatory power—its ability to explain the rest of the text, the context.

But is that not circular reasoning—the context explains the word, the word explains the context?

Yes, it is circular, it is the infamous hermeneutical circle mentioned earlier. But some circles mesh together to make a clock, something a single gear cannot do. Our surprise at this unexpected function, this added information, is what we call explanatory power. Explanatory power consists of the coherence that shows up at the semantic level of sentences, at the textual level of paragraphs, at the literary level of stories, and the largest extent, at the logical level of systematic theology. The general consensus is that one should resolve the meaning of a word/text at the smallest unit of coherence. However some problems are not resolved despite invoking ever larger contexts. This is invariably the case for verses that are used by warring denominations, such as this one concerning the magnitude of Noah's flood. So, in the few cases where they really matter, these rules of thumb are of little practical help. Historically, when many sought merely to win the argument, theology resolved (or more likely, escalated) the differences. That was the approach of the Reformation and the Wars of Religion, with many unfortunate outcomes.

Is there no escape from theologically assured devastation?

Yes, there may be a way to resolve differences of interpretation if we can postpone invoking theological arguments, which invariably introduce fallible interpreters and historical controversies. A great deal can be learned by focusing on the linguistic data and logical reasoning of the text itself—where I have broadened the definition of "data" to include (non-ideological) observations. This is the scientific method of hypothesis testing, a method that attempts to compare the data with several different hypotheses without dogmatic commitment to a particular one.

Allowing multiple interpretations to interact with each other without declaring a winner is simply a rediscovery of rabbinic *midrash*, an approach which permits several parallel "meanings" of the text, each based on a different set of dictionary definitions. For like poetry, *midrash* cherishes the text itself more than its many interpretations and will tolerate (and evaluate) many meanings as long as the sacred text itself is left pristine. By contrast, the Western prose tradition assumes that the intent of the text's author takes priority, and the text can be paraphrased and translated as necessary in order to convey the sacred meaning. No other religion takes such a cavalier attitude toward its sacred texts, and neither should we.

But what sense is there in treating Genesis like poetry, of withholding judgment and so fueling the chaos of post-modern relativism? Why would we not speak the truth if we knew it? Is not *midrash* simply a refusal to commit, a rejection of the basic concept of inerrancy?

There are many times when it is wiser to withhold than to dispense judgment. In a famous instance, Solomon was asked to choose the real mother of a baby (1 Kgs 3:16–28). In his case, and in many similar court cases, the truth was discovered later and premature judgment would have been erroneous. Sometimes, newly discovered evidence changes the case so profoundly that reconsideration is necessary, as in Nathan the prophet's legal protest (2 Sam 12:1–7) "*You are the man!*" This delayed evidence is also our situation with Noah's flood, as I discuss later. But *midrash* does more than simply delay judgment. Sometimes the consideration of the matter is more significant than its resolution, just as the uncertainty of future taxation is worse for business than the eventual implementation.[4] *Midrash* recognizes that interaction with the Hebrew text may be of greater lasting value than having a dogmatic answer which requires no knowledge of Hebrew; it is a restatement of the Psalmist's plea (Ps 34:8): "*Taste and see that the LORD is good!*" It is a plea for commitment to an empirical observation over a dogmatic assertion that needs no evidence.

Am I saying that the Bible is intentionally ambiguous? Would that not contradict inerrancy? How can two conflicting assertions both be true?

This is one of the great mysteries, as Paul tells us (Eph 3:5), that what was hidden for centuries can be revealed to a later generation. For the Bible

4. Glertz and Feldman. "Economic costs."

remains true and inerrant despite our ignorance and confusion, or perhaps I should say, because of our ignorance and confusion. For if we completely understood the Word then we would be masters and lords of a dead text, willing to cut it in half to protect our ignorance, rather than stewards and pupils of a living text, the Words of Life. Much remains uncertain until the time is ripe for its revelation; in due course, all will be explained. Until then it is prudent to hold lightly to theories and dogma, but firmly to His Word and Person, for there is salvation in no one else.

Therefore we will consider both theories, a world-wide catastrophe and a local Flood, to see which proves the more capable messenger of truth.

2.2.2 The Purpose: Genesis 6:11–13

The reason given for the Flood in Gen 6:11–13 is that "all flesh" on the whole earth is corrupted by violence. Corruption is not simply an act or an offense: it is a state of being. If changing this state of being necessitated a Flood, then the normal human and cultural resets of regime change, repentance, or death/rebirth that work for most other sins were not sufficient for this one.

What kind of pernicious corruption was this that required the death of "all flesh"?

We need to do a Hebrew study to find out. Table 2.4 shows the statistics on the word pair "all flesh" shows that *kol* H3605 (all) + *basar* H1320 (flesh) appear together 69x in the whole MT, 12/69x in the Noah story alone. Of the 3/69 ambiguous passages, Lev 17:14 stands out because the phrase appears three times, drawing a strong connection between animal blood and human life, which forms the basis of kosher butchering as well as the Christian doctrine of the Eucharist. Clearly it has some deeper significance than a material carcass. Without getting into the weeds in Leviticus, it is clear that when the phrase is not being used for deep theological analogies, "all flesh" at a minimum possesses the abstract meaning: "mankind."

kol+basar	in Noah	by chance	"mankind"	ambiguous	"sacrificial bull"
69	12	24	26	3	1
100%	17%	35%	38%	4%	1.4%

Table 2.4: NAS translation of כָּל־בָּשָׂר (*kol-basar*).

Because "mankind" implies a moral nature, in contrast to birds and beasts, this corruption goes beyond some material property like lice, but targets what it means to be human. If the corruption is genetic (e.g. Rom 5), the passage must be referring to Adam's descendants. It affected more than just Cain's descendants because Seth's descendant Methuselah was still alive, yet Genesis says only Noah was a non-violent man. Only Noah escaped the genetic disease of violence.

Do we have any scientific support for a genetic basis for violence that could have corrupted the race?

Most certainly, because violence is the trait that is bred for in pit bulls and in fighting cocks. It has also been linked with testosterone, being one of the known side-effects of taking steroids, whether for enhanced physical endurance or hormone replacement therapy (e.g., Mike Tyson and Lance Armstrong.)[5] Since sexual selection is a favorite evolutionary talking point to remedy the deficiencies of Darwinian natural selection, arguing that increased violence could become genetically selected is hardly novel.[6]

The text of Genesis supports this view, for Gen 4:7 reports that Cain's act of violence was predictable, as would be true of a character trait. Gen 4:23–24 reports that Lamech bragged about his own violent tendencies as exceeding those of his ancestor Cain. If, as we argue in this book, the Adamic race was well acquainted with genetics, then Lamech's boast is far more than testosterone-fueled braggadocio; it is an assertion of genetic superiority, a National Socialism of vengeance.[7] Then the commentary in Gen 6:3 sheds new light. The evil filling the land is a genetic evil, a desire to breed a more aggressive, violent race.

Is this a reasonable reading of "evil"? Does it not contain more than a little racism?

Yes, it is reasonable, and yes, it is "racism" in the old-fashioned sense, not the sense used in the media today. When we consider that Goliath was one of many giants to come from Gath, including a six-fingered giant (2 Sam 21:20) expressing polydactyly—a genetically recessive trait—then very likely human breeding programs were endemic in the ANE. Just as dog breeders can produce chihuahuas and great Danes through selective breeding, so also the ANE used selective breeding to produce a new breed, a new race of giants.

Are there different races of humans?

In technical terms, two species are separate if they cannot have fertile offspring. Races or breeds are subspecies because they (and their progeny) are not sterile the way a mule is sterile. Every human race on this planet is

5. Willis. "The Bite Fight."; Aubrey, "Lance Armstrong confesses."

6. Darwin. *The Descent of Man*.

7. Weikart. *From Darwin to Hitler*.

part of the same species because we can intermarry and have fertile children. What separates human races is the distribution of alleles or genetic variants, such as blue versus brown eyes. Because everyone has two parents (ignoring recent genetic engineering exploits), everyone also has two alleles from each parent for each trait, which can be the same (purebred) or different. But if an allele is destructive, such as the allele for sickle-cell anemia, then no one lives long with two copies of this allele and there can be no sickle-cell race. In this case, the sickle-cell allele is parasitic, only able to survive in the presence of healthy alleles. On the other hand, one can have a healthy purebred trait like black hair or brown eyes, and it is these sorts of traits that have been used to characterize the human races.

Is this the first step toward separation of human subspecies into species?

Both the recent migration of people groups (some 6000 years ago in the Neolithic) and the continual intermingling of humankind mean that none of these subspecies are showing any signs of turning into separate species. Therefore, the "racial purity" emphasis of the twentieth-century eugenics programs that greatly influenced the Nazi party is mistaken—there are no pure races, only statistical differences in the distribution of alleles. Let me put it another way: there is a trait not found anywhere else in biology, which all humans possess, the ability to talk. And with this genetically inherited ability comes self-awareness, consciousness, and abstract thought, in short, personhood. Personhood is so qualitatively different from whatever your dog communicates with his wagging tail and begging eyes that we cannot and must not think that talking is simply a continuum of communication, as if humans can be placed on a sliding scale with animals. As Gen 9:6 clearly states, the value of humankind is not on the same scale as animals, nor even on a sliding scale between races, but in their qualitatively distinct personhood "*made in the image of God*," so human blood should not be shed, not even that of Cro-Magnons. Perhaps this explains the apparently non-violent, incremental, 2500-year expansion of Neolithics into Aurignacian Europe.

What happens then when the breeding of humans produces qualitative differences? What happens when artificial means are used to create a parasitic allele purebred?

I conjecture that the command given to Joshua to annihilate seven Canaanite nations "devoted for destruction" (Jos 11:21) suggests a genetic defect introduced into those nations through breeding that required cleansing. Likewise, Genesis could be describing a genetic defect with consequences more profound than the hemophilia of Queen Victoria's inbred descendants, because it was a defect of character, something that apparently caused uncontrollable rage, perhaps like the trait bred into pit bulls. Given the ease with which inhuman upbringing can seriously damage a child's psyche, we must consider our mental consciousness, our sociability as a fragile equilibrium as easily disrupted by nurture as by nature. So breeding could very well be the evil discussed in Genesis, an inherited evil capable of destroying the species, a permanent "corruption" of the race.

Why in the world would anyone breed for a genetic defect like violence?

More than likely, violence was not the trait being bred for, but became closely associated with the primary trait. For example, Siamese cats are bred for their coat and eye color, and their schizophrenia is a closely associated but unwanted genetic side effect. Likewise, the degenerative spinal arthritis that affects German shepherds is an unwanted side effect of breeding large dogs. Thus it is likely that if Lamech is boasting of his increased violence, some other trait is being selected for. And from Gen 6:3 it seems that this trait is longevity.

For if the curse of Adam is known to all his descendants, then it would seem that foiling the curse, defeating death even without the miraculous fruit of the forbidden Garden, would be high on their priority list. After all, the longest-lived human was not Adam, as we naïvely might have assumed, but Methuselah (Gen 5:27). It is also highly suggestive that Methuselah died in the Flood, making him one of the people that God referred to as "corrupt." Therefore it would appear that this breeding program for long life was destroying the purposes God had for Adam's race, a bad breeding program which necessitated the Flood.

But to understand the human corruption that provoked such divine wrath, we must understand that curious verse, Gen 6:3.

2.2.3 Eternity, Genesis 6:3

> Gen 6:3 (NAS) *Then the LORD said, "My Spirit shall not [strive|rule in|abide] with man forever, [because|in his going astray] he also is flesh; [nevertheless|therefore|and] his days shall be one hundred and twenty years."*

I am using the NAS, putting the alternate translation from the footnotes back into the text. The first NAS footnote follows LXX in reading "strive," *diyn*, as "abide." Neither verb explains why a 120-year age limit is newly imposed, but let us follow our rabbinic directive to leave the MT unchanged and the verb as "strive" (which keeps us in John Calvin's company at least.)[8]

8. Calvin. *Commentary on Genesis.*

The next footnote points out that the English does not quite know what to do with "in his going astray," *beshaggam*, and tends to drop it in favor of a simple "because." As there are many possible meanings of the phrase and not all of them can be reduced to "because," we will put the full phrase back in.

Finally, the third footnote changes the causality of the last phrase from "nevertheless" to "therefore." The MT merely has a *waw*-consecutive for a connector, which really carries little if any causal force, so we replace it with the bland conjunction "and." It now reads:

> Gen 6:3 *Then the LORD said, "My Spirit shall not strive with man forever; in his going astray he also is flesh; and his days shall be 120 years."*

This hardly seems an improvement but for a recent novel by James Barney, *The Genesis Key*,[9] which suggested that the MT *'olam* (forever) was modifying "man" rather than the verb "strive," giving the translation, "strive with eternal man." It supports this reading because the next verse has the relative phrase "men who [were] of *'olam*." The novel argues that the 120-year limit is a genetic judgment transforming eternal man into mortal man. And while the novel displaces the arrival of genetic death from Adam's curse to Noah's flood (a big stretch!), the reference to genetic limits is intriguing.

Well, does *'olam* mean "eternal" or "forever"?

6:3 And God said,	וַיֹּאמֶר יְהוָה
My Spirit shall not strive with man forever	לֹא־ יָדוֹן רוּחִי בָאָדָם לְעֹלָם
because he also is flesh,	בְּשַׁגַּם הוּא בָשָׂר
nevertheless his days shall be 120 years.	וְ הָיוּ יָמָיו מֵאָה וְעֶשְׂרִים שָׁנָה

Table 2.5: Significance of עֹלָם (*'olam*) in Gen 6:3.

Table 2.5 shows the MT for this verse, a verse which has collected quite a bit of commentary as well as footnotes, indicating that the meaning is a bit obscure. Clearly there's something going on about Noah's (and prior generation's) 950-year life span and this new 120-year age limit, though the reasoning is not transparent.

Why would God's Spirit have something to do with long life? Does a shorter life span have something to do with genetic corruption?

I think it does, but some effort is required to explain the relationship, which once again shows that without a destination in mind, translation

9. Barney. *The Genesis Key*

can be hit-or-miss. That is, translation is not a value-neutral, objective enterprise, but like most goals in life, requires a road map. As we have done before, let us consult the dictionary for guidance.

A search on *'olam* (Strong's H5769) finds it 448x in the MT, where Gesenius's grammar defines it as "a long stretch of time (past or future)." But it will require more sophisticated tools than Strong's numbering scheme to determine if the word should be translated as an adverb "forever" or a noun "for eternity." Even the annotated Hebrew *Westminster Leningrad Codex* (marked WLC in many computer helps) can only tell us that both "man" and "forever" are labeled "ncmsa" (noun-construct-masculine-singular-absolute), which favors Barney's adjectival use. But understanding this odd sentence will take a yet more sophisticated tool, a syntax parser.

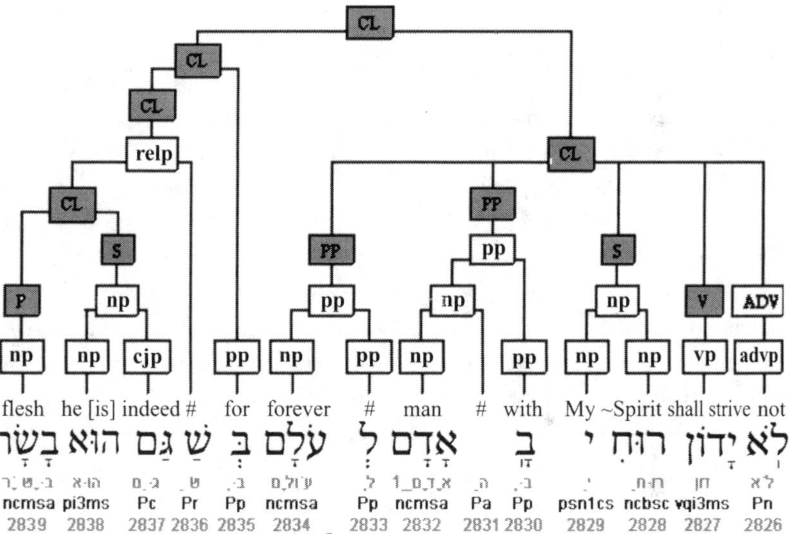

Figure 2.1: Gen 6:3 syntax diagrammed with WTS 2011 Tanakh ruleset and Emdros 3.4.

I used Hebrew syntax parsing software implementing the WTS Tanakh 2011 ruleset[10] with the graphical Emdros 3.4 display as shown in Figure 2.1, where boxed acronyms indicate parts of speech: np=noun-, vp=verb-, relp=relative-, cjp=conjunction-, advp=adverb-, and pp=preposition-phrase. Clause parts are labeled with capitals: S=subject, V=verb, P=predicate, ADV=adverb, PP=preposition, and CL=clause. Focusing on the words "forever" and "man," I find that these two words are the objects of two separate prepositions, two separate branches in the syntax tree. The nouns *'adam* and *'olam* are in two separate prepositional phrases, one that

10. Petersen. "Emdros" 1190–1193. Lowery. "Review of 'Emdros'" 332–339.

means "with/against" and another that means "about/concerning." The sentence diagram for the second phrase reads: [subject] *My Spirit*, [verb] *shall not strive*, [prepositional phrase] *with man*, [prepositional phrase] *about eternity*.

Does the second prepositional phrase modify the subject of the first prepositional phrase?

The WTS 2011 parser rule-set says no, they are in separate prepositional phrases, both modifying the main clause.

Why then does the English have only one preposition where the MT has two?

I turned to linguistics for help. Some verbs take no object, called "intransitive." These verbs would include "I think" or "I sleep." Other verbs take an object and are called "transitive" such as "I dropped the teacup." Some transitive verbs take two objects; for example, "I gave the girl the teacup." Linguists add a third category when the verb not only takes no object but requires no subject either, as in "It is raining." The sum of subjects and objects is called "valency," which is expressed as a number between zero and three.[11] The key to this verse turns out to be the valency of the verb.

Searching on "strive" (*diyn* H1777), we find that it appears with two somewhat distinct meanings: Gesenius's grammar gives it the meaning "rule" or "judge" 21/25x when it is in the active stem (*qal*) with a valency of two. But when in the passive stem (*niphal*), it is translated "strive" as in 2 Sam 19:9 and Gen 6:3, or "quarrel" as in Eccl 6:10. Each of these passive *niphal* uses has a formal valency of one but they also have two prepositional objects where one object explains "about" while the other explains "concerning." Linguists call these "oblique" arguments because any number of them can be added to the sentence. But if they are required, as appears to be the case here, then functionally they raise the valency to three. In contrast, KJV/NAS drop the second preposition in Gen 6:3 as if the valency were two (the one thing it is not!), making "eternity" into an adverb.

Are these the same? Is striving about eternity the same thing as striving forever?

Not if "eternity" is a genetic reversal of the curse: eternal life. Then my paraphrase of this verse becomes,

6:3 *My Spirit shall not quarrel with man about eternal life, indeed his going astray is in his genes and his lifespan being 120 years.*

So it appears that the Flood's purpose was not to kill animals nor start the creation over again, but to eliminate the corrupted genes that had begun to destroy the Adamic race, genes that, perhaps through breeding, had

11. Tesniere. *Elements of Structural Syntax.*

become a contentious problem. Genesis says Noah was the only righteous man, which we associate with a moral character. But perhaps there was a material reason as well. Perhaps, due to a very special trait, Noah was chosen to be the father of the line that would survive the Flood. He would become the genetic bottleneck that removed the contaminated genes. A genetic bottleneck occurs whenever a population is so decimated that all carriers for variant alleles (dominant or recessive) are eliminated, leaving only one allele to survive. In addition to eliminating this violent allele, Noah became the last of the 900-year old patriarchs (Gen 9:29), which suggests that the long-lived gene was also eliminated. Once again, this is evidence of a link between violence and long life.

How could we observe such a genetic bottleneck?

A genetic bottleneck can be detected by using genetic clocks, based on the rate of variations collected in the DNA genome. There are large stretches of DNA in which slight variations can and do occur without affecting the functionality of the DNA. Because these variations are inherited, we can study them statistically in the children to see how related two persons are and, by inference, how far back they shared a common ancestor. Now if we know the rate at which the genetic variation enters into the population (a big if!), then we not only know how related two descendants are but we have a good idea of when, in terms of number of generations, this bottleneck occurred.

2.2.3.1 *The Curse of Genes*

It cost $1 billion to sequence the human genome in 1998. By 2012, genomic studies had become much more affordable. With the advances in gene sequencing, the journal Nature reported a study of 2440 people looking at 500,000 distinct genetic variations.[12] When they mapped the chronology, they found that the genetic variation suddenly accelerated some 5115 years ago.

Could this be a signature of Noah's flood?

The Institute for Creation Research certainly thinks so.[13] While smaller populations can "fixate" variations faster, it still seems odd that a genetic bottleneck of eight people caused more variations rather than fewer, as would be the expected result. However, if at this time the Adamic race stopped in-breeding and started out-breeding, variations would develop quickly.

12. Stower. "Evolution."
13. Tomkins. "Human DNA."

Who would they have found as partners?

Gen 6:4 indicates that there were at least two subpopulations of humans. This is a highly controversial verse and we will tackle it later. For now, the new tools of genetics show something happened before 3000 BC, and I want to talk about that event. The genetic chronology is not well calibrated. That is both because we would need actual DNA from Carbon-14 dated fossils to get a better calibration, and because a more recent paper suggests that the rate of human variation is only half of the expected value.[14] In addition, the suspected pre-Flood in-breeding would have suppressed the rate of variation, so Stower's estimated date could easily be as long as 10,230 years ago.

This uncertainty should be noted carefully: Calendar dates in the scientific literature should always be taken with a grain of salt because absolute dates are often difficult to pin down, with one ambiguous data set used to calibrate another. The resulting interdependence in the calendars can undermine an apparent consensus. For example, David Rohl argues that the entire ANE calendar is rooted in Egyptian Dynasty dates, which in turn were determined by French Egyptologists at the time of Napoleon. The Egyptologists made a critical misidentification, thereby misleading scientists for 200 years. His proposed corrective technique, using ancient records of astronomical events, is brilliant because the stars are perfect timekeepers. But his conclusions are still controversial because so much theory was based on the old calendar.[15] Given the controversy over dating, we should focus on the dates in relation to each other, the ordering of events, holding many reservations about the absolute date.

Genetically then, we see that something happened to the human race near or after the dawn of literacy, which means we should have a written or oral record of the event. Noah's Flood certainly meets this criterion.

2.3 The Flood Size

Having established the textual and exegetical basis for the Flood, I come now to the scientific section of this chapter, where we can examine historical data to support the text. First, considering just what sort of Flood could "reset" the genetic havoc caused by breeding humans, I can discover only one candidate, the Flood. Written histories provide ample support for the Flood. As a consistency check, I review the rest of Scripture, where we find passages that had previously been treated as poetic describe the Flood quite

14. Callaway. "Studies slow the human DNA clock" 343–344.

15. Rohl. *Pharaohs and Kings.*

well. Finally, I turn to the scientific record, which provides much evidence but offers little interpretation. To my great surprise, the academic world is abuzz with controversial theories that mesh perfectly with our textually derived Flood.

2.3.1 Local Flood Achieves God's Purpose

If the purpose of the Flood was to eliminate corrupted Adamic genes, then it is not necessary to eliminate all the animals. It is only necessary to eliminate all the degenerate genes, or more precisely, all the fertile carriers of the genes. This is the first clue that we are dealing with a less than global flood.

How would a local flood manage to wipe out these virulent Adamic genes? Would people not just run to higher ground?

The response of the global Flood proponents is that there was no higher ground. However, it is also conceivable that higher ground was unattainable, or inhospitable, or both. All that is required for this Flood to succeed is that the carriers of the genes no longer reproduce, which could potentially be achieved in a local flood. Then the minimal flood that would satisfy Scripture requires a local flood to annihilate all fertile carriers of the genes, necessitates a boat for survival, and lasts for about a year.

Is that possible without a global deluge?

Yes, if the Flood plain were surrounded by impassable mountains, if those mountains were bare of food and shelter, and if the Flood never completely subsided. Then there might easily be no survivors. Many local flood advocates have proposed locations for their favorite version of that disastrous flood but I have always been skeptical.[16] There were survivors of the 2011 Japanese tsunami when a 5-meter wall of seawater penetrated miles inland.[17] There were survivors of the 1889 Johnstown flood when the failure of an earthen dam sent a fifty-foot wall of water roaring at forty miles-per-hour through the town.[18] There were even survivors of the 1963 Vajont dam flood when a wall of water 200 meters high washed over the dam in the Italian Alps![19] None of these disasters was cumulative or complete. The disaster would have to last a lot longer and be combined with plagues, earthquakes, or tornadoes in order to begin to approach the 99.999 percent lethality of Noah's flood. So if I am going to posit a local flood for accomplishing God's

16. Hill. "The Noachian Flood:" 170–183.
17. Wikipedia. "Dhoku earthquake."
18. Chisolm. "Johnstown Flood" 475.
19. Petley. "Landslide Information"

aim of purging the world of dehumanizing genes, it must feature higher mortality rates than all recorded local floods.[20]

Is such a flood possible?

It would need to take place in an escape-proof valley, preferably one surrounded by cliffs or high mountains. It would need to be of long duration, preferably as long as a year but, in any event, long enough that survivors of the initial flood had no chance of rescue. It would have to be vast enough that, say, a week of paddling about on a raft of driftwood would still not permit survival.

Where would one find the conditions for such a flood?

In the scablands of eastern Washington state, there is a landscape scoured by the emptying of a huge glacial lake, which was certainly powerful enough and long-lasting enough to annihilate civilization. But there is no reason for all the world's humans to be camped in this spot when the glacial dam gave way.[21] After all, if it was cold enough for a glacial dam, it was probably not the most favorable site for irrigated farming.

The warm Mesopotamian river valley of the Tigris and the Euphrates is one of the oldest civilized places on the planet. I find it easy to imagine that all humans of the day could have been concentrated on farms along the Fertile Crescent. But historically, the floods in this plain were easily survivable, lasting only a few days after they arose from the melting snow of the headwaters. Certainly humans could walk fast enough to escape the floodplain during such events.

Some have suggested that rising sea levels could have drowned a large farming community at the mouth of the Euphrates. But even the fastest global warming on record took years, not days. And even if it had taken mere days, there would still have been time to walk to safety. Even combining the two events does not seem to provide the destructive power of total lethality. For one thing, there are no confining cliffs or mountains around the Mesopotamian valley that would present obstacles to escape. In fact, none of the proposed local scenarios for Noah's flood feature this "confinement" condition, and that's a good reason to reject them all. Except for one.

20. O'Connor and Costa. "The World's Largest Floods"

21. Bretz. "The Channeled Scabland" 617–649.

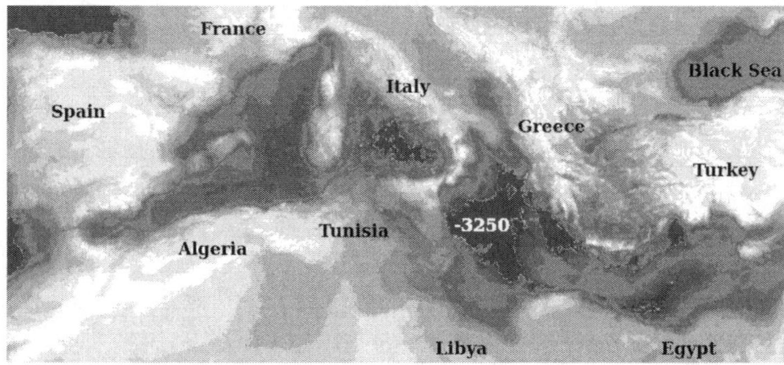

Figure 2.2: Bed of Mediterranean with sea level lowered -3250 meters leaving salt-lakes.

I first became aware of this option when I read that there are big blocks of salt on the shores of the Mediterranean Sea that were laid down six million years ago when tectonic forces (the geological forces that move the continents apart at the rate of centimeters per year) had once closed the Straits of Gibraltar, causing the sea to dry out (the Messinian salinity crisis.)[22] Further investigation revealed that all the rivers flowing into the Mediterranean—the Nile, the Danube, the Po—did not make up for the water that was evaporated from the surface of the sea. Even today, the difference continues to be met by Atlantic seawater, flowing in through the Strait of Gibraltar (Figure 2.3).[23]

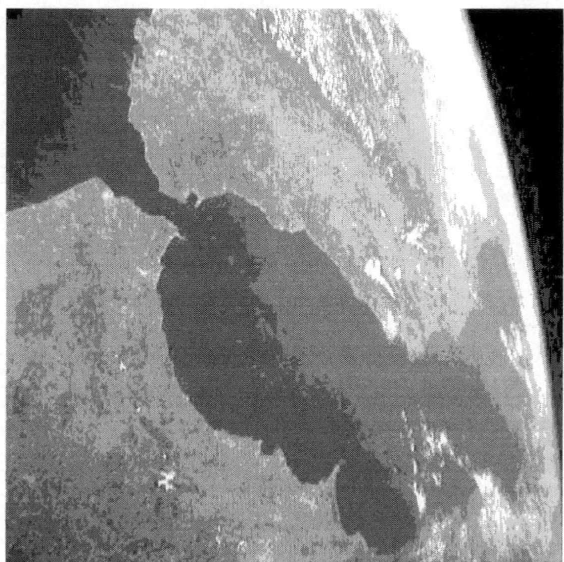

Figure 2.3: The Strait of Gibraltar from the Space Station. (NASA)

22. Cita. "The Messinian salinity crisis" 113–140.
23. Gall. "Atlantropa" 99–128.

In fact, when global warming was a major public concern about some years ago, it was proposed that a 13-kilometer dam across the Strait could block both the entrance of salty Atlantic water into the Mediterranean and the return flow of very salty water back into the Atlantic.[24] This super-salty return water sinks because it is more dense than the Atlantic. While sinking, it pulls warm surface water towards it, thus powering the Gulf Stream "conveyor belt." Because of this North Atlantic transport, England and Europe are constantly receiving tropical warmth. So great is the Gulf Stream warming that it fooled the Pilgrims into falsely predicting if London is at the same latitude as Newfoundland, Boston would have the weather of Rome! So, if the Strait were temporarily blocked, the Mediterranean would dry out and simultaneously, Europe would go into a deep freeze. This dam would make the Mediterranean sea bed into a dry, warm valley surrounded by ice-covered mountains and a glaciated Europe (as depicted in Figure 2.2).

We now have a location for the Flood that matches all our requirements. The breaking of the dam at the Strait of Gibraltar would begin an immense, unstoppable Flood that lasted far more than a year; it would entrap the citizens in a mountain-ringed valley because the bed of the Mediterranean is over two miles (3 km) below the rim; and it would come with violent stormy weather that compounded the disaster. It is likely that all humans would have been concentrated in this most fertile of valleys and they would require a boat to survive. The Flood would also place Eden for all time under two miles of seawater, hidden from view.

2.3.2 Local Flood in Historical References

After making this connection, I was gratified to discover that Greg Morton[25] and others had likewise identified the "Med bed" as a likely place for civilization, though few were interested in defending Noah; most were looking for the location of Atlantis. Tony O'Connell writes,

> "Strato (c. 335 BC), the philosopher, quoted by Strabo (c. 64 BC), spoke of a dam separating the Atlantic and the Mediterranean being breached by a cataclysm. This idea was reinforced by comment of Seneca (c. 4 BC) . . . The same idea was expressed by Diodorus Siculus (c. 90 BC), who said that Africa and Europe were joined and separated by Heracles. Such ideas could only

24. Johnson. "Climate control"; Johnson. *Secrets of the Ice Ages*; Cathcart. "Gibraltar Strait."

25. Morton. *Foundation, Fall and Flood*

> have arisen if there had been a Gibraltar dam far more recently than the conventionally accepted 5.3 million years ago."[26]

Pliny the Elder, in his *Historia Naturalis* (77), writes:

> Book 3, Intro, "The whole globe is divided into three parts, Europe, Asia, and Africa. Our description commences where the sun sets and at the Straits of Gades [Gibraltar], where the Atlantic ocean, bursting in, is poured forth into the inland seas. As it makes its entrance from that side, Africa is on the right hand and Europe on the left; Asia lies between them; the boundaries being the rivers Tanais [Don] and Nile. The Straits of the ocean, of which I have just spoken, extend fifteen miles in length and five in breadth . . . At the narrowest part of the Straits, there are mountains placed to form barriers to the entrance on either side, Abyla [Ximeira] in Africa, and Calpe [Rock of Gibraltar] in Europe, the boundaries formerly of the labours of Hercules. Hence it is that the inhabitants have called them the Columns of that god; they also believe that they were dug through by him; upon which the sea, which was before excluded, gained admission, and so changed the face of nature."
>
> Book 3, chapter 1, "I shall first then speak of Europe, the foster-mother of that people which has conquered all other nations, and itself by far the most beauteous portion of the earth. Indeed, many persons have, not without reason, considered it, not as a third part only of the earth, but as equal to all the rest, looking upon the whole of our globe as divided into two parts only, by a line drawn from the river Tanais [Don] to the Straits of Gades [Gibraltar]. The ocean, after pouring the waters of the Atlantic through the inlet which I have here described, and, in its eager progress, overwhelming all the lands which have had to dread its approach, skirts with its winding course the shores of those parts which offer a more effectual resistance, hollowing out the coast of Europe especially into numerous bays, among which there are four Gulfs that are more particularly remarkable."[27]

This geography was so widely known that Galileo, in his *Dialogue Concerning Two World Systems* (1632) has the foil Simplicio alude to it: "From the oldest records we have it that formerly, at the Straits of Gibraltar, Abila and Calpe were joined together with some lesser mountains which held the ocean

26. O'Connell. "Atlantipedia."

27. Pliny the Elder. *Historia Naturalis.*

in check; but these mountains being separated by some cause, the opening admitted the sea, which flooded in so as to form the Mediterranean."[28]

More recently, C. S. Rafinesque (1834) argues for the origin of Amerindians, "The clearest traditions point to the east, Africa and Europe then united at the Strait of Gibraltar, and the Island Atlantis as a stepping place."[29]

H. G. Wells (1920) suggests,

> "But if this reasoning is sound, then where today roll the blue waters of the Mediterranean there must once have been great areas of land, and land with a very agreeable climate. This was probably the case during the last Glacial Age, and we do not know how near it was to our time when the change occurred that brought back the ocean waters into the Mediterranean basin . . . The people of the Mediterranean race, may have gone far towards the beginnings of settlement and, civilization in that great lost Mediterranean valley."[30]

Skipping to more recent sources, Maltese author Joseph S. Ellul (1988) encouragingly interprets Gen 7:11 and 8:2 "*fountains of the great deep bursting forth*" as the collapse of the Gibraltar Dam.[31] David Hatcher Childress (1996) proposed a date of 9000 BC for dam collapse and flooding of a desiccated Mediterranean;[32] and Paulino Zamarro Sanz (2000) suggested "that a Gibraltar dam was created by silting when the Atlantic was very much lower during the last Ice Age and that it lasted until 7,500 years ago when it was breached and destroyed Atlantis."[33] As recently as 2006, Robert Sarmast led two expeditions to Cypriot waters looking for evidence of submerged Atlantis.[34] Other recent writers on this theory include Georgeos Diaz-Montexano, Alberto Arecchi, and Constantin Benetatos.[35]

This model also makes sense of a scene in the *Gilgamesh Epic* (c. 2900 BC), where the hero Gilgamesh is searching for eternal life. He is directed to the ancient survivor of a major flood, a Noah figure who tells him to pluck a leaf from a special tree at the bottom of the sea called "Old Man Grown Young, I will eat it myself and be again as I was in my youth! (XI 299–300)"[36] Now when multiple independent sources confirm a hypothesis, the result is

28. Galilei. *Dialogue.*

29. Rafinesque. *The American Nations.*

30. Wells. *The Outline of History*

31. Ellul. *Malta's Prediluvian Culture.*

32. Childress. *Lost Cities of Atlantis.*

33. Zamarro-Sanz. *De Gibraltar a la Atlantida.*

34. Sarmast. *Discovery of Atlantis.*

35. Diaz-Montexano. *ATLÁNTIDA;* Arecchi. "Atlantide"; Benetatos. *"Atlantis History."*

36. George. *The Epic of Gilgamesh.*

greater than the sum because the probability is the product of its parts. Thus a Med bed flood supported by both science and myth was strong confirmation to develop the hypothesis further.

2.3.3 Local Flood Explains Genesis 7:11

But what makes a good theory is not just the number of anecdotes or corroborating testimonies, but the explanatory power of the theory. A Med bed flood should illuminate other aspects of the story that otherwise have little or no justification on their own, and have therefore been treated as "metaphorical" or "poetic." Testing the hypothesis then, we look for a poetic phrase that is little regarded in the current interpretation, but offers extra information under the new hypothesis.

In Gen 7:11 we have just such a phrase: "*the fountains of the great deep burst forth, and the windows of the heavens were opened,*" a metaphor repeated nearly verbatim in Gen 8:2, "*the fountains of the deep and the windows of the heavens were closed.*"

Why is it that two different verbs describe the beginning of the flood and the rain, but a single verb describes their end? Do we close rain in the same way that we close fountains? And what exactly is a "fountain of the deep"?

Strongs #	in Noah	Elsewhere	Hebrew
H4599(fountain)	2/23	21/23 "spring"	מַעְיְנֹת
H8415(deep)	2/37	20/37 "ocean floor"	תְּהוֹם
		11/37 (opp. heaven)	
		1/37 "spring"	
+H7227(great)	3/8	3/8 "great waters"	רַבָּה

Table 2.6: The meaning of מַעְיְנֹת תְּהוֹם רַבָּה (*ma'yanot tehowm rabbah*) in Gen 7:11.

A search on *ma'yan* (Strong's H4599), "fountains," finds 2/23x in this Noah story, where the other 21/23x are translated "spring," designating the source of a creek or a river. Of those uses, 3/23x use spring metaphorically: Ps 87:7 "spring of joy," Isa 12:3 "spring of salvation," and in Prov 5:16 to refer to adultery. None of these uses invokes any sense of the meaning of the Flood story's "fountains of the great deep."

Likewise, the nearby word, *tehowm* (H8415) "deep," appears 2/37x in the Noah story, 20/37x corresponding to the bottom of the ocean, 11/37x referring to a counterpart of heaven, and 1/37x translated "spring." As can be seen from Gen 1:2, the opposite of heaven may not always be the solid earth but rather non-solid water, which often means a body of salt-water elsewhere.

Combining both terms in "great deep" (H8415 + H7227) narrows 37x down to 8x with 3/8x being exactly the same as Gen 7:11 and 3/8x featuring parallel constructions such as "the deep and its great waters." In these cases, *rab tehowm,* "great deep" always refers to a saltwater sea, in contrast to *ma'yan,* "fountain," which always meant a fresh water source for a river.

Therefore Gen 7:11 is combining the idea of "fresh-water fountain" with "salt-water sea," in a unique and paradoxical usage. If we search on the NAS English translation for "spring" and "sea," we find that the only other conjunction is in Job 38:16 "*have you entered into the springs of the sea*" with the very next verse mentioning "*gates of death.*" If we go back to the immediate context, we find Job 38:8, "*Or who enclosed the sea with doors When, bursting forth, it went out from the womb.*" So I conclude that Job 38:8 and Gen 7:11 are discussing the same "saltwater springs," which is also the conclusion of some recent scholarship.[37] And Job 38 associated that saltwater spring with doors or gates that can be burst open, apparently with deadly results.

Therefore the usage "*fountains of the deep*" in Gen 7:11 and 8:2 is not metaphorical but rather refers specifically to a saltwater dam or gate. This reading supports the hypothesis that the Flood was in part due to a rupture of the straits (or Gates) of Gibraltar (Figure 2.3).

Furthermore, the rain that falls from the "windows/doors/sluicegates of heaven" is causally connected to the saltwater gates. Thus when the saltwater ocean floods the hot dry plains, the resulting evaporation provides exactly the right conditions for a hurricane. That is consistent with Gen 7:11 where the floods precede the rains. But the cessation of flooding also means the cessation of salt water evaporating from the hot ground. The end of one is the end of the other. Other than a miraculous mechanism (which may be an oxymoron), the connection between rain patterns and a salt-water flood provides a causal connection that neatly explains these verbs. This unexpected synergy of hypothesis and new discoveries is an illustration of "explanatory power."

37. Rodriguez. "Genesis and Creation."

2.3.4 Local Flood Matches other data

One could raise many textual objections to this local flood interpretation, such as "mountains covered," "waters receding," or the need to put birds in the ark, and I will address them in due course. But first let us look at some scientific objections. If the Gates were closed before the Flood so as to make Eden a fertile valley, then there should be a recent geological record of a dry valley at the bottom of the Med, with large salt plains from the evaporated salt water.

Why have they never been observed? For that matter, if the Gates were closed and the Gulf Stream stopped, would not the glaciation record show cold weather before the Flood? Why then did the last global glaciation period end 20,000 years ago, long before the purported Flood narrative?

The salt plains of Eden may have dissolved with the Flood if they were not too thick. That is to say, if the drying out of Eden was geologically brief, lasting only a few thousand years, then the salt plains might never have been as extensive as those from five to six million years ago, and might therefore be rarely observed. Likewise, the rapid drying out and refilling of the Mediterranean basin would have prevented the erosion of shoreline that is the signature of a paleo-beach. And this is also the answer to the second objection: The most recent European glaciation, known as the Younger Dryas, was local and lasted only about 1300 years, from 10,900–9590 BC, ending with a very abrupt warming of less than a few years' duration.[38] The abruptness of the warming is unprecedented in the glacial record, and provides another clue that something catastrophic happened.[39]

Because the accepted opinion is that the 1300-year cooling was related to the stopping of the Gulf Stream, several theories have been advanced as to how this warm ocean current might have been abruptly turned on and off. Some recent papers suggest that weather changes caused by a meteorite impact that littered tektites (glass spherules) across North America and Britain may have stopped the Gulf Stream.[40] I suggest a more direct effect may have occurred if this fireball (c. 10,900 BC) hit the Atlantic near North Carolina, sent a tidal wave across the ocean, and/or made a direct hit in the Mediterranean itself. The following is a nutshell synopsis—further developed in later chapters—of the chain of events that I hypothesize created Eden and ended with the Flood.

38. Praetorius and Mix. "Synchronization" 444.

39. Broecker et al. "Putting the Younger Dryas" 1078–1081.

40. Firestone et al. "Evidence" 16016–16021; Wu et al. "Origin" E3557–E3566; Wittke et al. "Evidence" E2088– E2097; Petaev et al. "Large Pt" 12917–12920.

The tidal wave generated by the fireball impact into the Atlantic or the Mediterranean would have been directed by the Spanish-African coastline into the Straits of Gibraltar, where it may have raised rocks and earth to lift the Camarinal Sill 250 meters and block the Gates. Sea level was forty meters lower at the time, while the sill was higher and undamaged by the Flood. Alternatively, the near circular basin between Algeria and Spain (see Figure 2.3) could have been the result of a direct impact whose raised rim formed the Gates.[41] Either way, the consequent cessation of the Gulf Stream would have plunged Europe into a local ice age called the Younger Dryas and begun the drying out of the Mediterranean. This cooling European climate did not stop the warming that continued elsewhere across the globe, known as the Bølling-Allerød warming that preceded the Younger Dryas.[42] That warming precipitated superfloods on the Eurasian rivers that caused the Caspian Sea to overflow into the Black Sea and then into the Med bed. It also caused Lake Victoria to overflow into the Nile and then into the Med. Thus would the events of Gen 2:5 begin—the founding of the Garden circa 10,700 BC, with new rivers to water it and a new race to cultivate it.

The temperature at the bottom of the Grand Canyon is always 28F/16C warmer than at the rim because air compresses and heats (adiabatic lapse rate) when it falls 1600 meters into the Canyon. At 3000 meters below sea level, the Med bed would feel more like hell than paradise, for it would have been the hottest place on the planet, hotter than 131F/55C record-holder Death Valley, California at eighty-six meters below sea level. This scorching heat sped the evaporation of the Mediterranean from 1000 years to 200 years. It took the ending of the Bølling-Allerød warm period and a resumption of the cold European Dryas glaciation before the Med bed temperature was tolerable. The reduced rainfall/snowfall of the Younger Dryas, however, also meant that less water was available for irrigation. That was because the drying Black Sea dropped below the Bosporus sill and could no longer flow into the Med bed. Thus, the two main concerns of a prospective Edenite farmer would have been to avoid a saltwater flood from the Gates or a freshwater drought from the rivers. This fragile culture was brought to an abrupt end by Noah's Flood that refilled the Mediterranean in less than a year, restarted the Gulf Stream, ended the Younger Dryas glaciation of Europe, and scattered civilization to the four corners of the Earth.

Considerable scientific evidence seems to support a Med bed Flood at 9590 BC, which is, admittedly, older than both Bishop Ussher's 4004 BC date and the 3115 BC genetic date mentioned earlier. The Younger Dryas/

41. Westerman. "Seismic Circles."

42. Thiagarajan et al. "Abrupt pre-Bølling–Allerød" 75–78.

Pre-Boreal (YD/PB) transition for the Flood, however, is determined with multiple data sets, using both well calibrated Carbon-14 (C-14) radioactive dating, Greenland ice-cores, and soil sediment boundaries at multiple sites. Thus it is unlikely to shift very much.[43] Then I have two basic options to reconcile the accounts: Find reasons to push the textual and genetic evidence back six more millennia or search for other climactic events more recent than the Younger Dryas. Following the rabbinic *midrash* approach, I attempt to hold all possibilities in mind in order to compare and contrast their unique predictions.

Addressing the genetic uncertainty, I have already noted that the 3115 BC "genetic variation" date could perhaps be lengthened to 8230 BC, which places it very close to my Flood date and makes it consistent with the outbreeding (with Cro-Magnons) time period of Noah's grandchildren.

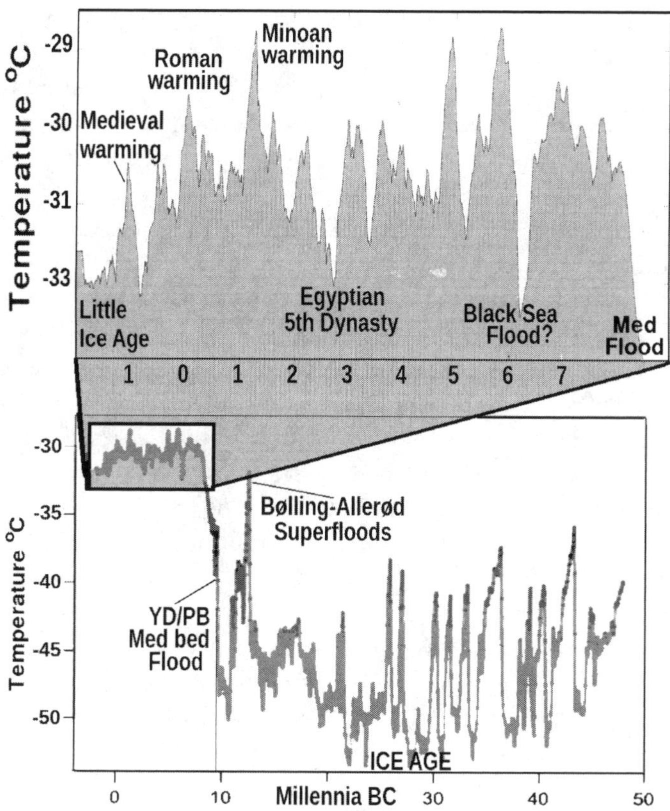

Figure 2.4: Greenland temperatures inferred from Oxygen-18 GISP2-ice core. (Wiki Commons)

43. Kobashi et al. "4±1.5°C abrupt warming" 397–407.

The text is also uncertain, for in the LXX, the Greek translation completed around 200 BC and a full 1000 years before the Masoretic tradition began to preserve the Hebrew text, the ages of the Noah's descendants are greatly expanded. The LXX adds roughly 1000 years and the extra generation of Cainan (which also appears in Luke's but not Matthew's gospel). Likewise, since the Messiah was often called, "the son of David," while kings were said to "sleep with their fathers," some scholars suggest that genealogies play fast and loose with terminology and might skip several generations, so that "son of" might often mean "great-grandson of," allowing for perhaps 4000 years to be inserted into the Genesis 10 genealogy.[44]

Another textual approach is the "gap theory." On that view, an undisclosed gap appears in the narrative, caused perhaps by the same name appearing twice in a genealogy and a later scribe skipping the intervening text. In that case, the gap is most conveniently located in Genesis 1:2, or in Genesis 10, during the time of linguistic diversification of Noah's descendants.[45] This is by no means an exhaustive list of critical approaches nor even an implicit endorsement of textual criticism, but simply an example of the methods used by even conservative scholars to reconcile the text with the data. I take it as encouragement not to abandon the Med bed hypothesis too quickly.[46]

Alternatively, I can assume scientific uncertainty and search for other climactic events that occurred more recently than the Younger Dryas. Two or three cooling events can be seen in the Greenland Ice Sheet Project ice-cores (GISP2) data of Figure 2.4 in addition to the unparalleled 9600 BC event: a 6200 BC event perhaps related to Black Sea flood and a smaller 2800 BC event. If they fit the text better, they fit the science worse because they tend to have C-14 dates more recent than the Neolithic Revolution, which I believe to be a post-Flood development. Others have focused on the 6200 BC event as having the potential to be the Flood. I believe that there are too many factors disqualifying it. For one thing its temperature disruption was less than a quarter of the size of the 9590 BC event and was less abrupt.

But what is more significant than selecting the appropriate climactic event is that the identification of Noah's Flood with a rupture at the Gates allows us to place Eden, the Garden, Adam and Eve, and the entire first six chapters of Genesis in the eastern Med bed approximately 6,000–10,000

44. Ham. *The New Answers Book.*

45. Madsen. "The Gap Theory"; Batten. "What is the gap theory?"

46. Poythress. *Christian Interpretations.*

years ago. And once we have a place and a time, we can start constructing a geological time line to fit all the events into one cohesive story.

Is this not at odds with archaeology and paleoanthropology?

Perhaps, or perhaps it is the fulfillment of them both. Science is mute and text is blind,[47] but together they can unite artifact and legend. Not only does this account unify many mysterious events of the Neolithic, it also explains that interval between the Neolithic and the Historic when stories were oral, history was myth, and myth history. We find that instead of Genesis discrediting myth, Genesis and myth work together to describe the countryside and conditions of the Flood. Not only does Genesis benefit from a cohesive chronology but so does myth, for then ancient myth becomes a coherent story of prehistory.

I began with a defense of Noah, and to my surprise rediscovered Eden, Adam, and the gods.

47. Einstein. *Science, Philosophy and Religion.*

PART 3

The untold story of blood.

Figure 3.0: Line drawing of bas-relief of Rhea & Cronus from Capitoline Museum. (Wiki Commons)

CHAPTER 3

Cain and Abel

3.1 Kanu's Rule

A LOW GREEN HILL BEGAN the rolling foothills of a tree-clothed ridge that climbed ever higher eastward shading into green, brown, and purple until it merged with snow-covered mountains in the hazy distance. All was now lit by the setting sun. To the west, the hills gave way to plains covered in tall golden grass, rippling outward to a flat horizon that seemed to meld into a reddened sky. Patchy clouds etched by the now horizontal light floated leisurely against a dominating blue sky that yielded only to fixed mountain clouds in the west. A human figure, small against this majestic backdrop, climbed the first hill, then stood motionless amid the swaying grass.

Kanu had climbed the last rise without even breaking into a sweat, and he took in its beauty with a calculating eye.

"A meter of rain at least," he said to himself, "and meltwater streams to tap. No danger of flooded fields. Mines lie within a day's journey. Good hunting too, near mountains, plains and deserts. This is a place a man can ever live and never leave!"

Taking his walking stick, he stretched up to his full height and drove it, two-fisted, a meter into the soil.

He examined the stick. "Yes," he said,"it is rich. It will be the new garden, the new Eden. No, more than a garden, it will be a garden of the minds, a garden of knowledge, of the future when I am gone. It will be my child's garden, and my child's child's garden, dedicated to the future of my race."

With his heel pressing into the soft turf, Kanu dug out one line from the walking stick toward the setting sun, another east toward the mountains, another north and the last one to the south. Suddenly dropping to his knees, he laid his forehead on the walking stick and pressed it against his ridged scalp. "El," he said, "May you bless this spot with your presence, and may your wisdom never depart."

Rising to his feet he abruptly turned and raced the shadows down into the valley from which he had come.

Years later the mountains still looked majestically over the grassy plain, but a double-tracked path could be seen arriving from the west. Upon rising from the plains, it became wider and was paved with stone. Soon it was a shady boulevard with trees spaced twenty meters apart approaching the hill. Once the road began to climb, the trees gave way stone pillars, rectangular rocks marching up the hill. As the road crested the rise, the standing stones parted to encircle a structure that appeared to be made of tall slabs of stone, almost as if the mountains had leaned down to grace the hill with cliffs. Inside this circle of stones was a stone portico, whose columns and lintels nearly surrounded a flagged, open courtyard. Each of the pillars was carved in intricate bas-relief; one with a leaf, another with a head of grain, then a four-footed animal or serpentine lizard.

In that courtyard, on colorful blankets or straw-covered stones, was a noisy market. One blanket might offer a mound of wheat while another displayed pottery bowls. Here and there, lay a few animals tethered by coarsely woven fiber ropes. A scrawny sheep shared a straw-covered mat with what appeared to be a mangy wildcat. The cat, at least, was not taking the matter peacefully. Its hissing and spitting prompted bystanders to give it a wide berth. Some blankets held trinkets, and others featured wooden farming implements. There did not seem to be any overall organization to the layout except that animals seemed to usually be near a corresponding animal pillar and grain to be near a pillar decorated with sheaves.

But more striking than the almost random sorts of wares for sale were the people who wandered about or tended to the animals. Some were short and stout, with black beady eyes looking distrustfully out from under bushy eyebrows and mats of dark hair. Their shapeless clothes seemed functional but unadorned. Mixed in with them and equally numerous was a two-meter tall, fair-skinned race with high foreheads, blue eyes and wildly fashioned hair: long auburn braids, braided beards, twisted mustaches. Their clothes were as bizarre as their hairstyles, with fabrics made of hair or hide or twisted rope, dyed all manner of natural colors— black, brown, burgundy, yellow, red, and ocher—and decorated sporadically with colorful stones and bits of mica. Yet common to both groups were stone blades, tucked into their belts or hanging on a thong around their necks. The thick, rounded stone backs were often blackened with age and crusted with use.

And here and there, sprinkled like nuts among the fallen leaves, were the People. They did not appear to be a race because no two of them looked alike, but there was no mistaking their identity. Their faces looked old and young at the same time; they had bronzed skin with lines about the eyes, yet their cheeks were still plump with youth. Their eyes might be black, blue, or green and their wide faces sparkled with life. Yet they also seemed weary and easily distracted. But what attracted the most notice was their height. All were over two and a half meters tall, and several approached three meters, which meant they often had to couch to deal with with much shorter people. But they were not misshapen; it was a graceful gigantism that produced slender women and heroic men. Their hair and beards were carefully trimmed, their clothes, whether skin, fabric, or metal, were as carefully fashioned as the others were not.

It was the People who moved about the market, examining goods, calling out numbers or conferring among themselves. The shorter tribe was mostly silent, though occasionally someone exclaimed loudly, creating a brief ruckus in the immediate vicinity. The middling tribe, on the other hand, was loud but not communicative. They would hum or sing repetitive songs, abuse each other and assail the shorter ones with musical shouts. One needed a loud voice to be heard over the clamor.

A peculiar order could be discerned in the chaos. Wherever the taller People went, they became the center of attention, as if they were buyers and everyone else a seller, except that nothing seemed to change hands.

Occasionally, there would be a commotion, and after some lengthy negotiations, a little knot of people would move away from the market, over the crest of the hill toward some low buildings on the other side. Although the buildings were the most prominent structures, they were not the only structures spreading around and down the back of the hill, keeping the market between them and the plains. This was clearly more than a trading post, it was a city. It was the City and it had a name, Enok.

Enok had been Kanu's first son. He had died of a genetic disease. No one was sure what the disease was but his death had become the universal explanation for nearly all the indecipherable decisions trickling down from the town council. For example, it was decided that domesticated animals—cows, sheep, cats—should never be eaten, but should be "under-citizens" of the city. The sheep provided wool, the cows provided milk, and the cats provided intolerance of everything else alive. This food taboo completely mystified the middling race, who evidently had acquired quite a taste for meat, but Kanu was firm—no domestic meat, ever. Rumor had it that eating meat had killed Enok, and an even darker rumor held that meat had nearly killed Kanu. It was partly the ban on meat that caused the middling race to settle far from Enok, although what they had was hardly much of a settlement. They lived high up in the mountains in caves and fortresses frequented by mountain goats and eagles, it was said, and only visited the market for a few days before vanishing again into the hills.

It was the shorter race of cragmen that had settled in Enok, or at least in the outskirts of Enok. They cultivated the fields of wheat and barley, built the stone buildings and aqueducts, cleaned the streets and marketplace, and raked the muck from the stables and irrigation ditches. Enok was always enlarging its fields or trying out new types of agriculture and it was the ever cheerful cragmen who did the work. Communication was not easy; the Adamites gesticulated and play-acted to make their wishes known. It was not that the cragmen were mute, but rather that many had a very limited vocabulary, perhaps a hundred words, of which most were nouns. A complex project would often take almost as long to explain as to finish. But the effort was usually worthwhile because the cragmen attacked the task with such dedication and perseverance it was often necessary to physically restrain them at times.

With such a willing labor force, Kanu had only to provide food and shelter, though that proved more difficult than it first appeared. In the early days of Enok, the fields produced little grain. The stems were weak, the heads were tiny, and the amount collected barely repaid the effort involved. A late rainstorm might rot the grain resulting in many deaths from the poisonous ergot. Before the aqueduct was functioning, a summer drought could take the whole crop. Even now, with the expansion of the grain fields, there were years when the water supply was insufficient and some fields went without water. When these disasters struck, the population of Enok would shrink, as the cragmen drifted back to the plains or the hills, searching for wilder food. Often it would be years before Enok attracted them back, so the Adamites were faced with a chronic labor shortage.

Kanu solved this himself, "without El's help," he would add, by fashioning collars for his steers and teaching them to drag a plow. And while all the Adamites learned to plow before they could run, none of the cragmen showed any ability with animals. The efforts would always devolve into a shouting match, the steer going one way and the cragman the other to the voluble amusement of all. It wasn't that the cragmen could not understand the plow or the purpose of plowing, it was rather that they could not understand the cow. Or as Kanu would grimly say

"You can't plow an eatin' cow."

After the plowing, the second hardest task was reaping. The grain had to be gathered when it was ripe, for if it lay in the fields too long, the rains, locusts, or black rot would finish it first. Kanu had to teach the cragmen to go through the fields stripping the seed heads into a basket. It was a hopeless task at first. The cragmen collected little because the seeds would either be too green and difficult to strip or too ripe and already falling off the stalks. He tried wooden "stripping hooks" and multiple passes through a field but each pass resulted in more trampled grain. In the end a worker collected no more grain than he consumed during the rest of the year. If it were not for the wild game, which emptied Enok of cragmen throughout the spring and fall, the city would have never have grown larger than a trading post.

Kanu and the council worked hard to solve this problem. They needed many citizens for survival. They could offer housing, clean water, and security but in those early years, there was not sufficient food. Of course there were warehouses and storage bins, with many dedicated felines to eliminate pests, and yet most years would still end with everyone on half-rations, hungrily awaiting the early barley harvest. And in bad years, the plowing had to be done by weakened workers with withered thighs, hardly able to handle the plow or the rambunctious teams, so that many fields went unplanted. A short string of bad years, Kanu knew, would annihilate his life mission along with Enok, his child.

As with most things in his life, Kanu would recall with bitterness, the answer did not come from El. Instead, he was out watching the harvesters when he saw a cragman get out his stone blade and cut four or five stalks of trampled grain. Holding the stalks in one hand, he pulled the stalk over the hand holding the stone, dropping the seeds into the basket. It wasn't a particularly efficient way to harvest, but Kanu was inspired. If one cragman went ahead and cut the stalks, then another could collect them without trampling ripe grain into the mud. Then they could be stored safely away from the rain until there was time to strip the seed heads and remove the husks. All he needed was a better way to cut the stalks.

Kanu tried to use the stone knives but the tough stalks needed sawing, requiring a second hand to grip a handful of straw. And while it was slightly faster than seed stripping, the rough handling shook many seeds loose. Besides, the small hands of the cragmen made them so slow as to be almost a hindrance to the Adamite reapers. "Of course I can send every able-bodied man into the fields," Kanu said in the council, "but it is not right to feed the cragmen on the sweat of our brow, for how then will it benefit Enok?"

The cragmen had another tool in their kit, though one they rarely took outside because of its weight. It was a stone blade several times larger than the hand-held version, sporting a notch carved into the blunt side that permitted a wooden handle to be strapped on. When a job needed force, such as breaking the thigh bone of a slaughtered ox to get at the marrow or retrieving firewood from dead snags, this was the preferred tool. It was called an ax or an adze by the Adamites depending on the angle at which the handle was strapped to the blade, though the cragmen made no distinction. Kanu had them use their adzes in the field, but to cut through the tough stalks, the blade had to be swung with such speed that it completed a full circle over their heads. Not a few heads of all sorts were lost.

After several years of experimentation, Kanu finally hit upon a design that worked for both cragmen and Adamites. It was thin like a knife, though longer and notched like an adze, so that it could be secured by a handle. But the real innovation lay in the blade, which curved inward like a crescent moon. When it encountered the tough stalks it would drag them toward the center and simultaneously saw them. With a little practice, the stalks could be cut in an easy, horizontal motion of the arm, and the grain heads bunched together as they fell, for ready retrieval. The cragmen were delighted. Attaching a long handle meant that the Adamites need not stoop, so even Kanu could enjoy an afternoon of reaping with his stone sickle. But more importantly, the city could be fed, and once again Kanu could return to the pursuit of the cure for the curse.

A rectangular building with many columns supporting its shallow peaked roof was the most prominent structure among those that clustered around the hill. A group of three tall men and a small woman stood inside, at the foot of a large stone seat occupied by a white-haired man. Kanu looked over the candidate with jaded eyes. "What have you discovered today, Shammi, a blue-eyed singing maiden or a dumb giantess?"

The words were light-hearted but the intent was serious. Everyone knew that Kanu had spent his life on this project, that failure was not an option, for as he often repeated, failure meant certain death. And of course, everyone also knew just how many failures, how many decades he had devoted to it. The centuries had not been kind to Kanu; while his back was straight and his step was firm, the lines about his eyes were chiseled deep into his face. He did not have many more decades left. It was a race against time, or rather, a race against the ravaging of time.

Shammi shifted his weight and answered carefully, "My Lord, it is most peculiar. We bring you a maiden from the South. We rescued her on the borders of the desolate sands, where she nearly died of thirst. She had traveled in the company of five men and three women from the dark coast of much disease and her companions had perished on the way. Yet behold, she is clean and without fever. Could she be in possession of our Mother's blessing?"

Kanu shifted his gaze to the woman, and for a short instant held her eyes before she blushed and lowered her face. For a few moments he stared at her before declaring as if to an unseen hearer, "She has worms, malaria and possibly smallpox scars. Has my essence become too cheap?"

Shammi stammered. "But, but, my Lord, even our Mother had no protection against such assaults. There is no immunity to worms. And those aren't smallpox scars. Look at the lines, they were made by human hands. Yet this is hardly the wonder that caused me to bring her to you. It was the speed of her return from the shores of death. We had no sooner given her water than she lifted up her head and begged to be permitted to carry our water skins, if she could travel with us. We have been traveling for weeks since then, yet she has never flagged for strength."

Kanu did not reply for several long minutes but rather fixed his eyes on her feet. They were bare and calloused, obviously accustomed to harsh terrain and long journeys, and very unlike the soft, sandaled feet of Shammi and the Adamites. Finally he broke his silence with a sigh.

"Put her in Building 7. There should be room today after the weekend births. And start her on the wormwood. You know the routine."

A dozen long, low buildings, clustered around the back of the hill, served as dormitories. Some were for newcomers, and they were harsh and bare—their stone floors easily washed down with water from the aqueduct coming down from the mountains. Others were more elaborate. There were comfortable arrangements for the expectant mothers and well-equipped facilities for birthing. But it was clear that the highest priority, at least in buildings, was for children. There was a nursery for the infants, a playground for the toddlers, a kindergarten, and a gymnasium for the pre-teens. There was even a college for the youth to train and induct men and women into citizenship in the city of Enok.

"How is it that time has become our enemy and not our friend?" Kanu would begin his lectures to the young initiates. "Long ago, before I was born, our Mother lost the power to transmit to her children the blueprint of El, to repair the errors that in the course of time crept into El's infallible design. She passed on this corruption to her children. If she had not lost this ability, El's image would have remained unchanged through many generations. And perhaps I would have been happily tilling the soil of Eden with our Father today. But as El willed it, this was not to be. Instead, every child, every generation of the blessed ones has been collecting mistakes that are destroying our heritage, our birthright. We are discovering diseases, mutations, defects in our own offspring that are not even found among the benighted cragmen. Before long we will be unable to prevent our degeneration into the mute ones even were we able to find the cure to our Mother's curse. Therefore we must use the methods that El gave us to repair the methods that El took away. If He will not permit proper propagation of our bodies, then we will use our minds; if He will deny us repair, then we will learn recreation; if He will corrupt physical replication, then we will sanctify manipulation."

It was easy for Kanu to preach to the initiates from a position of age and experience; it was much harder to convince his relatives. "Kanu," Raya pleaded while removing her coat, "You can't undo the curse of El. Give it up. Surely there are sufficient tasks left in the taming of this world to amply reward your efforts."

Raya, like Kanu, stood head and shoulders above the cragwoman who silently took her cloak while another brought her a platter of fruit. She smiled her thanks, and the woman beamed with pride while backing out through the doorway. But Raya was still much shorter than Kanu, and softer. In contrast to his angular form and lined brows, her round face seemed filled with dimples, or would have been if it had not been drawn haggard by lack of sleep. For it had been a long trip, and judging from the thickness of her cloak, it had taken her up into the highlands of the cragmen.

"You cannot tame the past," she said while smoothing her tunic to sit on a stone bench padded with rushes, "Why do you insist on taming El?"

"No man tames El," Kanu almost growled, "but every man must tame himself. How else can we fulfill our destiny?"

It was a worn argument and well-traveled, but Raya was not going to rest until she had made her point. She spoke intensely. "Look at yourself!" Kanu's hand jerked instinctively but he willed it back to his side.

Raya continued. "You are thin. You are old. And you still think you need taming?"

"You know what I mean, Raya. It is the blood line. It is the inheritance. It is the children who grow wild and untamed."

"Children!" Raya half rose from her bench. "What do you know about children? You treat them as, as your subjects, as your cragmen, as your precious plow teams! Filling their heads with nonsense, demanding their allegiance to your project, your obsession. And what has all this," she swept her arm in a half-circle, "this city ever done for our children? Has it made them strong and swift? Has it made them glorious and proud of their inheritance? Has it made them as wise as our Father or as content as our Mother?" She dropped her voice to a half whisper.

"Has it pleased El?"

Kanu flushed, which turned his scar crimson. He opened his mouth but shut it again without saying anything. Then after a long moment he turned and looked out the window that admitted the rays of the setting sun. The fields were a patchwork of golden grain and stubble, all lit up by the orange sunset. Several tall reapers could be seen out in the field wielding their scythes, followed by a short army of gleaners, bent double to their tasks.

"You've been to the Cretan Mountains, haven't you." he said after a while.

"Yes."

"Getting cold?"

She nodded her head.

"And the baby . . .?" his words trailed off.

"Died." Her face was expressionless.

He turned and stared at her intently. "You should have stayed here. We have the best trained midwives . . ."

"Bah!" she spat. "Trained in what? Trained in sorting puppies! Trained in killing babies!"

Kanu spoke slowly, "We don't kill babies."

"You might as well have been." Raya remained defiant.

"You should have stayed."

"No. I would rather be with my maidens, with Mother's people."

"But he died anyway?"

"Especially on that account."

Kanu sighed. After a while he turned and asked, "Where is he, now?"

Raya met his level gaze but said nothing. Their eyes battled silently, until finally Raya turned to the window. The sun had set and the western sky was a mass of purple and salmon clouds. The field workers, now like smudges of charcoal, were trailing back into the city.

"I came as soon as I was strong enough for the journey" she finally replied. "Mosin made the baby a box, a soapstone box. It's in—he's in the donkey basket."

Kanu stood in the dusk, staring at Raya until she dropped her head. Then without a word, he strode out of the room. Raya sat quite still as the echo of his footsteps faded. Then her shoulders began to shake, and shook for a long time in the dark.

* * *

It was the beginning of another beautiful day in Enok, which had added more fields and another acre of buildings in the two decades since. The sun had just broken free of the mountains to the east, and daylight was spilling sideways over the city, lighting the green fields to the west while leaving the city in morning shadow. The angled sunlight illuminated a trickle of smoke rising from behind the hill, creating a blue cloud over the city that rested almost motionless in the still morning air. Surprisingly, a large crowd was standing on the pavement. What was equally surprising, was that it was completely silent. Everyone was straining to listen to a tall man mounted on a fallen pillar at the east side of semi-circular marketplace.

"It was foreordained." Kanu spoke evenly, but with strong emotion. "My own son has lifted up his hand against his kindred. You have all seen what he has done to our city. He has broken its pillars, burned the Houses of Knowledge, and killed those in the Houses of the Repaired. Today he has undone all that we have accomplished, all that we strove for, all–" And then Kanu stopped, for what had come from his lips was a deep cry, ending on a strangled note. His throat was constricted; his forehead was lined with crimson. After a brief pause, he began again in a quieter voice.

"We have been betrayed by Raya. Even now she has fled to Crete with that wild son of hers, Zeru. She deceitfully raised him there and filled him with malice for our work. They hate Enok without reason, without limit, and will ever strive to see it utterly destroyed."

"What shall we do?" Shammi asked. "Can we prevent them from further destruction? Can we lock them away in the Houses of Mercy?"

"I do not think we can overtake them, or even if we could, that we can stop them or bring their wild band back in bonds."

"What then is to be done?"

Kanu bowed his head and was silent. The crowd began to murmur but ceased as he finally lifted up his face. "There is no counsel that can change them. No words that will convince them. They are beyond reason, beyond help. They have chosen their lot with the beasts, and as beasts they shall be to us. They must be broken as a heifer to the plough. They must be tamed as an ass to the bit. They must be chained to their deeds . . ."

Shammi shouted, alarmed. "My Lord, they are not cragmen! How can you tame Adam's blood?"

Kanu shouted back, "From blood to blood, if needs be! There will be no cure without the shedding of blood."

"My Lord, how can this be? Will you not become like those you rule? What then will separate us from the fate of the red-heads in the wilderness?"

"Listen!" Kanu's eyes were bright and his words came louder and faster. "If they behave as the red-heads with their ambush and their spears, then we will be their lion. If they come against us with boys, we will answer back with men. If they are filled with passion, we will conquer with reason. If they claim our Mother, we will bring our Father. If they conspire to destroy us, we will plan their defeat. If they take our children, we will take their grandchildren. If they avenge seven times, we will avenge seventy-seven—"

The sun rose in strength, as did their voices until the mountains echoed back their angry shouts. A breeze picked itself up from the fog covered plains. The pillar of blue smoke trembled and shook and then, like a breath, vanished into the east.

3.2 Viruses, Genes, Sin

In the previous chapter I looked at the many reasons why the Flood had a global purpose despite a local size, focusing on some of the geological evidence for a catastrophic event. In this chapter I make the case for why genetic corruption was such a heinous crime against humanity and what must be done to correct it.

Theologically, there has been a tendency to apply a thermonuclear exegesis to Genesis and attribute every putative evil condition on the "Fall," which conveniently eliminates the need for further explanation. But this dogmatic reductionism greatly oversimplifies both the cause and its cure. While this theme is not developed in Genesis 3, we get a lengthy account in Genesis 4 of fratricide, of Cain killing his brother Abel, a story that puzzles many theologians and preachers alike.

What happened that would cause a man to murder his brother? Where in human nature does such violence originate? Why does God appear so passive in the story? And if the story of Cain and Abel is a primeval account of the origin of human conflict, what are we to make of all these references to other humans (Gen 4:14)—are they likewise participants in the strife?

Convinced that genetics provides the interpretive key, in this chapter I reexamine Genesis 4 for the message it tells us about genetics, and about sin. I found it surprisingly difficult, partly because I kept stumbling on over-interpreted words like "sin," which took a great deal of effort to pry from the death grip of theologians. I think that the story of Cain elaborates on the consequences of Genesis 3 and sets the stage for Genesis 6. Strangely—for one educated with the usual neglect of the classics—I found the causes of the Fall and the Flood are amply recorded in myth, and even emphasized by interpreters such as Plato. It puzzled me, why should myth understand the Fall and explain Cain?

The answer came as a sudden insight—because myth also remembered Eden!

In that case, we have multiple accounts, multiple memories of this most egregious of sins: the epigenetic degradation of our race.

3.2.1 Genesis and Mythology

We need not go very far into Genesis before we hit stories that are echoed by ancient mythology. For mythology is the same story of our origins but told from the opposite viewpoint. It is the losers of Genesis who are the heroes of myth. And that alone should alert us to the significance of the Genesis account. For centuries, for millennia, it was the victors who wrote the stories, it was their exploits that motivated men, that subordinated women and indoctrinated children. And so, for thousands of years, we have had stories about the great men and women who lived between Eden and history, between the perfect and the present, between high knowledge and deep ignorance. They founded cities, redirected rivers, and plowed plains. They climbed mountain peaks and forded river gorges, they settled frozen steppes and traversed scorched savannas. In a world filled with wild herds, with dangerous predators and treacherous brutes, with demons who could not speak yet carried wicked knives, they conquered and named its inhabitants. So it is with respect that I repeat their names: Odin and Thor, Zeus and Herakles, Indra and Vishnu.

We ought not to approach the classical myths with condescension; rather, we must look beneath the colorful tales of mythological beasts and heroes with understanding. For all men everywhere want to know who we are, where we have come from, and why we no longer live on Olympus, in Asgard, or in Eden with the Immortals. And despite all their accomplishments, despite all the deeds they inspired in the lesser men that followed them, the heroes were unable to bring back the idyllic contentment they so longed for, the Paradise where one could talk with God and laugh at Death. And that is why this forgotten story, rewritten by an exiled Egyptian prince wandering the Sinai wastes, stoops under the weight of glory. For it tells us what no other story ever could. It tells us what God intended for Adam, for Cain, for us. It tells us where we have come from, why we are here, and how we can rediscover Eden to once more walk with God, so that like Enoch, we may never taste Death.

If Genesis is the greatest story ever told, why was it so late in coming? Why was it not told and retold like the sagas and epics of old? Could it be that it is just reworks those old stories, retells the same exploits?

It would be a marvel indeed if, in the millennia that preceded Moses, no one had rediscovered Eden, and yet by accident a recent mash-up of old texts should reveal it! No, a student is not greater than his master (John 13:16), and the copy is no more true than the original. For there is more than the ring of steel in the Genesis account, there is the edge of truth. Retold stories exaggerate details, they make the good heroic and the bad demonic.

In epic accounts, style is as important as substance where, as in an oft-photocopied letter, the gray becomes a stark contrast of black-and-white. In the Genesis story, however, there is a mixture of good and evil, often without elaboration. The contrasts are so pale that rabbis resort to the Talmud, and preachers to the New Testament, to find its subtle evils. If anything, Genesis most closely resembles a compressed message, a telegraph cable with scant explanation or commentary. In centuries past, commentators thought many embroidered filigrees in the account resembled myth, but today each of those details has become a blade that cuts, separating joints from sinew.

This is because today, for the very first time, we have other accounts of Genesis, accounts written in flakes of stone, in coals from a hearth, or in genes extracted from bone. Today we have traced the long untold migrations of peoples across the savannas by tracking their C-14 ashes, their spear points, their DNA variants. After many millennia, hidden messages, like Sumerian cuneiform tablets dug out of the mud, are finally being deciphered. The results are astonishing, for the messages not only corroborate myth, but also Genesis. They shed light on ancestors and communities of long forgotten people groups and—even more exciting— fill in details about which Genesis is silent. In those supposedly extraneous details are entire stories trimmed to their moral lesson.

For example, that may be the reason that the origin of Cain's wife (Gen 4:17) is never explained or why we are told little of Cain's descendants despite their great importance to the Noah story. And why Cain is the beginning of Greek myth. For the story of the one is the anti-story of the other, and the villain of the one is the hero of the other. On this account, mythology and Genesis part ways, only converging when something as dramatic as the Flood happens to both.

Attributing the story of the Flood to a discredited myth does injustice to both. Neither is derivative of the other, for both present authentic viewpoints on the most dramatic event ever to shape human history. They are independent corroborations of a geological event that we are only now beginning to unravel. But rather than take the mythological flood accounts as validation of the Genesis text, I am now prepared to take the Genesis text, along with recent scientific discoveries, as validation of the essential truthfulness of myth. With Genesis as my guide, I can sketch the outlines of Greek myth. I can not only find in Cain the anti-story of the Greek Kronos, but find in his murder of Abel the reason for Kronos's mythological offspring. These offspring appear in the Germanic Beowulf legend, in Norse mythology, in Akkadian Gilgamesh, in Sumerian Atrahasis, Egyptian pyramid texts, and even in the Hindu Vedas.

3.2.2 Genesis 4:1–6 The two trades

Turning then to the text, I find in Gen 2:15 that the very first task assigned to Adam was the tending of the Garden. One would assume that this included watering, weeding, pruning, and picking of the fruits of the Garden. The second job assigned to Adam in Gen 2:19 was the naming of the animals. This does not seem like such hard work, but naming is always the first task of any trade. I'll never forget planting my front yard in Switzerland with "wildflower seeds," then hearing my neighbor complain about the weeds. "Which ones?" I asked innocently, because none of them had flowered yet. "*Alles es umkraut!*" she replied with exasperation. So if Gen 2:15 describes the task of the gardener naming weeds, then Gen 2:19 describes the task of farmer naming breeds. And when in Gen 4:1 Eve gives Adam two sons, it is significant that the elder gardens, and the younger raises animals. Their careers are prioritized in the order in which God had assigned these tasks to Adam.

But does this prioritization have a hidden significance? I had been taught that it was an extraneous detail, a moral lesson about God's arbitrary preference for animal sacrifice over grain offerings. But was it arbitrary?

Paleontology tells us that gardening and grain preceded raising sheep and later cows. Pigs and chickens, the staple of Polynesian settlers, came even later. But what made the Nile river the breadbasket of Egyptian dynasties was not the domesticated cow or sheep, for when Joseph brings his family to Egypt, he instructs his kinfolk (Gen 46:33–34) "*When Pharaoh calls you and says, 'What is your occupation?' you shall say, 'Your servants have been keepers of livestock from our youth even until now, both we and our fathers,' in order that you may dwell in the land of Goshen, for every shepherd is an abomination to the Egyptians.*" Rather, it was grain that began the Neolithic Revolution, grain that permitted farmers more leisure for weaving linen, and grain that founded the cities of the ANE. Sheep and goats could turn inedible grass into wool, milk, and meat, which expanded the habitable areas to include the less-watered grasslands far from Nile irrigation. But we must not forget that it was grain that begat the Neolithic. Herding always seemed suited to rustic nomads, grain to urbane civilization.

Myth supports this interpretation. Kronos is identified with a stone sickle,[1] while the food of both the Greek and Vedic pantheon is from a plant: *ambrosia* and *soma*. Therefore, Cain was given the more privileged task, as befitting the eldest son, and Abel the less privileged one, as demonstrated by the attitude of the Egyptians.

1. Leadbetter. "Cronus."

But if Cain's was the more important task, why then does Gen 4:3–5 recount "*In the course of time Cain brought to the LORD an offering of the fruit of the ground, and Abel also brought of the firstborn of his flock and of their fat portions. And the LORD had regard for Abel and his offering, but for Cain and his offering he had no regard.*"? How can it be that the more important task is treated "with no regard" (KJV "with no respect")? What does it mean to give a job but withhold regard/respect from its completion?

As noted in the preface, permeating Genesis is a record of genes and genetic inheritance that we are only now beginning to decipher. If the reader has borne with me this far, grant me the liberty to draw out the genetic implications of these verses. In the spirit of *midrash*, I am not denying the more obvious meanings of Scripture, I am simply enriching the significance of the text by exploring its other meanings—meanings that until this half century were opaque.

When I was young, during the summers, I would visit my cousins in Iowa and endure the long hours of driving through miles and miles of rippling corn-covered countryside. The mile-long fields were harvested by combines the size of houses, for farms had long since been transformed from a single family's livelihood into huge agribusiness conglomerates. Dividing up the fields every mile, like a precision watch, were gravel roads or barely paved ones marking off the sections of 640 acres each. "A quarter section," my cousins assured me, "will make you a millionaire." As we stared out the back-seat window, rolled down to keep us cool, we saw other, more frequent markers among the otherwise indistinguishable corn. Two or three times along a section, there would be a little sign in the shape of a triangle or a corn cob saying "Pioneer 631" or "DeKalb 6603." My cousins explained, "Oh those indicate what variety of corn is planted in that section. No, farmers don't grow their own seed corn anymore. Everything is a hybrid. And you can't get seed corn from a hybrid." That was why my cousins got work every spring in the Pioneer or DeKalb fields, detasseling corn so that it would not self-pollinate. That enabled the breeder to cross-pollinate his trademark hybrid seed. All this work was well worth it, for hybrid corn would out-grow and out-produce purebred strains.

The reasons for this "hybrid vigor" are somewhat obscure, having to do with the genetic machinery of corn. But all are agreed that the effect vanishes in the next generation, requiring farmers to buy fresh hybrid seed corn every year. That is why you can search the web for Pioneer or DeKalb corn and find hundreds of patented varieties of hybrids, specially tailored for any need.[2] There are just so many it is hard to keep them straight, hence the demure little signs that mark out the fields with coded numbers.

So, in addition to knowing the difference between *kraut und umkraut*, a prospective farmer must know how to breed his plants. He must know what is purebred and what is hybrid. He must even know how to make hybrids on demand. And every year is another chance to experiment, to enlarge, to increase the yield of produce over the previous year. The first cultivated strains of wheat or barley were hardly an improvement over the wild grasses. But over the years breeding caused the seed count in each head to increase, the volume of the seed to increase, and the strength of the stalk to increase—for heavier heads of grain need sturdier stems to hold them. This is the sort of skill the Neolithic farmers learned, as they spread out of the Middle East and fanned across Europe in the great Neolithic Revolution. This was Cain's task. And it was no small task either. The success of Cain led to the founding of cities, and the failure of Cain led to the migration of peoples.

Therefore, when Gen 4:5 says "*God had no regard*," I take it to mean that Cain's breeding efforts had failed. He was not able to improve on the gifts that God had given Adam, his father, while Abel apparently had been very successful in his breeding program for animals.

Why might that be?

We might attribute it to personality; perhaps Cain was indolent and Abel industrious. But impugning Adam's son reminds me of Jude's warning about the disputation of Michael (Jude 8–10), who would not rebuke his superior. Criticizing Cain risks brazenly playing holier-than-thou to men who so greatly surpass us in knowledge and intellect. No, it more than likely related to the difficulties of their respective tasks.

Despite their lowly position compared to animals in human thinking, plants have far more complex genetics. They can even behave like animals. A recent article entitled "The Intelligent Plant" lists animal-like behavior that plants must pre-program into their seeds.[3] After all, a plant cannot move, yet must find a way to maximize unreliable resources, repel mobile pests, and fertilize distant kin. It accomplishes these tasks with remarkable ingenuity—chemical warfare, root network communication, symbiotic bacteria, addicted pollinators, and one other lesser known feature—complex genetics. The reason all those hybrid seed varieties are patented is that it takes a lot of knowledge and effort to develop a useful new variety of corn.

2. Dekalb. "Dekalb hybrids."

3. Pollan. "The Intelligent Plant."

Imagine then that you are Cain and you have crossed your two best varieties of wheat, producing a bumper crop. This year you planted the seeds from that hybrid, hoping for another bumper crop. But all that appears are spindly little plants that collapse before their heads ripen. What if you had done this year after year, only to be disappointed every fall. Meanwhile, your younger brother has been breeding sheep. And they are getting fatter and woollier every year. You know he isn't as experienced as you, you know he's even a bit slow learning his logarithms. So why is he doing so well using the techniques he learned from you, his elder brother? You might reason, "Clearly, this has something to do with God's plan in giving me the more difficult job. But surely, surely He will eventually give me success! Surely He will reward me for my exhausting loyalty!"

Perhaps it finally occurred to Cain that he might spend his entire allotted 900 years without ever matching the accomplishments of his younger, slower brother. That is not to say that Cain had no success but the small improvements in grain production seemed pitiful in comparison with Abel's progress in breeding sheep and cows. It felt completely unfair, yet it was entirely God's doing.

> Gen 4:6 tells us, "*The LORD said to Cain, "Why are you angry, and why has your face fallen? If you do well, will you not be accepted? And if you do not do well, sin is crouching at the door.*"

This passage is generally read as a moral lesson in anger management. But considering the importance of grain to the Nile river civilization, surely something more than personal jealousy is under discussion here, perhaps the threatened mass starvation of the first city, the first civilization. This may be why Cain's face fell.

3.2.3 Genesis 4:7 Cain's Choice

At this point, we first encounter the word "sin" in the MT (*chatta'ath* H2403), which the New American Standard (NAS) translates Gen 4:7 "*If you do well, will not your countenance be lifted up? And if you do not do well, sin is crouching at the door; and its desire is for you, but you must master it.*"

Now we have all heard sin described as a "breaking of God's command," for example when eating the forbidden fruit. Yet strangely, we have no record of God forbidding Cain or anyone else from killing another, so strictly speaking, Cain has not broken any command of God by contemplating murder. Even more strangely, despite the tragic consequences of Adam's disobedience, it was not termed *chatta'ath*, sin. But here, in this passage about Cain's anger, the word first appears. So the disobedience (of Adam) is not a sin, and the sin (of Cain) is not a disobedience.

Why then is *chatta'ath* translated "sin"?

Stem	Gesenius	HALOT
Qal(active)	miss,incur guilt	miss,offend,be culpable,wrong,sin,commit sin
Piel(refl.)	bear loss, purify	bear loss,offering,purify
Hiphil	miss mark,induce sin	miss mark,cause sin,bring guilt
Hitpael(refl.)	lose/purify self	wander,purify

Table 3.1: Verbal noun senses of חָטָא (*chata'*).

Granting that the word is defined as "sin" in later Scriptures and that Scripture interprets Scripture, bear with me a moment, or better yet, give *midrash* a chance to elaborate. Consider the interpretive principle, "What the Old conceals, the New reveals." Could this principle not apply to any chronologically ordered section of Scripture? Could we not say, "What the Torah conceals, the Ketuvim reveals?" or even "What Genesis conceals, Exodus reveals?" We are often given progressive revelation, especially about words. So, if the word *chatta'ath* appears here for the first time, perhaps it has a softer, less black-and-white meaning than when it is used later. Does not David speak for all of us (Ps 25:7) when he prays "remember not the *chatta'ath* of my youth"? If sin hardens with age within us, could it not also be green with the sap of youth in Gen 4:7?

What am I getting at?

Simply that in Gen 4:7, disobedience is not *chatta'ath*, and *chatta'ath* is not disobedience, not yet. When God commands Noah not to shed the blood of men, (Gen 9:6), thereafter disobedience and sin coalesce. But God's message to Cain warns against something that goes beyond unjustified anger against Abel. It points to something that makes Abel more than a victim, but a prophet and a saint. And it forces Cain to choose.

What is this thing, this sin-that-is-not-disobedience, that is crouching at the door?

The question turned out to be a harder nut to crack than I had bargained for. Perhaps because "sin" is such an important theological word, or perhaps because Hebrew has more words in this "word cloud" than in any similar concept, or perhaps because even the Rabbis agree this is Gen 4:7 is hard to translate, many have avoided discussing the term "sin" in Gen 4:7.

Nevertheless, as I hope to demonstrate, there is meat in this nut that will reward the effort. Let us get out the really big hammers and go at it.

From Gesenius's grammar, we learn that *chatta'ath* is a feminine noun derived from the verbal root *chata'*. From Table 3.1 we see that the verb has a nuanced meaning depending on stem (where a stem is somewhat like the passive/active/reflexive "voice" in English). The more up-to-date HALOT Hebrew dictionary gives more meanings for *qal*.[4] Note how the reflexive stems of the verb (*piel, hitpael*) carry the opposite meaning, "to unsin," which suggest that "incurring guilt" is a better translation for *qal* than "missing the mark" because we can not easily "unmiss the mark" but we can "remove guilt." The inclusion of "miss" may be due to the preference of the LXX translators for *hamartia*, to miss the mark. Their views from two centuries before Christ is of great value but, as we argue below, their mistranslation misses the mark.

Linguistic grammars use a completely different jargon from the grammar we learned in grade school, perhaps because they must describe widely different languages. But no matter the jargon, every language recognizes the same property of sentences and verbs—they have an actor, which is subtly different from a subject. Thus it is very significant that *chata'* has a strong dependence on the actor, so that when we *chata'* others it is bad, whereas when we *chata'* ourselves it is good.

chatta'ath	verb	noun	fem.part.
595	239	356	293

fem.part.	Gen	Exo	Lev	Num	Deu	Jos	1Sa	2Sa	1Ki	2Ki	2Ch
293	4	9	66	41	3	1	6	1	16	15	9

Table 3.2: Location of חַטָּאת (*chatta'ath*) in NAS.

Such a usage is unusual.

For example, Jesus's proclamation of the second Greatest Commandment (Matt 22:39) was: "Love your neighbor as you love yourself." If the verb had been *chata'*, he would have needed to say "don't *chata'* your neighbor as you *chata'* yourself." While this pattern is rare, we can find verbs that fit it. Paul says (1 Cor 9:27) "I bruise my body and make it my slave, so that after I have preached to others, I myself will not be disqualified." Certainly, bruising others would be considered a bad thing to do. Other examples might include personal hygiene as well as asceticism, a class of activities that one does only for oneself, not others. In this case, the "badness" is not conveyed

4. Koehler and Baumgartner. *Hebrew and Aramaic Lexicon*.

by the verb alone, but by the combination of "actor + verb + object," which is an important clue.

In the discussion of Gen 4:7, I am not dealing with a verb but with the noun *chatta'ath* derived from the verb, so we might translate it as "incurred guilt," somewhat like staining the carpet. HALOT gives two meanings for this spelling: sin, or sin-offering. The noun is feminine, which implies that it is the recipient of some action, and not the actor.

Everything in the account points to a very passive incident of *chatta'ath* like a carpet stain. But then why would this "mark of the miss" be crouched at Cain's door, as if it featured some actor or personal quality?

Ignoring the dictionary and the confusing etymology, we can go directly to the usage of the term in Scripture. From the *Theological Wordbook of the Old Testament* (TWOT) we learn that *chata'* appears 356/595x as a noun and that 293/356x are the feminine participle *chatta'ath* alone.[5] From Table 3.2 the word appears for the first time here in Gen 4:7, but by the fourth or fifth occurrence in Exodus, where Moses is atoning for the golden calf, the word seems to have settled down into its traditional meaning of 'incurred guilt." Its usage peaks in Leviticus which the NAS translates 51/82x as "sin offering." Now recall that when the verb is reflexive, "actor + verb + self" the result is good. That is precisely the action performed in a sin offering that features so largely in the pages of Leviticus.

Semioticians, who study the signs and symbols by which we communicate, are always telling us that the meaning of a word is more in what is excluded than in what is included.[6] Leviticus specifies many kinds of offerings other than sin offerings. Commentators divide these other types of offerings into mandated "involuntary" and optional "voluntary" sorts. Sometimes the voluntary offerings are called "thank" offerings, and I would suppose that after a drought or a flood, one might be forgiven for omitting them. But the two mandated offerings are the sin offering and the guilt/trespass offering, which must be presented every year. Since even the highly esteemed HALOT has collapsed "sin" and "guilt" into its definition, I cannot use a dictionary to distinguish between them. But to understand the significance of *chatta'ath* we will need to understand why Leviticus has two distinct mandatory offerings: *chatta'ath* (sin) and *'asham* (guilt).

The guilt offering is easy to understand. It is required when a command has been violated and guilt incurred. It is often associated with making reparations, so much so that *Vine's Bible Dictionary* suggests,[7] "In one

5. Harris et al., *Theological wordbook of the Old Testament.*

6. Saussure. *Cours de linguistique generale.*

7. Vine. *Vine's Concise Dictionary.*

respect the sin offering differed from the guilt offering in that the former was required where the harm done could not be undone or measured." Vine goes on to further separate the two. "The former [sin, *chatta'ath*] relates to personal condition, the evil nature, the latter [guilt/trespass, *'asham*] to the effects, evil actions." Despite Vine's attempt at semantic separation, *chatta'ath* is used for trespass that occurs through ignorance (Lev 4), which is eventually discovered, and reparations are made. Note that Leviticus 4 uses the *qal* stem (active voice) of *chata'* for the verb of sinning, whereas the act that incurs guilt, and the reparation of that sin involves the reflexive, a *hitpiel* stem of *chatta'ath* to undo the *qal*. Nevertheless, the distinction from *'asham* seems clear enough: *chatta'ath* involves violating an unknown command, or possibly, doing something whose effects cannot be undone.

Now the division between guilt and sin offerings is more complex than, for example, the difference between murder one and manslaughter; it is not simply the attitude or mental state of the perpetrator. For example, when a leper (a person with either skin disease or Hansen's disease) is healed, he must offer two animals, one for a sin offering and one for a guilt offering (Lev 14:31)—all this for a disease contracted unwillingly! So perhaps it is better to view these two types of offering as responses to two aspects of the same deed; the guilt offering responds to the consequences, while the sin offering responds to the causes. Notice how this captures the "actor+verb+object" distinction: *chata'*, where a sin offering focuses on the actor+verb; and *'asham*, where the guilt offering focuses on the verb+object.

Therefore, I argue that if the guilt offering (*'asham*) is clearly for a subject/actor's trespass and willful breaking of God's law, then the sin offering (*chatta'ath*) is for everything else that results from the evil event: from a violation committed in ignorance, a violation committed unwillingly, or perhaps even a violation imposed upon us. This captures Vine's "evil nature" usage because we either inherit or absorb our evil nature at a young age without moral consent. We note that the Talmudic rabbis also find this meaning for *chatta'ath*, among other ones, quoting from the second century Genesis Rabbah commentary on Gen 4:7,

> "Said Rabbi Abin, 'Whoever indulges his impulse to do evil in his youth in the end will be ruled by the evil impulse in his old age . . .' Rabbi Hanina said, 'If your evil impulse comes to make you laugh, put it off with the words of Torah: "The evil impulse, when near you, you shall combat." (Isa 26:3)' "[8]

8. Neusner. *Genesis Rabbah*. §XXII.6.

There was meat in this nut, for using these definitions in our translation of Gen 4:7, we find God saying to Cain, "*An evil nature crouches [or couches] at the door, and his desire is for you.*" God is warning Cain that if he continues in his anger, he will be forever chained to the desires of the body, subjected to Paul's lament in Rom 7:24 "*wretched man that I am, who will deliver me from this body of death?*" This leads us to a theological dilemma because it would seem that Cain already had an evil nature, having been descended from the fallen Adam.

Why would God be warning Cain about something that has already happened?

My proposed interpretation is this: What for centuries had appeared to theologians to be one event can now be seen in the light of new discoveries to be two closely related events. Adam had poisoned his progeny by eating the fruit but had otherwise not acted violently or rebelliously toward God. Cain was to be the first to begin the cycle of violence that eventually necessitated the Flood. Anticipating later discussion, Adam's curse was genetic, but Cain's epigenetic.

Therefore, when God gives Cain a warning about sin, He is describing more than simply "the knowledge of good and evil," which Adam acquired by eating the fruit, but something more akin to "a violent temperament" or "evil nature," acquired by immoral behavior. By using the word *teshuwqah*, desire, He is saying that this "evil nature" will act like a street-walker, "couching at the door," producing evil progeny or implicitly, infecting progeny. This interpretation may also explain the grammatical irregularities of having a feminine noun, *chatta'ath*, take two words with masculine endings, "his" and "couches," because the 'street-walker" will be in control, as revealed by the usage of *teshuwqah* in Gen 3:16.

How can this be? Does not an evil nature look more like a genetic trait rather than a bad behavior? After all, how can one inherit "a bad attitude"?

The explanation has been the surprise provided by twenty-first-century biology. The twentieth-century neo-Darwinists had insisted that the environment had no effect on genetics. To say otherwise was to follow Lamarck, who was completely discredited by the experiments of Weismann, having supposedly cut the tails off twenty-two generations of mice with no effect.[9] (He might have spared himself the trouble by consulting the owners of Rottweilers.) The twenty-first century has not been kind to neo-Darwinists, however, because many environmental factors have been found to be inherited, not in the DNA, but in changing "markers" on the DNA.[10] Therefore

9. Wikipedia. "Lamarck"; Wikipedia. "August Weismann."

10. Carey. *The Epigenetics Revolution.*"

it is not only material causes that have material effects; immaterial causes can also produce long-lasting material effects. Cain's violence did change him and *chatta'ath* did pass on to his children. For his desire birthed the escalation of violence that is reported in Lamech's boast (Gen 4:23–24) and became the cause of the Flood.

3.2.4 Genesis 4:10 Abel's blood

Before I turn to twenty-first-century biology to understand how this street-walker can produce such monstrous progeny, let us look at the bright hope this text offers. For there is more to this tale than simply the back story to Noah. Otherwise, Abel would not have received a shout-out in two gospels (Matt 23:35; Luke 11:51) and two commendations in the letter to the Hebrews (Heb 11:4, 12:24). Three passages mention his blood and one mentions his faith. Like the other *midrash* in the Letter to the Hebrews, more is said about Abel later than what Moses reports earlier. Genesis 4 tells us only that Abel was second-born, tended sheep, made a sacrifice, and spilled his blood. Yet somehow in the later writings, these events made him a prophet, a priest, and a type (or precursor) of Christ.

If genetics links Cain with the generation of Noah that received the great judgment, does genetics also link Abel to Christ?

In every culture there is a saying of the sort we find in Lewis' *The Horse & His Boy*—blood is thicker than soup—which means that relatives are more important than friends, baptisms, or legal affiliations.[11] Genetic relatives are always separated from marriage bonds or adopted relations by the term "blood relatives."

But why blood? Why not say "flesh relatives" or "birth relations"? When did blood become synonymous with genetics?

I think the answer is Abel. There is more in this story than simply a murder, and it has something to do with blood, Abel's blood in particular, crying out from the ground. Once again, I want to emphasize that Genesis is sparing with words. There is nothing extraneous or poetic or embroidered about the text. If Abel's blood cries out, a very important concept or story is being summarized. With modern forensic tools, we know a lot more about Abel's blood than we used to, filled as it is with RNA and cellular communication vesicles.

In the 1980s we used blood-types to trace the historic migration of Adam's descendants across Europe, now repeated and validated with

11. Lewis. *The Horse and His Boy.*

mitochondrial, nuclear, and Y-chromosome marker studies.[12] That extra information suddenly transforms the meaning of Abel's story, which has been the emphasis of *midrash* throughout this book. There is often a lengthy period before full revelation, a period when one feels the significance of a detail without pin-pointing what it is. That is the case with Abel's blood.

3.2.4.1 *Typology versus midrash*

Now it does not help to do what many theologians do, and call my hunch a "symbol," and then go on to say that the point of the story is symbolic. This is just circular logic for saying "I do not yet know why it is obviously important." Nor does it do much good to trace symbols through the Bible to demonstrate their significance.

Why not, what is wrong with typology?

A problem arises when we do not know what the symbol points to, with the result that our "significance" explanations are just long lists of usage. For example, suppose that I was learning electronics and I ran across the word "impedance." I look it up in a conversational dictionary, but the definition does not really address electronic circuits. So, I say, "This is a symbol that engineers use a lot." Then I go on to list how many times the word appears in various electronics textbooks and that it is often represented as the letter "Z." I even find examples of malfunction because the "impedance" was wrong or mismatched.

Am I then entitled to conclude that impedance is a form of a sin especially connected to electronics simply because I do not understand electricity? And if this approach is unhelpful in electronics, why should it be helpful in Biblical scholarship?

Well, there may be an answer to this last question. God made our brains superior to computers, so that we often sense things we cannot express, or as Blaise Pascal wrote "The heart has its reasons that Reason knows nothing of."[13] As it turns out, many of the great discoveries of science and literature are of this nature—which is why Arthur Koestler entitled his biographies of twentieth-century scientists, *The Sleepwalkers*.[14] And just as scientists can "sleepwalk" their way toward the truth, so also in Biblical scholarship we can converge on the truth without massive ANE textual "help," hence the mantra, "Scripture interprets Scripture."

12. Cavalli-Sforza and Bodmer. *The Genetics of Human Populations*.
13. Pascal. *Pensee 28*.
14. Koestler. *The Sleepwalkers*.

The method was developed by Rabbis two centuries before Christ. It is variously referred to as "2nd Temple exegesis" or *midrash*. To the uninitiated, it sounds like a blend of free-association and linguistics, but it follows rather strict rules, as spelled out in the seven *middot* of Rabbi Hillel.[15] It can be and has been misused (e.g., *Zohar*), but then so has traditional grammatico-historical scholarship (e.g., JEDP). Despite its bad reputation, every seminary student has been exposed to it when they study Paul's letter to the Romans or Galatians, or the letter to the Hebrews. Given our present ignorance of genetics and the apparent symbolism of this passage, this will be our approach to the significance of Abel's blood.

In one sense, I am not actually engaging in *midrash* because I am analytically reverse-engineering the *midrash* of Genesis. But in another sense, the Talmud is full of comments about comments, so reverse engineering is also *midrash*. I leave for you to judge whether I succeed or fail—thereby including you in the *midrash*—because it's not just the destination, it's the journey too, just as it was for Noah.

3.2.4.2 *Midrash on Abel's name*

Gesenius traces Abel's name, *hebel* (H1892) to the word for breath or vapor, or in its poetic usage, vanity.[16] It is a very odd name to give someone. The root word first appears much later in Deut 32:21. The usage in both the KJV and the NAS is given in Table 3.3. From the size of the word cloud, I think it would be fair to say that the exact meaning of *hebel* is somewhat nebulous.

KJV	**72**	**NAS**	**54**	**NAS**	**11**	**NAS**	**5**	**NAS**	**2**
vanity	61	vanity	25	breath	3	emptily	1	vain idols	1
vain	11	futility	14	emptiness	2	nothing	1	fleeting vapor	1
altogether	1	idols	6	fleeting	2	useless	1		
		mere breath	6	delusion	2	vainly	1		
		vain	3	worthless	2	fraud	1		

Table 3.3: Translation of הֶבֶל (*hebel*).

In fact, I would go so far as to say that the meaning is intentionally ambiguous. For example, all but two of the NAS "vanity" translations occur

15. Jewish-Encyclopedia. "Middot."

16. Gesenius. *Hebräische Grammatik*.

in Ecclesiastes—principally because the KJV translation of Eccl 1:2,14 is famous, "vanity of vanities, all is vanity" and "all is vanity and a striving after wind." The NAS does not like that English translation but, lacking any better way to ascertain the meaning, stuck by the KJV's choice, which makes my point. Because the word does not have a sound, clear dictionary meaning, the NAS uses parallel constructions to find the "meaning" contextually, leading to a superabundance of word equivalents—something the NAS usually avoids. Yet when there is no parallel structure, as in Eccl 1:2, it falls back on the KJV's ambiguity and hopes for the best.

But is this the best we can do?

Let's go back to the root meaning and retranslate Eccl 1:2 as "*breath of breath, all is breath and striving after spirit.*" Is that a mantra of despair, or of hope?

Let us capitalize the last word (a translator's gimmick, but done in Gen 1:2 for example), and read it again. "*Breath of breath, all is breath and striving after Spirit.*" Sounds a lot more optimistic, no? Strangely, capitalizing a word can change its tone.

What is the meaning of this word *hebel*? Is it gloom and despair, as the NAS seems to think, or something hopeful, something associated with Spirit, *ruwach*?

Because if it is, then the more common *ruwach* (H7307, appearing 378x) has already made an appearance in Gen 1:2, 3:8 and the controversial 6:3. Contrast Abel's name with that of his older brother. Cain can be translated as "spear" (H7013), and from the text of Gen 4:1, it is also a pun on the verb "acquire," "buy," or "possess." A breath can neither be bought nor used as a spear, but a spear is used to destroy breath. On the other hand, a spear is difficult to hold and throw without extensive aerobic training, which requires plenty of breath.

This pair of "spear" and "breath" is neither complementary nor antagonistic. More like "rock, paper, scissors," it is asymmetric. Spear needs breath but destroys breath. Breath strengthens spear, but can also weaken it. A more familiar example of this asymmetric relation is the common complaint, "Women! You can't live with them, and you can't live without them!" And so we get in Gen 4:1–7 the working out of the *teshuwqah* curse of Gen 3:16—your desire shall be for your husband, and he shall rule over you—now is transposed into sibling rivalry.

Because these names seem to typify the story in which they appear, some have wondered if Abel is really just a metaphor for two sides of Cain's personality, making this story more of a psychological drama than a fratricide. But if we look further, we may find another reason. Drawing upon the connection to *ruwach* and to its meaning as Spirit or mind, perhaps *hebel* implies something more like "knowledge" or "planning." (Ecclesiastes, in my view, hints at this interpretation.) In that case Cain would be the brawn and Abel the brains.

3.2.4.3 *Midrash on Abel's blood*

These are much better word complements than many that are offered and one might be tempted to reconstruct Genesis 4 into a psychological drama of one character. But my goal is to look for genetic interpretations, which play little role in psychology. On that note, the second most important feature about Abel is his fraternal relation to Cain, which is mentioned seven times in this story, only one fewer time than his name. This pattern is the key to understanding his odd name that appears so asymmetric to the name "Cain." We started by asking how "blood" came to mean, specifically, "relation," and here we see "brother" tied closely Abel.

Is there a connection between "brother" and "breath"?

The book where *hebel* appears most often also features the only verse where both concepts are mentioned. Eccl 4:8 suggests that a person without brother or child is a "breath," because he is all alone. In that case, when Cain killed Abel, he became Abel. What ties all these verses together is genetics, relations, fecundity, or children. Because Cain and Abel were the very first children in the world, they represent more than simply all brothers everywhere, but all children everywhere, all kinfolk everywhere.

And that is why Abel's blood is not just the first murder and hence the blood of all murderers everywhere, but also the breaking of family bonds, the death of relatives, the destruction of all families everywhere. Abel's blood represents the promise transmitted from Adam, the genetic and epigenetic treasure that made Adam "*a little lower than the angels*" (Ps 8:5). Abel represents all the promises of God in Adam—His Spirit, His plan, His breath, His treasure—and Cain willfully, knowingly, after being warned, ended all of it.

But it gets worse.

At this point in history, God's plan for the world was represented by three unique men— Adam, Cain and Abel—each fulfilling the direct commands of God. Adam's first task of cultivating the garden had gone to Cain, his second task of naming the animals had gone to Abel. And now Adam had been given a third task (Gen 1:26 and 2:24)—filling the Earth with children by Eve. If one considers how long Adam lived, the time frame does not seem at all unreasonable. Nor had this task been given to Abel or Cain, for presumably God would eventually answer their need for wives as He had answered Adam's. Three jobs but one blood, a trinity of God's tasking.

I will elaborate on this trinity of tasks later on, but let me begin by looking at the three aspects of Cain's career. First, he was given Adam's gardening job, keeping alive the lineages that God had given Adam. Second, he was applying his brain, his intellect, to improving those lineages, thereby starting the Neolithic Revolution. And then there was a third, seemingly incidental gift: He was given a little brother. The first gift was material, the second informational, and the third spiritual. That is, satisfying God's plan required more than simply doubling or tripling the yield of primitive cultivars. Satisfying God's plan also required getting along with his younger sibling. From such small beginnings one can foresee tribes and nations, governments and churches, and ultimately, the New Jerusalem, the City of God. One can only guess how different the world would have been if, despite Adam's sin, Cain had fulfilled all God's plans. Instead, Cain killed his brother, destroyed the trinity, and seemingly gave in to the *teshuwqah* for hatred, thereby permanently contaminating the epigenetics, the bloodline of Adam. One violent act, but thrice deadly.

This is why Abel's blood cries out. It cries out with breath, the resurrection of Spirit in the place of Spear. It cries out for purity, for regeneration from epigenetic sin. It cries out for justice, for restoration of family bonds, the reversal of spiritual sin. It cries out for unity, for the restoration of the trinity. It cries out to us, on account of the ruin we must all inherit. It cries out to God for a redeemer of all mankind.

3.3 Epigenetics

I have introduced the genetic sin of the Fall in terms of Cain's disobedience and violence. Until recently, no scientist took the idea of inherited behavior very seriously. An animal's inherited behavior is an instinct, but instincts were thought to denigrate people, lowering them to the level of unthinking beasts. Yet a discovery of the past twenty years that is revolutionizing biology (and challenging Darwinism's "sola DNA" orthodoxy) is that there is a mechanism in all animals including us, that can pass on learned behavior to children and grandchildren. It is called epigenetics, and Genesis has a lot to say about it. This chapter is about that scientific discovery and its application.

3.3.1 Weismann's barrier

Can Cain's bad behavior be inherited by his children? Now if someone had asked me this question immediately after Biology 101, I would have said "No, that's Lamarckism, a discredited theory." For, as every textbook recites, Darwin had rejected the erroneous belief that environmental effects could be inherited: Giraffes did not acquire long necks because generation after generation of giraffes stretched their necks to reach the high leaves at the tops of trees. I was told that August Weismann disproved this theory by demonstrating the existence of a "Weismann barrier" which prevented the environment from affecting genes. (We were warned that allowing Lamarck would allow the problems Trofim Lysenko caused in the Soviet Union, resulting in a lost generation of Russian biologists.)[17] The gene, our textbooks informed us, is the master of our fate, the captain of our self. Evolutionary biologist Richard Dawkins has even gone so far as to say that a human is just a gene's way of replicating itself.[18] So following from this logic, nothing Cain did could affect his genes, and therefore *chatta'ath* cannot be inherited (Figure 3.1)[19]

Figure 3.1: Jean-Baptiste deLamarck, August Weismann, Trofim Lysenko, and Richard Dawkins (Wiki Commons)

The last two decades of genetic research, however, has been an earthquake to this Jericho of gene orthodoxy. We have found multiple mechanisms by which the environment triggers genetic changes. Lamarck's explanation of giraffe necks may not be true for giraffes but it has been shown to be correct in many other situations. Lee Spetner, one of the earliest

17. Wikipedia. "Weismann barrier"; Wikipedia. "Lysenko, Trofim."
18. Dawkins. *The Selfish Gene.*
19. Jurvetson. "Richard Dawkins."

proponents of environmental inheritance, reminds us of findings from thirty-five years ago:[20]

> In 1982 Barry Hall reported on an experiment in which he prepared a strain of E. coli bacteria lacking the beta-galactosidase gene lacZ, which normally hydrolyzes lactose [digests milk sugar]. When these bacteria grew and multiplied on another nutrient, but in the presence of lactose, they gained the ability to metabolize [digest] lactose, an ability that proved to be heritable. The gained ability was found to be due to the presence of a new gene. The new gene encodes a new enzyme that can perform the function of the beta-galactosidase, enabling the mutant bacteria to metabolize lactose. The gene was present all the time, but in a dormant state. It was turned ON by two mutations that occur in the presence of lactose and do not appear in its absence. Hall declared that the "normal function" of this gene is unknown, and he called it a "cryptic" gene.
>
> Neither of these two mutations alone gives the bacterium any advantage, so there could not have been any selection for them separately. For the cryptic gene to become active, both mutations have to occur. In the absence of lactose, these two mutations are independent. They can occur together only by chance, and will do so with a probability of only about [one in a billion billion] per replication. If they occur at random and independently, the expected waiting time for one of these double mutations to occur in Hall's population would be about 100,000 years. But in the presence of lactose, he detected about 40 of them in just a few days! One can conclude that the lactose in the environment was inducing these mutations . . .

What Hall discovered, and Spetner reports, is that random mutations cannot account for how bacteria switch on crypto-genes when they need them. Rather, organisms edit their genetics in response to their environment. As Nobel Prize winners Jacob and Monod showed, the genetic control system senses the presence of an unused food source and turns on the gene that encodes the digestive enzyme.[21] This genetic control system, which can turn genes on or off in a few generations as they are needed, is called epigenetics. It is epigenetics that permits the organism to thrive during specific short-term food supply changes in the food supply.

In another study, female agouti mice were fed methyl-rich supplements such as folic acid and vitamin B12, which resulted in dramatic, visible

20. Spetner. *Not By Chance.*
21. Monod. "Jacques Monod"

changes in their pups, including darkened coat color and decreased weight gain. The changes persisted for two generations.[22] In another, cocaine-addicted male mice passed on to their descendants (two generations) an inherited suppression of a brain neurotransmitter.[23] Another famous study found that Swedish and Dutch boys, starved before puberty, passed on a lowered risk of mortality (e.g., heart attacks) to their sons' sons but not to their granddaughters, whereas starved girls passed on lowered risk of mortality to their sons' daughters, but not their grandsons. Maternal grandparents had no effect on their grandchildren's mortality at all.[24]

Why is there a gender difference in epigenetics?

To be heritable, a switched-on gene must occur in the cells that are essential for reproduction, in the gametes. For women, life experiences do not affect the eggs because they have already undergone meiosis and are in a condition of suspended animation long before puberty. And while changes that occur in the womb after conception are heritable, as in the agouti mice, they are also less persistent, perhaps because the baby's cells are already differentiating. For men, however, sperm cells are formed continuously and can respond to a life experiences via chemicals in the blood. Therefore many heritable switches (methyl-tagging, RNA imprinting)[25] have been traced to the father's environment, including alcoholism, cocaine addiction, and exposure to cancer-causing agents (carcinogens).

Epigenetic changes do not depend on whether the gene exists but whether it is turned on or off. The Swedish boys still had the same gene for cholesterol regulation but the switch was changed by the environment and the changed switch was inherited by the next generation. This process is called epigenetics because "epi" means "above" and the changes occur "above" the genes. Traditional "Mendelian" genetics, as learned in school, concerns only the inheritance of the genes and the on/off switch had yet to be discovered.

Just today, a newspaper headline reported, "Epigenetics: How to alter your genes."[26] The article's subtitle went on to explain "We've long been told our genes are our destiny. But it's now thought they can be changed by habit, lifestyle, even finances. What does this mean for our children?" The article answers its own question. "And thus your worst habits—smoking, overeating—are the ones that can be passed onto your offspring, and even

22. Wolff et al. "Maternal epigenetics" 949–957.

23. Vassoler et al. "Epigenetic inheritance" 42–47.

24. Pembrey et al. "Sex-specific" 159–166.

25. Epigenetics-Society. "What is it?"

26. Bell. "Epigenetics"

further down the hereditary line. Or, put another way: your grandfather was making lifestyle decisions that affect you today."

From its controversial discovery thirty years ago to the bold new frontier of biology today, epigenetics is now believed to be the key to twenty-first-century genetics. When the Human Genome Project completed the transcription of the entire human genome at a cost of $3 billion in 2003, it was trumpeted as the key to understanding cancer, disease, and the causes of senility.[27] Yet here we are fifteen years later, and we still have no cures for cancer, disease, or senility.

What happened? Was the $3 billion spent in vain?

3.3.2 Cain's Epigenetics

What we have discovered is that there is a whole lot more to DNA than we thought when we began the Human Genome Project. It would be as if we paid $3 billion dollars for an Egyptian hieroglyphic dictionary but discovered that we still could not read the Rosetta Stone because we did not understand the grammar. When we read the human genome, we discovered to our amazement that fully 90 percent of the 3 billion "words" (codons) were never turned into proteins. They were not "genes."

At first, evolutionary biologists were elated because they saw this discovery as proof that the genome was an evolutionary train wreck, full of "junk DNA."[28] But in 2012 the ENCODE study showed that, at a minimum, 80 percent of that DNA was being processed into even if the RNA was not being translated into proteins. But they had no idea why.[29] Little by little, we are learning why: The non-coding RNA is controlling the DNA. A recent paper called this junk DNA, "an operating system."[30] It is supplying the grammar that makes sense of the DNA: It regulates the production of other proteins, it responds to the environment, and it turns around and modifies the DNA. Far from being the mute messenger of a DNA tyrant, RNA is the bureaucracy that surrounds the emperor, acting and reacting to the events of empire.

And like a bureaucracy, RNA implements changes that last for years, sometimes for generations. RNA is responsible for tagging sections of DNA with methyl groups, to turn genes off and on. Sometimes the tags go onto the DNA directly, sometimes onto the histone "spools" that wind the DNA

27. Collins. "*The Human Genome Project*"
28. Wells. *The Myth of Junk DNA*.
29. ENCODE-Consortium. "ENCODE."
30. Dimond. "What Junk DNA?"

up into its compact storage form. The operation is complex enough that researchers call it a "methyl-tag code" that is read, transcribed, and duplicated by the cell. A decade ago we thought that all of epigenetics was in this methyl-tagging, but now we know of many other "codes" in the cell: RNA variants, DNA-codon-variants, introns, spliceosome switches, polymerized sugars, and tubulin-structures, to name just a few. Some of these codes last for minutes, some for weeks or years, and others for generations.[31]

Why such a super-abundance of codes, why so many different kinds of biological "memory"? Why could DNA not just do everything?

Control theory, the mathematics behind automation, provides an answer but everyone is familiar with the basic way it works from experience.[32] When I was seventeen and a new driver, I wrecked my father's car by "over-correcting" on a mountain curve sprinkled with gravel. When I felt the car sliding, I spun the wheel too far in one direction, and then tried to compensate by turning too far the other direction. Each time I "corrected" the car's direction, I made things worse until the car went spinning out of control and into the mountain. Because the car had springs and momentum, it could not respond instantaneously to changes of the wheel. But in my naïvete, I thought I should turn the wheel a bit further instead of waiting for the car to respond. My reaction was quicker than the car's and caused the accident. From bitter experience, I know that a safe driver must react no more quickly than the car can. In science jargon, one must match the forcing frequency to the resonant frequency to achieve stable control. Applying this mathematical insight to biology and humankind, we can see that our bodies need a way to respond to a changing environment at the right speed or frequency. Some adaptations, such as "altitude sickness" require a few days or weeks, whereas others, such as the tall, dark, and skinny bodies of tropical races, may take several generations to adjust. Just as each type of environmental change, from weather to seasons to climate, has its own timescale, so each type of adaptation has its own matching timescale in order to prevent "over-correction" and extinction.

Genes and genetic inheritance lie at the low-frequency end of a great spectrum of heritable adaptions to our changing environment, making epigenetics the overarching explanation, teleology, or purpose of heredity and adaptation. (And that in-built purpose is why Darwin's heirs hated Lamarck.) It also makes epigenetics the key to understanding Genesis. We have dug up Neanderthal bones more than 40,000 years old, examined their DNA, and found it widely different from ours, thereby demonstrating that

31. Wells. "Membrane Patterns" 1–28.

32. Kirk. *Optimal Control Theory*.

Neanderthals were not human, and, in all likelihood, could not interbreed with humans even if they had overlapped in time. We have also dug up Cro-Magnon bones around 15,000 to 25,000 years old, and found their DNA to be 100 percent modern, demonstrating that they were human and could interbreed with us.[33]

If Eden existed 12,000 years ago and Adam and Eve its first occupants, then what sets them apart from the tens of thousands of Aurignacian Cro-Magnons that populated the world before them?

Epigenetics set them apart. And now we have grasped the point of Gen 4:7. For if Adam was created epigenetically for the glory of God, Cain can likewise epigenetically destroy that glory to his (and our) lasting shame. For what crouched or couched at Cain's door was the opportunity to change his progeny through his actions. If he lifted up his face to God by doing what was right, his children would inherit the full blessings of Adam. But if he gave in to anger, if he translated the anger he felt into action, then the brain chemicals he created would imprint themselves upon his genes and be transmitted to his children. As psychologists have long understood and neurologists now concur, anger changes the way our brain functions, and the effect travels down the generations. I have been told that psychologists can spot grandchildren and great-grandchildren of alcoholics by the way their brains operate.[34] In fact, all seven of the deadly sins have this quality of changing our bodies and changing our children, as indicated by the proliferation of "12-Step" groups for all manner of family dysfunctions. This is surely the meaning of God's self-description to Moses on Mount Sinai (Exod 34:7) "*I am a jealous God, visiting the iniquity of the fathers on the children and the children's children, to the third and the fourth generation.*"

There is mercy even in God's judgment, for notice the timescale—three or four generations. That is precisely the timescale of methyl-tagging or epigenetic changes in the genome. If the behavior that caused the methyl-tagging is not repeated, the effect wears off in about a century. By contrast, Adam's sin and its resulting mortality is with us still, some 14,000 years and 700 generations later. So, Cain's anger need not have created the level of irreversible harm as Adam's disobedience did because his grandchildren would have an opportunity to escape "the cycle," as 12-Step groups put it.

But if Cain's rejection of God's warning was in some sense less lethal than Adam's, it was also more acute. Perhaps because Cain and his children lived so very long, or perhaps because Cain willfully continued in his

33. Green et al. "A complete Neandertal" 416–426; Caramelli et al. "A 28,000 Years Old" e2700.

34. Hemfelt et al. *Love is a Choice.*

disobedience, this epigenetic inheritance could not be erased. Given Cain's longevity, his anger would be directed at his son, his grandson, his great-grandson, his great-great-grandson, and so forth for over ten generations of continuous dysfunction. That perhaps accounts for Lamech's apparent desire to vindicate Cain (Gen 4:24). For what was mercy to us, was merciless to Cain. Somehow, the cycle had to be broken. And that is what the story of Lamech and the story of Noah tell us—how pernicious the inherited sin had become and why the Flood was the necessary cure.

3.3.3 Cain's Redemption

If the cycle can be broken and was broken by the Flood, can it also be repaired? Can Paradise be regained?

That is the promise hidden in the fall of Cain. For just as epigenetics can destroy our children, so it can also redeem them. If we do the opposite of Cain, if we control our anger, if we control our lust, then our great-grandchildren will be born with those switches turned off. Or if we are fortunate to be born into a "good" family, a family with a heritage of godly grandfathers and fathers, we have the privilege of passing on to our children a godly heritage (Mal 2:15). This heritage has a name, to distinguish it from wealth, power, and prestige; it is called holiness.

Seen in this light, the story of Genesis is the story of the loss of holiness and the path to its recovery. We might see in Joseph—the story that ends the book of Genesis—the antithesis of Cain. He was a man who valued his brothers, who treasured his blood, who resisted lust and violence, and thereby saved his family. But the story of Joseph does not end with an ascent back to Paradise. We have been given a long history that continued for another 1000 years, to the days of the prophet Malachi. And if I include the New Testament and the founding of the Church, the story has continued for another 2500 years to the present.

Well, if the descent of Cain was so sudden, why then has the ascent been so long?

In the final analysis, only God knows. Certainly, the apostles were hopeful that the return of Christ would come in their generation. But if we understand the Fall to be both a genetic and an epigenetic destruction, we may be able to understand why God's timing is so slow, and yet so inexorable. For if the sin of Adam was genetic, then the sin of Cain is epigenetic. Because Cain founded the first city, the sin became societal. Societal sins persist long after they are first committed. They contaminate persons who did not commit them; like a virus, they spread the infection further and further. Not only are they persistent and ubiquitous but they are passed down from father to son, producing a lineage of sin and infection. So perhaps the best way to grasp the magnitude of the problem is by examining the way it infected the human line.

My dating of the Flood to 9590 BC suggests that Cain's murder dates to about 10,600 BC. In that case, it took almost 1000 years for the effects of Cain's revolt to contaminate the entire race of Adam and require a Flood to erase it. By symmetry, I would expect at least 1000 years for decontamination, and in fact, that is nearly the time from Abraham to Malachi.

But what of the intervening years? What was happening between the Flood and Abraham?

The MT gives us about 250 years. But, as I have argued in this book where the Younger Dryas glaciation corresponds to Eden, the time span is about 7500 years from the purge of the Flood to the rebuilding of holiness through the line of Abraham. Much was happening in this time period, so it was not time wasted, though it does seem to be a long time. Perhaps, however, the correct clock is the "genetic" clock, the time it takes for variants to slip into or disappear from the population, making the time not linear but logarithmic. Finding the correct "clock time" must then include the large field of "population genetics," the mathematics of gene flow. Population genetics is undergoing tremendous upheaval at the moment, as it reels from the gigabytes of human genome data that are pouring in.[35] I mentioned previously that recent data show a dilution event some 5100–10,000 years ago. However, what is clear to everyone, whether they acknowledge it or not, is that the clock does not run at a steady pace. Rather, sizes of populations, diversity of populations, and migrations of populations vary the rate of change.

So what is the right clock?

The evidence is somewhat muddy, relying as it does on historical rather than biological data.[36] Recall that it takes four generations to undo an epigenetic tag, or about a century of clock time. It is also a familiar saying that it takes seven generations to make a priest after the first conversion. I would even argue that it may take forty generations to make a priestly culture out of a tribal one, basing this on the time between the Christianization of Europe and when that culture began exporting missionaries. But once the

35. Gillespie. *Population Genetics.*

36. Stark. *America's Blessings.*

culture has made the transition, it does not appear that it ever goes back to the blood-thirsty tribal behavior of its roots.

This may help us understand the apparent delay of the day of the Lord: the cleansing of Adam's blood is not yet complete. I think that when our society and culture get to that stage, we will be like Cain, able to see the *chatta'ath* crouching at the door, forced to make a choice; and the choices of that day will usher in the final stage of man's ascent.

What are we becoming; what are we ascending toward?

The best answer to this question is to examine where we started. So let us examine the first human and his condition.

PART 4

Ecce homo.

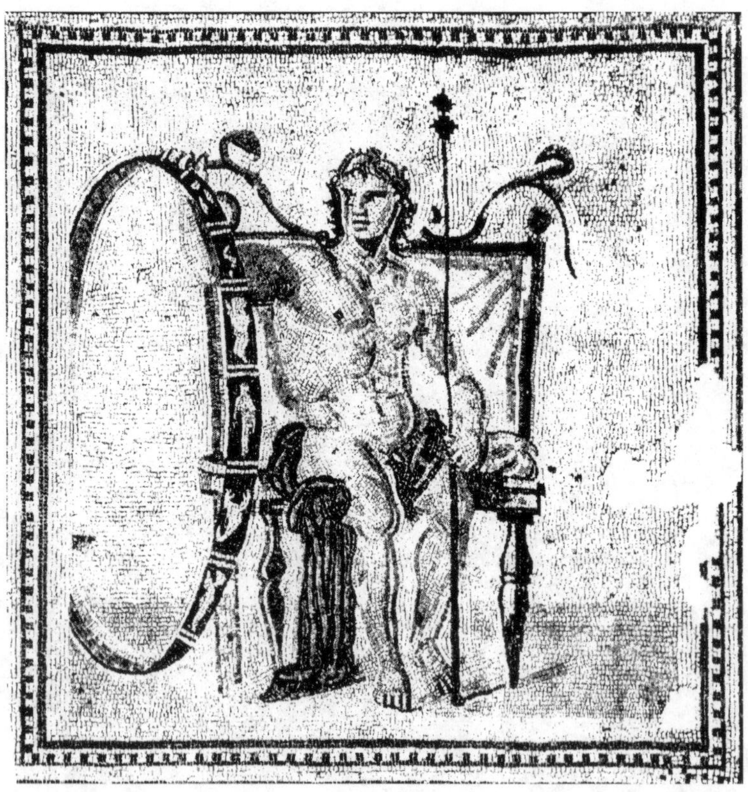

Figure 4.0: Aion, protogenetos, 3rd century AD mosaic from Arles, France. (Wiki Commons)

CHAPTER 4

Adam

4.1 Adam's Task

It was hot. Really hot. Adam felt as if his lungs were on fire. The hazy sky glowed around the sun as if it had been set ablaze in the heat. The air was cooler under the banana palms but even they were having a hard time, their wide leaves wilting in the strong sunlight. Adam dragged himself down to the river and sat for a while on the bank under a large-leafed tree, then plunged into the water. He cupped his hands and poured it over his head and face. The cool water refreshed him and he could think clearly again: When was the last time it was this hot?

Adam tried to remember. It was so far back, he hardly could count, at least 342 nights ago. That was not counting the nights when He talked. There was no accounting for that time. Time just stopped or perhaps ran forwards and backwards, but whatever it was, it could not be measured.

Measure. Now there was a worthy activity. Adam paused to count the leaves on the tree above him, the twigs that supported them, down to the branches, and finally the single trunk with its ridges of bark that ran zigzag up its length. Multiples of 13 and 21, he calculated, but easily explained as sums of the previous two. He counted the giant dragonflies as they zoomed over the sparkling water, and tried to correlate their number with the number of sparkles. But both were changing so quickly he found that it was the ratio of the changes that stayed the same.

Adam laughed. How like Him to hide the numbers from me by putting the answer in the changes! But perhaps He hides them twice? Adam quickly calculated the changes in the changes. The leaf number matched the bark number, which is exactly what Adam expected. Trees are just giant calculators, forever adding and adding in the same tree-ish way. But the sparkle numbers went back and forth, neither growing nor shrinking yet changing nonetheless. What was going on?

Adam chuckled. They were water numbers! Without the sap of life, they simply sloshed back and forth forever. How He loved to play those games, hiding and revealing, drawing and erasing His lines. He had talked about counting a fortnight ago, and for three days Adam counted everything. It was not just for the fun of it, for Adam knew that, when he had mastered the secret, the next evening He would explain something new. Adam wanted to show Him all the things he had found out about numbers, and sums within sums would be part of the report.

The sun beat down on Adam's head, causing him to look up at the tree. The sun had moved five of its diameter in the time he had been doing sums, and he was no longer in the shade. Which reminded him of his first calculation. The sun had not been this high in the sky since at least 342 days ago. Its latitude had risen and fallen in the meantime, just like the water sparkles. Perhaps the sun was like the water numbers, endlessly repeating?

But why would the sun and the water be alike? Adam pondered this paradox. One is hot and the other cold, one discrete and the other continuous, one singular and the other multiple. What made them grow and wane together in such regular patterns? Unless, unless the sun was like the sparkles on the water—a ripple, a wave in the great ocean of the sky, reflecting a greater glory. Adam looked up at the hazy sky and remembered the stars—23,081 last night— that moved like the sun. The water of the sky that carried these sparkles was very distant and more transparent at night. He must be floating the sun and the stars in the same sea that fills the heavens. It was the sea above and the sea below, with the trees and the clouds and himself in between. Adam laughed again, cupping his hands and splashing water into the air. How He likes to surround me with His hands, lest I fall off the edge of His good earth!

But does a ball have an edge? Adam's eyes twinkled. What a good question for Him tonight! I wonder what He will say. If He says yes, then I will promise to fall out of Eden, and if He says no, then I will ask Him for a walk in the heavens! Yes, it will be a wonderful question. He never gives a straight answer, but He makes it a key to unlock new rooms, to discover new treasures. Adam remembered with delight the evening He answered his question about where the river comes from. "Where does it go?" He had asked in return. Adam said that he supposed it rose as mist, and collected in the clouds. "And when the clouds get too heavy?" He asked again. Adam struggled with that answer for a long time, finally proposing that it must fall on distant lands. Adam had never seen rain, but He explained that it was like the dew, though fuller and more refreshing.

Adam thought a while about rain, splashing some water from the river onto the bank. The ground grew dark, and then pushed the water away. It ran back down the bank and into the river again. Does it rain in heaven? Adam wondered. What would it do to the stars, or to the messengers? Yes, he decided, that will be my second question.

Now the sun was ripening into a golden orange, and the air was just tolerably hot. Adam stood up from his seat in the river, stretched, and shook off the water from his tall, slender frame. It had cooled off enough that he could get some work done before the evening visit. What was it He had asked me to do? Water the fruit trees, prune the branches, and that third thing. Something about the dirt. Hoe, that's what it was called. I'm to dig the dirt up and put it back for the dew to settle. As Adam headed for the plot of land that jutted out into the salt-lake, he reviewed all the things that He had told him about this land and his duties.

Adam learned that long before Eden, He had made men that looked like Himself, the Wordless Ones who had been sent before him to shape the world and to fill it. It had taken them forty millennia, but they had tamed the wilderness and, more important, filled it with men who, like the land itself, expressed the manifold and eternally varying thought of their Creator. Some men were tall, some short, some light, some dark, but all knew where the lion gets his prey, or where the ostrich makes its nest, for all knew that His hand clothed and fed them. Finally the time was ripe for His greatest creation, one who not only shared His image, but also shared His breath. But the land was not ready.

Therefore, His messenger had closed the Gate and prepared the land. When Eden had thoroughly dried, another messenger opened the Hiddekel and the Gihon to water it and remove the salt. And when that task was done, He had planted the trees and awakened Adam, breathing into him His Spirit. Then, walking beside him in the evenings, He would teach Adam all the things he needed to know to properly care for the trees, for the Wordless Ones, and especially, for the world. Because this world was His gift to Adam, who was to prepare it for His own coming when He would live here too.

Adam marveled. If He strode across the ocean of the heavens, calling out His stars by name, if He formed Eden, sending forth His flaming messengers from the Abyss, where would there be room for Him in Eden? When Adam confided his doubts, He laughed. At first Adam thought he had said something foolish but His laughter was contagious, and soon Adam was laughing too. "I will fit," He had said. "Look at the heavens, which I made to hold My world. Look at the world, which I made to hold My Eden. Look at Eden, which I made to hold My offspring. Look at yourself, Adam, which I made to hold My breath. Look at My breath, which I am to be Me."

Adam was not sure what He meant. He had never seen His breath, he had only heard His words. Was there something hidden in His words? And how could His words become visible, become solid? Adam's puzzled face told his thoughts for He laughed again, teaching Adam a new word. "A mystery is a seed that holds its future within, a fruit that is not yet ready to eat, a child that cannot wait to grow up." And then He had given Adam his second task.

"You must find the name of every creature," He commanded. Adam knew it was both a test and a task involving mystery. For if only he could hear their voices, he would know their names. But not every creature spoke. If he knew how the visible features determined their voices, however, then he could find their names by observation. He would need to learn and practice how their bodies become a word, so that he would also discover how the word becomes a body. And once he knew that, then he would also know how He could fit in Eden. It was a challenge, but Adam wanted to master it. What a glory it would be to spend, not just evenings, but all day with Him!

It was not too difficult to discover the name of the first creature he saw, for it was continually calling it out. "Bird," Adam said, trilling the "r." A bright flash of silver in the river caught his eye but it had disappeared by the time he turned his head. All he heard was the splash of the creature's return. "Fish," he said, drawing out the "sh." This was fun, Adam thought, but what will I name a creature that is silent? Surely, He will expect me to find its hidden name. Adam resolved to find out all the secrets of the animals, to find out what they eat, where they nest, and how they move, in order to extract their silent names.

* * *

Adam was tired, and not only from the heat. He wiped his forehead and looked at the building he had just finished. It was not much, three walls made of stone and mud plaster, with leafy branches for a roof. But it would provide shade from the sun and a break from the hot winds that dried his skin and cracked his lips. It had taken him most of the week, what with finding the stones down by the river and hauling the mud. But the house was not for him, it was for the animals He had brought together the previous fortnight.

They stood there in the shade, gratefully lapping up the water that Adam had brought them in a gourd from the spring. Funny-looking animals they were, splaying out their four spindly legs, muzzles buried in the trough he had provided. Neither as fierce as lions, nor as graceful as gazelles, they looked rather awkward, pitiful actually. It was as if they were as dependent on Adam for survival as Adam was on the fruit trees. And the trees depended on the irrigation and the irrigation depended on Him. The little ones had fur beginning to curl around the edges of their wrinkled skin, while the bigger ones were covered in a glossy black hair. Adam had not been able to find their names yet. For one thing, they were still young and seemed to change every day. For another, they did not seem to know who they were either with their big black eyes following Adam as he walked through their barn.

Their arrival was as solemn an event for Adam as it had been for them. Adam thought back to the night when he had brought up the matter of the heaven with Him. He had replied that he could not fall out of heaven but that heaven had fallen into him. He said that the red-eyed Bull and the bright-heeled Hunter were not just images in the ocean of the heavens but rather were icons of Eden, mysteries for him to seek. It had been a very different sort of conversation than Adam expected. It was then that He had explained about the farm and the animals.

Adam had objected, of course, that he was completely satisfied with the Garden and the trees, and had no more desire to hunt gazelle than a lion had to hunt fruit. But He explained about family, about community, about ecosystems. For just as heaven had come to earth in order to make earth into heaven, so earth only held Eden so that Eden would become the earth. The animals were not just Adam's responsibility, they were his freedom. The Bull and the Hunter were alike in both the heavens and the earth, each depending on the other, each fulfilling the other.

Adam looked at the creatures in the barn. None of them looked anything like the Bull. Adam chuckled, when he realized that he did not look anything like the Hunter either. But He did imply that His plans would take time to develop, the way a fruit takes many nights before it is ripe. "What will these poor creatures ripen into," Adam wondered, "something as fierce as the Bull?" The black one made a low noise, and Adam saw that its water trough was empty. He measured the distance to the spring with his eyes. "If I start to work on it now, by tomorrow I can have a ditch bringing water directly to the barn," he calculated. "First the trees, and then the animals. What will He bring me next?"

One of the smaller ones was bleating now, and Adam went over to scratch her behind the ears. "I'll get you a drink," he said, "but you mustn't complain. We are all in Eden together, and we'll all survive the heat together too."

Now Adam's days were full. Mornings were spent filling the feeding trough, running the water into the drinking trough, and mucking the stable. By the time the sun had cleared the eastern mountains Adam was out in the Garden, watering the trees, or tending the young shoots from the seeds that He had brought. Every week it seemed there was a new seed to sow with instructions on when to water it and what purpose each plant would serve. Adam found the succulent plants to be quite tasty in the heat of the day, taking a siesta by the river while he waited for the temperature to drop. But the grasses were harder to fathom. He had said that they were even more important than the greens, but so far Adam had found them bitter and stringy, fit more for the animals than for him. He had even smiled when Adam suggested they would make good animal feed, and replied that the good is the enemy of the best. Adam interjected, "A mystery?" "Yes," He had said, "but a brief one."

Every day Adam checked on his Brief Mystery, which grew visibly taller, changing from a grayish shoot to a brilliant green blade of grass with a swelling tip. The animals were growing fast too, in both size and number. Lower and Bleater had been joined by a menagerie He had brought: big birds and small creeping animals. Adam had to make a fence of tree branches buried in the dirt to keep them from falling into the river or trampling the Garden. Really, the day was not long enough to finish all the chores and Adam soon found himself inventing more and more short cuts and special tools to assist in their care and feeding. Evenings grew later and later, and Adam found that he could whittle fence posts or shovel handles by the cool blue light of the waxing Moon. Then there came a night when the full Moon arrived before the Sun had set and lit up the farm so brilliantly that Adam worked through the entire night, wondering if there would be a visit. He did not come that night, but when the Sun arrived and the animals began to ask for breakfast, Adam was surprised by how sluggish he felt. His body had never been this way before. So it was almost with relief that evening when he saw the late arrival of the waning Moon, knowing that He sent the darkness for Adam's rest.

"Adam. Adam." It was late. Adam opened one eye. The Moon had risen over the Eastern mountains, waning from its fullness the night before. He was standing in the Garden, calling to Adam. All Adam could think was that the Lowers had eaten through the Brief Mystery patch. He scrambled to his feet, rubbing his sore eyes. "Adam, come here." Adam stumbled more than once as he followed His voice to the Life tree. He was standing under a massive limb, looking at the fruit that seemed to erupt from its trunk. "Adam," He spoke without moving, lifting only His eyes, "Would you like a helper?"

As always, Adam never was not sure what His first words meant. "Did I fail to complete Your tasks?" he asked, "Or do You have more tasks to complete than I can finish?"

"Adam, You have done well, and you are doing well. Do not be downcast, look up. Look at the sky. The Hunter is not alone in the heavens, see who follows at his heels. Nor is the Bear alone, for night after night she brings her family wherever she goes. Your task of bringing the heavens to earth is not a short one, but longer than you know. It will require many hands, many helpers."

Adam thought back to all the Wordless Ones he had met on his travels through Eden. They had been quite shy, and tended to keep to themselves in their caves or encampments by the cliffs where they collected their food and cooked it. But they practically worshiped the ground he walked on, hindering whatever task he was engaged in, whether it was harvesting branches for the fences or finding flint for the tools, reaching out to touch him or the tools hanging from his belt. If he were not so much taller than they, he would have had a hard time outpacing them. As it was, Adam could just walk faster to escape their unwanted attention. Not only did they have to run to keep up with him but they rapidly overheated and dropped behind. If it were not for their fear of crossing the narrow peninsula with its steep cliffs, falling 100 meters down into the Salt Lake, the Garden would long since have been trampled.

"Do you mean the Wordless Ones?" Adam asked. "I do not think my fence would keep them in, nor would it keep them out." The thought of the "Brief Mystery" being trampled, and the fruit of the Life tree being stripped gave him a shudder.

"No Adam, I did not mean the Wordless Ones, that will come later. Would you like a helper who is like you, that you can talk with, that will work alongside you?"

Adam felt his insides churning, he did not really know what to say. "But I want to talk with You." he said, "I can talk to myself just fine. If you taught me more about gardening, I think I could finish in the daylight. And how will I learn anything if I talk to someone else? If I just get these tools made, I believe I can do everything you asked. And what if the helper just wants to talk to You instead?"

Before Adam could take another breath, he was interrupted: "Adam. I will never leave you nor stop talking with you. I will teach you much more about gardening as well. But not everything can be learned by listening, some things must be learned by doing. One of those things is teaching. I do not speak with everyone as clearly as I have spoken with you. Just as you have taught the animals to come for milking, or taught the earth to receive the dew, so you must teach the Wordless Ones to speak, to count, to perform all the tasks that I have taught you."

Adam was silent. He could hardly keep up with the tasks of gardening and animal keeping, and now He was adding another task. But it was a different sort of task. It was the opportunity to become like Him. As He was to Adam, so Adam must become to the Wordless Ones. In order to bring Him into Eden, Adam would have to make Eden into heaven, with everyone speaking the words of heaven. Yet Eden was so huge, more than thirty days' journey to reach the Gates! And Wordless Ones also lived outside Eden, in the cold mountains and desert plains. Three hundred days, three thousand days, thirty thousand days just to find them all and teach them. Yet none of the Wordless Ones lived for thirty thousand days—by the time he had taught them all, he would have to start all over again!

Adam looked up at the sky, where the Moon's light washed out most of the stars except for the brightest three, the summer triangle. The Hunter was not visible yet but the red eye of the Bull peered over the horizon at him. The Bull was only apparently alone, for Adam knew how many companions he had after the Moon had set. Adam thought back to the day when Lower and Bleater had come, and imagined them as patriarchs, towering over their herds in the river pastures. Adam turned toward Him, his face a wordless question.

This time He did not answer, and Adam knew that he was expected to find the answer. He looked up again, toward the north where the stars turned around the Man with a Club. It might even have been a hoe or a shovel so he could have been named The Gardening Man. The Man was nearly flat on his back now, perhaps overcome by the heat of summer, yet staring up toward the bright Pole star and beyond, toward the Goose in full flight over the Milky Way river. He is no more able to stand than I am, Adam thought. And why is it he looks forever at the Pole star, morning and evening, winter and summer? And why does that Pole star outshine him, rivaling the Moon for unsetting glory? And why is the Goose and the Bull, yes, even the Hunter so far away, beyond Heaven's river? Could it be that He will bring me a star that will lift me to my feet, someone who comes before birds, before irrigation, before animals, a light that shines when all other stars have faded and set?

Adam lowered his eyes to the Life tree, and the brightness of His eyes said "Yes."

"Even brighter than me?"

"Of course," He said, "the job of the Pole star is to be bright, to be seen, to be a guide. But you were given a different task: to prepare Eden for Heaven, for My coming. Are you willing to be outshone?"

Adam looked at the gibbous Moon, reflecting the light of the Sun. It was bright enough to see the colors of the green leaves and red fruit of the

Life tree, yet cool enough to lure him back to work. It was not a demotion to be a lesser light, it was simply a different task. The Sun ruled the day, and the Moon ruled the night. But why then had He made Adam first? Surely the greater light has priority of time as well as space?

"Adam," He said, "when you prepare Eden for Me, will not the greater come after the lesser? In my Creation, that which is first must always come last, and those whom you serve make you the master. You have been preparing Eden for more than Me, you have been preparing it for her. For it will be through her that I shall come to live in Eden."

Adam's head was spinning. So many things to reconsider, so many new responsibilities. But at the same time, the new ones replaced the old ones. He would no longer have to hoe the Garden if he could teach the Wordless Ones to do it. Nor would he be teaching alone, but she would be with him, talking to them, talking to him, doubling his voice, doubling his strength. And had He not promised to place her closer than the animals, even closer than the irrigating river? Had He not promised to make her a never-setting star to guide him through Heaven, to guide Heaven to Eden?

Adam looked once more at Him, standing in the shadows cast by the Moon. "But why will I need a guide when You are here?"

"Adam," He said, "You will not always see me. Nor will you always hear my voice. But where the two of you are, I will be there also. That is what a guide star does."

Adam thought about waiting through the hot, heavy hours of the day, waiting for Him to come, waiting for the pleasure of talking with Him. If she were there, the waiting would be shorter. A bit of Heaven come to Eden. First the River and the Hunter, then the Bull and the Goose, and now like the Bear and the Dog, a companion and guide. But unlike all of them, a star of dazzling brightness, a star that never set. Not a light that rules like the Sun or reveals like the Moon, but a light whose task is to guide the travelers of Eden through the waters of heaven, to guide the denizens of Heaven to their Eden home. The thought of sharing Eden, of sharing speech, of sharing Him filled Adam with a strange happiness that was also a familiar joy.

"Yes," he said at last, "I will."

4.2 Linguistics of Eden

In the previous two chapters, we looked at the geological and genetic origins of the Flood, where I argued that it took such a catastrophic destruction to undo the genetic mess introduced by the two separate Falls of mankind: the genetic and the epigenetic. In this chapter I have go back to Genesis 2 and look at the creation of Eden, Adam, and Eve. To understand the need for such a catastrophic Flood, we must understand how place, person, and purpose intertwine in Genesis 2. First, we see the historically special place called Eden. Then we look at the epigenetically unique makeup of Adam. Finally, in a tantalizing glimpse of the New Jerusalem, we look at the promise of Eve. This section examines Genesis 2 somewhat as a commentary would, but using all the exegetical tools we developed in the previous two chapters: linguistics, genetics, and geology.

4.2.1 Genesis 1 is not Genesis 2

Genesis 2 is a key chapter in the theology of man, because it describes him before sin came into the world. If we want to know what we were made for and how we are to recover our heritage, we must turn to Genesis 2. It is the foundation of biblical anthropology and the lightning rod for current theological disputes on sin, repentance, sanctification, and many other issues. When you read a title of a sermon or a book that uses the words "Historical Adam," you can be sure it is about Genesis 2. This approach addresses controversial issues. For Adam was historical, living about 10,500 BC in a location not far north from Benghazi today. He was apparently quite tall—I suspect over seven feet—and probably had brown eyes and dark hair.

We know so much about him because we have multiple accounts of him, as discussed later. But we must not misunderstand what Genesis 2 is telling us. And the greatest misunderstanding has come from conflating it with Genesis 1.

While the devout see no problem in having two accounts of the same exciting story, Julius Wellhausen had the exact opposite reaction, finding the difference a profound challenge to his faith.[1] Ignited by these two chapters, Wellhausen developed his JEDP "*décollage*" theory of formation of the MT text that has dominated Biblical studies for over a century.[2]

The nuances of identifying anonymous contributors by their vocabulary usage I leave to the armchair amateurs. What about the elephant in the living room: Why are there two chapters in which man and several other living creatures are created, but in different ways?

1. Encyclopedia-Britannica. "Wellhausen."
2. Theopedia. "JEDP theory."

Wellhausen and "higher critics" who hold a high view of their scholarship said it was because two (or more) people wrote the accounts of one event. Conservative Bible scholars, who hold a higher view of the text, have suggested that one person wrote both chapters about the same event, but in a non-chronological order, with variants entitled "literal," "framework," "analogical," or "complementary." Typical of such analyses is that of theologian C. John Collins:

> "Since Gen 2:7 recounts the formation of the first human (cf. verse 6 which says there was not a human up to this point), we cooperate with the author by taking it as complementary to 1:27. In doing so we note that the formation of the woman, which is given in the same verse in the broad stroke account of chapter 1, is in chapter 2 separated from the making of the man by several events."[3]

Collins cites both similarities and differences, but believes it is our duty to focus on the former rather than the latter. But there may be a third option: Chapters 1 and 2 are written by the same person about different events. In fact, there is good scientific evidence that the events of the two chapters are separated by about 40,000 years, roughly the extent of the Upper Paleolithic era. This should not appear too surprising because many "gap Old Earth Creationists" think the first chapter accounts for some 12 billion years between the Big Bang of Gen 1:1 and the creation of mankind in Gen 1:26.

How could there be a few thousand years' gap between Chapter 1 and Chapter 2?

Well, one argument against gaps is that if the details in Chapter 2 are non-chronologically interspersed with events in Chapter 1, then it would be impossible to pull the Chapter 2 story away and leave a temporal gap. Collins continues his argument:

> "The making of the woman is preceded by a declaration of 'not good' in 2:18, indicating that at that point we have not yet come to the 'very good' status of everything in 1:31. We note further that Gen 2:19 describes the formation of the animals. All of this suggests that the story line events of 2:5–25 are events of the 'sixth day' of 1:24–31."

Collins is saying that if God declared mankind's creation "good" in 1:31, then it would be a contradiction for Gen 2:18 to say it was "not good" a little later. Presumably then, the 2:18 statement had to chronologically precede the Gen 1:31 statement, to show that God had fixed the problem, making

3. Collins. "Discourse Analysis" 269– 276.

2:18 temporally out of order. Likewise, 2:19 talks about creation of animals that had already been made and declared good, so once again, why would God redo a successful work, unless the text was a flashback. Collins's logic hinges on the unchanging nature of God, who would not or could not declare His work both good and not good at the same time. I agree.

However, why must we assume that God is addressing the same creatures? What if two different men are being addressed, and two different animals being created? Could the first man have been good and the second not so much?

If the words are addressed to different people, then we must explain why we are given two separate beginnings. Not only would Adam have had separate beginnings (where "*adam*" is a generic attribution for "man"), but so would Eve, as well as cattle, beasts of the field, birds of the air, and some special trees. Such explanations become unnecessary in the "non-chronological" interpretation. Following William of Ockham's dictum (Occam's Razor), *pluralitas non est ponenda sine necessitate,* we should prefer the explanation that "uses the fewest arbitrary assumptions," also known as the law of parsimony.

Which interpretation is simplest, most parsimonious; which is most "natural"?

This question turns out to be highly contentious, for without some way to weight assumptions, counting is entirely subjective. For example, does the "non-chronological" assumption count as one hypothesis or five or six, one for each instance of a flashback? Conversely, does the "gap" assumption count as one hypothesis, or five or six, one for each repeated creation? Historically, the non-chronological assumption was taken as the simpler one and a second set of creations denied. As discussed earlier, however, progressive revelation means that tradition need not always be complete; rather in the fullness of time new information could and should enrich our understanding of Scripture. So in the spirit of *midrash*, let us cling to the text but hold both interpretations loosely to see which has the greater explanatory power. For if the two events really are separate, then the details should also differ.

Tabulating the differences in Table 4.1 we see that Gen. 1:26—2:3 is both impersonal and general, it could take place by delegated action, whereas Gen. 2:4–25 is both personal and specific, it had to be accomplished in person. It is always possible to tell a story in generalities and then to go back and fill in details, which is how most "non-chronological" commentators account for the differences. But in several instances the details do not fit into the general story. For example, male and female are created simultaneously in Genesis 1, but sequentially in Genesis 2. And they are instructed to fill the earth in Genesis 1, but told to cultivate Eden in Genesis 2, which would prevent them from wandering about.

Topics	Genesis 1:26—2:3	Genesis 2:4-25
Rhetorical intro	"Let us make"—continuity	Toledot—new chapter
Materials	Imper. w/o means, *ex nihilo*	Pers. w/dust of Earth,w/rib
Human names	Imper. male & female	Pers. Adam and Eve
Act of creation	Imper. *bara*–create	Pers. *yatsar*–formed
Post-creation	Imper. *bara*–create (repeat)	Pers. breathed into nostrils
God's name	Imper. Elohim	Pers. YHWH Elohim
God's command	Imper. be fruitful, multiply	Pers. name animals, wife
God's purpose	Gen. dominion over creation	Spec. cultivate Eden
Man's location	Gen. fill the earth	Spec. Eden of four rivers
Man's food	Gen. All seed-plant,tree-fruit	Spec. Garden trees but one

Table 4.1: Comparison of the creation accounts of Genesis chapters 1 & 2.

There are other inconsistencies between the stories that are not individually significant but, taken together, give pause for thought. Everything in Genesis 2 has a name—God, man, woman, four rivers, the garden, even two trees—whereas nothing is named in Genesis 1, all designations are generic. Something that goes beyond filling in details is apparent in this story, something about names themselves. Then we find out in Genesis 2 that this is the first job of Man: naming the four rivers, naming the trees, naming the animals, naming his wife. Only after the naming, do we get the first prohibition in the Bible, which is itself only possible if distinctions (names) can be made. So what the lumpers take as mere details in two identical accounts becomes of primary chronological significance for splitters, which means it is more than a detail, it is a difference between the accounts.

And if these details are different, where Genesis 1 is the creation of the first man and Genesis 2 the second, then we should separate the acts of God, we should separate the blessings of God, we should even separate the foods of men. The text remains silent as to how far apart the two chapters lie. But science gave us a hint when we learned that the DNA of Upper Paleolithic Cro-Magnon bones was 100 percent identical to that of modern man.[4] Genetic clocks also place the separation of "ancient modern man" from "last common ancestor" some 50,000 years ago, placing the first creation of Gen 1:26 approximately 50,000 BC.[5] But in this section I examine the second creation of Genesis 2 line-by-line to show how separating the two chapters gives us new information about Eden, Adam, and Eve.

4.2.2 Genesis 2 Creation

As Table 4.1 demonstrated, everything in Chapter 2 is specific and particular. If we are not forced by our interpretive method to generalize God's second creation, there is information to be learned from the specifics. And the first specific piece of information is the climate, often overlooked when the text is interpreted as symbolic.

I am indebted to many commentaries[6] on Genesis—particularly Cassuto and Kidner—but they are all textual commentaries, focusing on the literary meanings and implications of the Scripture genre.[7] Our discussion, however, is not focused on the literary and moral significance of the text but on the scientific content of Genesis. In the past, a scientific critique was shunned because it brought in non-Biblical criteria, with the result that only internal textual criteria (Scripture interpreting Scripture) was allowed. That approach misses the strength of science because external observation is potentially objective, unlike the necessarily subjective interpretation of texts. In this way, science provides a control, a hard limit on interpretation because it requires consistency with visual data (Ps 19:1–2). For this reason, I refrain from heavily footnoting the following translation lest it be confused with a textual commentary, which it manifestly is not.[8]

4.2.2.1 *The Preparation of Eden*

> Gen 2:4 *These are the generations of the heavens and of the earth when they were created, in the day that the LORD God made the earth and the heavens . . .*

4. Caramelli, et al."A 28,000 Years Old" e2700.
5. Rieux et al. "Improved calibration" 2780–2792.
6. Best commentaries. *Bestcommentaries.com*
7. Cassuto. *Commentary*; Kidner. *Genesis*."
8. Sheldon. "A Scientific Survey."

The phrase "these are the generations," *towledot,* is a semantic separator indicating a summary of what preceded and a transition to what follows. Gesenius's lexicon gives it two meanings: generations, or history. It indicates that the story of creation is concluded, and a new story is beginning. And remarkably, the first personal name in Genesis begins the new section, the tetragrammaton, which is the personal name of God, usually translated with capitals: LORD. As with Moses at the burning bush, this usage indicates that something special is about to happen because God is doing it in person.

> Gen 2:5 *Now no shrub of the field was yet in the earth, and no plant of the field had yet sprouted, for the LORD God had not sent rain upon the earth, and there was no man to cultivate the ground.*

The phrase "shrub of the field" (*siyach ha-sadeh*) suggests "of the sort in cultivated land," because fields are not usually wilderness. More specifically, it tells us there has not yet been cultivation of wild grasses or wild legumes, because the singular "shrub," *siyach*, when followed by the phrase "of the field," *ha-sadeh*, implies domestication, as I discuss later. The phrase "in the earth" uses the same MT word, *'erets*, used of the global Earth in Genesis 1, but ties it to the man's cultivation of the ground, a regional effect. In that case, the reason for the lack of domesticated crops in this particular region of the globe is that it has a dry climate and lacked a gardener.

If we assume that the Med bed is being described, then this verse also tells us other things. It tells us that the Med bed is now exposed ground after 200 years of the Younger Dryas glaciation that brought drought to the Mediterranean. But it is still very dry, much like Death Valley, and likely to be saturated with salt. Then either the salt or the desert heat is making it impossible for even wind-blown weed seeds to sprout.

> Gen 2:6 *But a mist used to rise from the earth and water the whole surface of the ground.*

If Gen 2:6 is a transition from the previous verse, then land that was too dry for seeds to sprout is now getting water. And it is not just a bit of water near the rivers; the entire bed of the Med is affected.

What does this mist do?

It precipitates on the surface, where it dissolves the salt and carries it downward into the soil. As in many dry regions of the world (e.g., Imperial Valley, Calif.), the deep soil has a lot of salt as a result but the shallower soil, the soil that seeds would sprout in, is now sweet. This is not irrigation, because the difficult part of irrigation is finding a way to spread the water evenly over the ground. Modern circular irrigation systems use sprinklers to approximate a mist. But natural mist is indeed found in many dry areas of the world. One famous location is a desert in Namibia that receives a warm wind off the ocean every morning when the land is still night-cold, causing a mist to fall on its sand dunes.[9]

In order for the mists of Gen 2:6 to "water the whole surface," the Med bed would need large salt lakes, which would evaporate large quantities of moisture to condense on the night-cooled soil. But unlike those of Namibia, these lakes are 3500 meters below sea level, with 50 percent greater air pressure and 50 percent more moisture. As a result, the atmosphere can hold up to seventy cubic centimeters of water per cubic meter of air, producing a very thick fog. So Gen 2:6 is telling us that something had changed in the climate, and a desert next to a warm-water lake is now being prepared for agriculture.

4.2.2.2 The Epigenetic Second Creation—Adam

> Gen 2:7a *Then the LORD God formed man of the dust of the ground . . .*

Unlike Genesis 1, God's revealed name is used here, making this creation more personal. God's unique name (not the more generic Elohim) is described as forming (*yatsar*) man (*'adam*) from pre-existing material as an artisan forms a clay pot, not creating (*bara*) man *ex nihilo* as in Genesis 1. Now if God is referred to by his personal name, man cannot help but be personal too. Instead of using the generic "man," the translators should have capitalized it "Adam" as they do later in the chapter.

Likewise, the personal nature of dust is also implied. Dust is certainly used to signify non-living material, as distinct from life, but there is no indication what this dust is composed of. Dust generally lacks the carbon and hydrogen elements that make up most of our bodies, so if God is not *ex nihilo* transmuting the elements in the dust, then He is using some very special organic dust, perhaps what Job has in mind when he reminds us "*to dust we shall return.*"

Why are we told about the formative material at all?

Because, as I will argue later, Cro-Magnon man was the Gen 1:26 creation of the bodily *Imago Dei*, this clause emphasizes for us that the Edenic creation includes something different, something more than an *ex nihilo* material creation. Genesis 1 told us about the creation of the materials, but Genesis 2 is telling us about something else. If the *yatsar* of Chapter 2 is

9. National-Geographic. "Africa's Skeleton Coast" 54–85.

using the *bara* of Chapter 1, then I might loosely paraphrase this verse: *the LORD God formed personal/named/Adam from the material of bodily man.* In this interpretation, Adam would then have the same genetic material as Cro-Magnon man, but organized or shaped differently. He is an epigenetic creation—for as we shall see, unlike Chapter 1, everything in Chapter 2 is an epigenetic creation.

Gen 2:7b *and breathed into his nostrils the breath of life.*

With this act, we see another personal commitment not present in Genesis 1. Here, God stoops down and exhales His *neshemah chayyim* into Adam, giving him life.

What is this *neshemah chayyim*, this breath of life?

The more common MT word for "life-spirit," *ruwach*, which can apply to animals, is not used here. Instead, we encounter the more personal word, *neshemah*, a quality possessed only by God and Man. It would be tempting to view it as a "life-force," but then Adam would be merely a bodily creation, no different from the Genesis 1 creation of Cro-Magnon man. Nor can animals be vessels of God's breath simply because they move, eat, and breathe, which would amount to pantheism. The clear separation between Genesis 1 and 2 indicates that the personal creation of Adam is distinct from the bodily creation we saw in Chapter 1. The two creations are meant to be separated by a vast gulf.

God did not just bequeath Adam a generic *ruwach* life-spirit, but His own breath, in a very personal act. For the MT *aph*, which KJV translated "nostrils" here, is translated "face" in most of the remainder of Genesis, making it seem that God's action is like the CPR lifesaving technique where one pinches the nostrils shut and breathes mouth-to-mouth. God's breath is not simply inflating the lungs, but is passing through the lips, teeth, and vocal cords along the way. That is why there is something very personal about breathing God's breath, something related to language and conversation that goes beyond simply providing oxygen for a material body. That immaterial something is the focus of this chapter.

Gen 2:7c *And man became a living being.*

After this very personal act, Adam becomes a *nephesh chayyah*, a living being. The KJV translates it "living soul," though the same word pair appears previously six times in Genesis where the KJV translates it "living creature" instead. So it would appear that this term is not personal, but a generic attribute of any animal, no more than *ruwach*, an enlivening spirit. There are good reasons for the KJV to translate it as "soul," however, because it begins to be used that way in Lev. 17:11 and throughout the remainder of the MT. The point is not that man became alive, although he could hardly do otherwise, the point is that he became a holistic body-soul, a *nephesh chayyah*. This creation, unlike the bodily creation of Genesis 1, is an immaterial creation of the *neshemah chayyim*. If the point of the account of a personal creation in Genesis 2 is to distinguish it from Genesis 1, this verse also reveals a continuity between the two creations—it seems that God's enlivening breath also requires a living body-soul.

But it is significant that the Aramaic translation of the Hebrew, translated sometime around the time of Christ, uses a different explanation of the *nephesh chayyah*. The less flowery *Onqelos Targum* from the eastern tradition of Babylon,[10] as translated by J. W. Etheridge [1862] says: "And the Lord God created Adam from dust of the ground, and breathed upon his face the breath of lives, and it became in Adam a Discoursing Spirit."

The Western tradition, as represented in the *Yerushalmi Targum*, amplifies this further:

> "And the Lord God created man in two formations; and took dust from the place of the house of the sanctuary, and from the four winds of the world, and mixed from all the waters of the world, and created him red, black, and white; and breathed into his nostrils the inspiration of life, and there was in the body of Adam the inspiration of a speaking spirit, unto the illumination of the eyes and the hearing of the ears."

It is encouraging that both of these ancient translations preserve the meaning that we have so laboriously recovered—the gift of speech.

> Gen 2:8 *The LORD God planted a garden toward the east, in Eden; there he placed the man whom He had formed.*

The third personal name we discover in Genesis is that of a special place, Eden, in which a garden is located. The directions suggest that the first cultivation was just east of a lake or sea. The word for garden, *gan*, carries the idea of an enclosed space. It may be a peninsula or a valley with a body of water on the western side. Alternatively, this might be a reference to the more eastern of the two basins of the Med bed, the one named (by Adam) Eden.

Just as Gen 1:27 repeats the word *bara*, created, so Gen 2:8 repeats the word *yatsar*, formed. The clause "whom He had formed" modifies the noun, indicating that "forming" is what is special about the man. Unlike the

10. Targum, transl. J. W. Etheridge.

Cro-Magnons who were created *ex nihilo*, the Adamic man was formed. Forming implies personal attention like that of an artisan, just as specific as the placing of the man in Eden. But more importantly, forming adds information, the way an artisan takes a shapeless thing of pure potential and gives it a specific, personal shape.

It is only after the forming of Adam that we encounter our first proper place name in Genesis, that of the garden, Eden. Although this detail would not arouse much interest if it occurred later in the book, the fact that no place names have been used at all up to this point is significant. Likewise, when the animals are named, it is not God who gives them their names. So, it would seem logical that Adam named Eden and its four rivers also. If that be so, then we are being told something very significant. First, God does not name even landmarks; Adam does. And second, if anthropologists are correct that Cro-Magnon man existed 40,000 years previously, then Cro-Magnon man had never named the garden or these rivers either.

> 2:9–10a *Out of the ground, the LORD God caused to grow every tree that is pleasing . . . . Now a river flowed out of Eden to water the garden;*

Trees require a great deal of water, but if the surface soil is dry, they may flourish where herbs cannot because their roots go deep. The last verse suggests that some time has elapsed since Gen 2:6; God (or Adam) is indeed irrigating what would otherwise be a rather dry region. But more significantly, this verse describes how the Med bed was prepared for the Garden.

The geology and hydrology of Eden will be a topic in Volume 2, but here is a brief chronology. First, in Gen 2:5, the Gates had to be closed and the Med bed dried out. The same dam at the Gates shut off the Gulf Stream, started the glaciation of the Younger Dryas over Europe and the Urals, and reduced the river flow into the Med bed. The high temperatures of the Med bed kept rain from falling there as well. So the Med bed went dry after about 200 years of drought, accelerated in the last few decades as the shrinking sea caused the air temperature over the lake to rise very high (as seen in the C-14 signature of the Greenland ice cores). But the soil was still saturated with salt, heated extremely hot, and completely unsuitable for farming.

Then there was a swift reversal, possibly prior to Gen 2:6, which caused the Gulf Stream to flow and Europe to thaw. This "Bølling-Allerød" warming was thought to derive from shedding Antarctic glaciers raising the sea level and restarting the conveyor belt that brought heat to Europe. The result was a mega-flood in Northern Eurasia caused by flooding over impermeable permafrost. As a result, the Caspian Sea overflowed into the Black Sea, and the Black Sea overflowed into the Hiddekel, thence into the

Med bed. At the same time, and perhaps as part of the same event, heavy rains caused Lake Albert in central Africa to overflow and cut a channel into the northward flowing pre-Nile that drained from Egypt into the Med bed. Dumont reports on the recent C-14 dating of Nile river mussels "The results demonstrated that the present flow regime of the Nile was re-established 15,000 years ago, when the abrupt return of the summer monsoon precipitated the overflow of Lakes Albert and Victoria in the Ugandan headwaters of the White Nile."[11]

The result was the connection of a short, annual, pre-Nile river to a year-round, constant headwater source, producing for the first time, a constant flow of fresh water through the Sahara and into the Med bed. The overlap of the radiocarbon dates from the two branches of the Nile sets this event between 11,900–11,200 BC, which is very close to our mega-flood date for the establishment of the Hiddekel. So, both rivers, the Hiddekel and the Gihon, were created and directed into the Med bed at the same time, as Genesis 2 records—the Garden was finally being watered.

This influx of fresh water into the Med bed would create brackish lakes, whose evaporation would generate the morning mists discussed earlier. The mists falling on the ground as dew would wash the salt out of the soil into the lakes, make the ground sweet, and prepare the Med bed for agriculture. But as long as Europe was warm, the Med bed was hellish, over 54F/30C hotter three kilometers lower according to the adiabatic lapse rate of dry air.[12]

suwm	put	make	set	lay	appoint	give	set up	consider	turn	brought
585	155	123	119	64	19	11	10	8	5	4
yanach	leave	up	lay	suffer	place	put	set	-down	let alone	-him
75	24	10	8	5	4	4	4	4	4	2

Table 4.2: Translation of שׂוּם (*suwm*) and יָנַח (*yanach*).

At this point, a third event occurred, described in Gen 2:10. The Antarctic stopped shedding glaciers, the Gulf Stream stopped bringing warm water, Europe cooled (the Younger Dryas glaciation), and the temperature of the Med bed became tolerable for habitation. As discussed in the next two volumes, the four rivers of Eden still flowed despite the drought: the Hiddekel still flowed out of the reservoir of the Black Sea through the Aegean bed, and the Gihon/Nile still flowed out of the reservoir of Lakes Albert and Victoria. Both provided a reliable source of irrigation water for the Garden

11. Dumont. "The Nile" 70.
12. Wikipedia. "Lapse rate."

even as rain ceased in the region. This is the significance of Gen 2:5, 6, and 10; they describe a sequence leading to a reservoir-fed irrigation system for a fertile valley with a Mediterranean climate—not unlike the Imperial Valley of California with its elaborate network of water redistribution.

> Gen 2:15 *Then the LORD God took the man and put him into the garden of Eden to cultivate it and keep it.*

After describing the four rivers of Eden that are now providing irrigation water, Genesis returns to the story of Adam. Once again, there is an unspecified gap between Adam's creation in Gen 2:7 and his first job description in Gen 2:15. I take this to be a period of maturation or education. This gap may also explain the approximately twelve centuries that the Younger Dryas lasted versus the thirteen centuries given in Genesis before the Flood because Adam was 130 years old when Seth was born (Gen 5:3).

In both places, the KJV translation uses the verb "put" for how Adam arrived, but MT uses two distinct words: Gen 2:8 uses *suwm*, while Gen 2:15 uses *yanach*. From Table 4.2 we see that *suwm* focuses on the action of making/putting, whereas *yanach* focuses on the state of the object—it remains. So Gen 2:8 operates on Adam as if he were a rock, whereas Gen 2:15 requires Adam to consent, to remain where he was left. In between lies the maturation not just of Adam but of language itself. Adam not only consents to be left in the Garden but is given verbal instructions on how to take care of it.

By the time we reach Gen 2:15, three climate shifts have made Eden hospitable, with irrigation water running into Eden via the four rivers. Like the Nile floods that powered Egyptian civilization, this water is partially seasonal; however, unlike the water in Egypt, it has no outlet. It must evaporate in the salt lakes or salt pans of the Med bed. As a result, during the flood season, the salt lakes would expand, returning damaging salt to the rinsed plains. Careful water management would be essential for keeping Eden fruitful. And that appears to be what Gen 2:15 is telling us about Adam's role.

Trees' root systems enable them to handle water distribution problems—desert mesquite trees, for example, are quite drought resistant due to their enormous root systems—so Adam was not merely taking care of the trees in the Garden. The staple food crops that a farmer irrigates and cultivates are herbaceous plants, especially annual grasses. Archaeology of 21,000 BC Upper Paleolithic habitation sites show that the inhabitants collected and processed wild grass seeds but did not cultivate them.[13] In contrast, the Neolithic Revolution included the spread of farming of specific cultivated grasses: barley, rye, wheat.

13. Powell. "Harvard researchers."

The seed yield of those first grass cultivars was so low, that planting them would hardly pay except in an irrigated, sunny location, with much better chances of a harvest. Even after the Flood destroyed the homeland of agriculture, the three most ancient civilizations were still based in dry, sunny, irrigated locations: the Nile, Tigris-Euphrates, and Indus River valleys. So, the connection between irrigation and the beginning of cultivation, repeated in this passage, is the significance of Adam being placed in a garden—he was to be a farmer.

The following verses discuss the Prohibition, where God commands Adam not to eat a certain fruit. Understanding the Prohibition requires us to understand Adam's makeup, his strengths and weaknesses, which are elaborated in the verses that follow the Prohibition. Skipping over the Prohibition for now, we have the curious case of the cause separated from the creation of Eve by several verses.

> Gen 2:18 *Then the LORD God said, "It is not good for the man to be alone; I will make him a helper suitable for him."*

Many commentators have taken the compound prepositional phrase "like opposite him," found only here, to mean "complementary help," help that differs from and complements his inherent capabilities. I conclude the opposite because this is the first time in Genesis that God says "not good." What is not good is "aloneness." Now if the Paleolithic creation of man had preceded the Adamic one by 40,000 years, Adam should have had many Paleolithic friends and perhaps potential mates. Yet Adam is alone. This suggests that whatever new existence Adam possessed was unique and set him apart from the prior Paleolithic creation. It also suggests that it is not mere incompatibilities (they proved no hindrance to Cain's or Noah's descendants as we see later) that set Adam apart. Rather, one or more of the attributes listed above: cultivated plants, language, or God's breath made him unique.

> Gen 2:19 *Out of the ground the LORD God formed every beast of the field and every bird of the sky, and brought them to the man to see what he would call them; and whatever the man called a living creature, that was its name.*

It is peculiar that after Gen 2:18 announces a problem, man's loneliness, we are not told of a solution but of another task for Adam—naming the animals. Rather than speculating on God's motives for this *non sequitur* or rearranging the text, we might find an explanation in the task's effects. Adam had been alone, so God made creatures to bring to Adam.

What effect did these creatures have on Adam?

Not too long ago, a bachelor colleague came into my office late—he had just been to the vet to put down a "borrowed" cat. The cat had been abandoned when her owner had suddenly died. After trying to find a new home, my friend reluctantly became the owner of his first pet. Now, eight months later, he was sorrowfully recounting the last week of ministering to a cancer-ridden cat. Adam was a bachelor too, and God brought him pets. But these were not urban pets, free-loaders kept for emotional support; these were animals with distinct jobs to do.

How can we tell they were working farm animals?

Ref	Type	#	Ref	Type	#	Ref	Type	#
Beast of the field *sadeh*			**Beast of the earth** *'erets*			**Bird of Air** *shamayim*		
Gn2:19	animal.non-bird	s	Gn1:24	non-cow, -creep	s	Gn 1:20	generic	s
Gn2:20	animal.non-cow	s	Gn1:25	non-cow, -creep	s	Gn 1:26	domestic	s
Gn3:1	animal	s	Gn1:28	non-fish, -fowl	s	Gn 1:28	domestic	s
Gn3:14	animal.non-cow	s	Gn1:30	non-fowl, -creep	s	Gn 1:30	d+edible	s
Ex 23:11	herbivore	**P**	Gn7:21	non-fowl-cow-creep	s	Gn 2:19	domestic	s
Ex 23:29	ambiguous	**S**	Gn 9:2	non-fowl, -fish	s	Gn 2:20	domestic	s
Lv 26:22	carnivore	p	Gn 9:10	non-fowl, -fish	s	Gn 6:7	generic	p
Dt 7:22	ambiguous	p	Gn 9:16	terrestrial	s	Gn 7:3	domestic	**P**
2Sa 21:10	carnivore	p	Lv 11:2	edible	**P**	Gn 7:23	d+generic	s
2Ki 14:9	(herbivore)	s	Lv 25:7	owned non-cow	s	Gn 9:2	dread	s
2Ch25:18	(herbivore)	s	Lv 26:6	evil	p	De 28:26	carrion	p
Jb 5:23	(carnivore)	p	1Sa17:46	carnivore	p	1Sa 17:44	carrion	p
Jb 39:15	wild(ovi-vore?)	s	Jb 5:22	dangerous	p	1Sa 17:46	carrion	p
Jb 40:20	wild(herbivore)	s	Ps 79:2	carnivore	p	2Sa 21:10	carrion	p
Ps104:11	wild(herbivore)	s	Ez 14:15	evil	p	1Ki 14:11	carrion	p
Is 43:20	wild(carnivore)	**S**	Ez 29:5	carnivore	p	1Ki 16:4	carrion	p
Is 56:9	carnivore	p	Ez 32:4	carnivore	p	1Ki 21:24	carrion	p
Je12:9	carnivore	p	Ez 34:25	evil	p	Jb 12:7	generic	p
Je27:6	wild ambiguous	p	Ez 34:28	carnivore	**S**	Jb 28:21	generic	p
Je28:14	wild ambiguous	p				Jb 35:11	generic	p
Ez 31:6	(carnivore)	p	**Bird of the Air**(cont)			Ps 79:2	carrion	p
Ez 31:13	(carnivore)	p	Ez 29:5	carrion	p	Ps 104:12	generic	p
Ez 34:5	carnivore	p	Ez 31:6	generic	p	Ec 10:20	domestic	s
Ez 34:8	carnivore	**S**	Ez 31:13	carrion?	p	Je 4:25	generic	p
Ez 38:20	(carnivore)	p	Ez 32:4	generic	p	Je 7:33	carrion	p
Ez 39:4	carnivore	p	Ez 38:20	generic	p	Je 9:10	domestic	s
Ez 39:17	carnivore	**S**	Hs 2:18	generic	p	Je 15:3	carrion	p
Hs 2:12	herbivore	p	Hs 4:3	generic	p	Je 16:4	carrion	p
Hs 2:18	(carnivore)	p	Hs 7:12	generic	p	Je 19:7	carrion	p
Hs 4:3	(carnivore)	p	Zp 1:3	generic	p	Je 34:20	carrion	p
Hs 13:8	carnivore	**S**						

Table 4.3: Singular v. plural animals in: "bird/beast of the sky/field/earth"

Look at the words used to describe their origin. They are not "created," *bara*, but "formed," *yatsar*. This term was identified earlier as referring to a personal, epigenetic creation, in the same way that farm animals are systematically bred. The object of the verb is *chay sadeh*, "beast of the field." It seems odd that "beast" needs the modifier "of the field" except to distinguish it from some other kind of beast. And if so, the phrase implies the same distinction in plants. Gen 2:5 modified "herb" in the same way, *siyach sadeh*. Because the location is a garden, it seems reasonable to think of the phrase *sadeh* as meaning "domestic" or "cultivated."

But if *chay sadeh* means a "domesticated animal," then would not the next phrase, "bird of the sky," mean domesticated birds, such as geese or chickens?

This question prompted a *blueletterbible* search on three word pairs: "beast of the field" (*chay sadeh*), "beast of the earth" (*chay 'erets*), and "bird of the heavens" (*'owph shamayim*). Occasionally the modifier was separated from its noun by a relative clause, as in Gen 1:20, but if the meaning is the same as the word cluster, I included it in the exhaustive list of Table 4.3. I also characterized the type of animal described in the verse as herbivore, carnivore, or ambiguous. Often the animal is described as wild rather than domestic. If the animal appears in a list with a carnivore, then I put parentheses around its name to indicate "guilt by association." I also flag whether the name appears in the singular or plural. Birds listed can be domesticated edible, carrion, or generic/wild. Most plural uses of the word refer to wild carnivores or generic carrion birds, where I boldface the exceptions (see Figure 4.1).[14]

I argue that the key distinction is "dominion." A carrion bird dominates its prey and a wild bird has dominion over its land, but a farmyard bird has dominion over neither; it is dominated by man. Usually word pairs in the singular are dominated/domesticated and word pairs in the plural are dominate/wild. The significance of the modifier "field, earth, heavens" is not simply an aesthetic touch but a "specifier of domination."

Because this is an important point, I must quantify just how accurate the statistics are for what we usually find (singular dominated; plural dominant). That is, there are many reasons why exceptions occur but if one cherry-picks the data to "improve" it, one can get just about any answer desired. Thus I include the entire data set of 89 word pairs which, with 9/89 exceptions, is 90 percent reliable. It is least reliable for "beast of the field" and most reliable for "bird of the air" which features but one exception in

14. Iliff. "Greylag Goose"; Nandy. "Egyptian Vulture"; Palmer. "Sheep"; Shepherd. "Lioness hunting."

thirty-nine instances. Jeremiah's usage for "bird of the air" is instructive because 5/6 of his plurals are carrion birds with 1/6 ambiguous, and the lone singular is clearly a farmyard bird. We can conclude that this usage difference is not merely a personal word preference of Moses, but a lexical difference that persisted for almost a thousand years until Jeremiah's time.

To my astonishment, this same plural-wild/singular-domestic distinction shows up in a cuneiform Akkadian version of the Flood written in the same time period (second millennium BC).[15] The similar usage suggests that the distinction is highly persistent in space, time, and language across the ANE, making it a reliable inference. Now that we are alerted to this distinction, notice there are only two plural word pairs in all of Genesis, Gen 6:7 and 7:3, and both pertain to birds.

Because these pairs occur in Noah's story, we must ask, do they reference wild or domestic birds? In Gen 6:7, God is planning to destroy "man, beast, creeping thing, and birds of the heavens." The plural form appears in a list of generic categories that lack specifiers, so the word pair can reference wild birds. In Gen 7:2, Noah is given a series of instructions about saving domesticated animals: God commands that seven sacrificial or "clean" animals are to be loaded rather than the usual two. Then in Gen 7:3, the category of sacrificial animals is extended to birds, so that seven "birds of the air" are to be loaded. This plural may be the result of syntactical agreement with the number seven, where the domestication specifier has already been given in the previous verse, as well as assumed for sacrificial animals. On the other hand, it may be a reference to the wild raven that we hear about later.

Therefore, with the possible exception of Gen 7:3, I conclude that the entire Genesis story is about domination and domestication, about appointing Adam as the Gardener. And the purpose of the domestic animals epigenetically formed by God in Gen 2:19 is to provide Adam with a farm, as well as give him opportunity to domesticate (name) them.

15. Finkel. *The Ark Before Noah.*

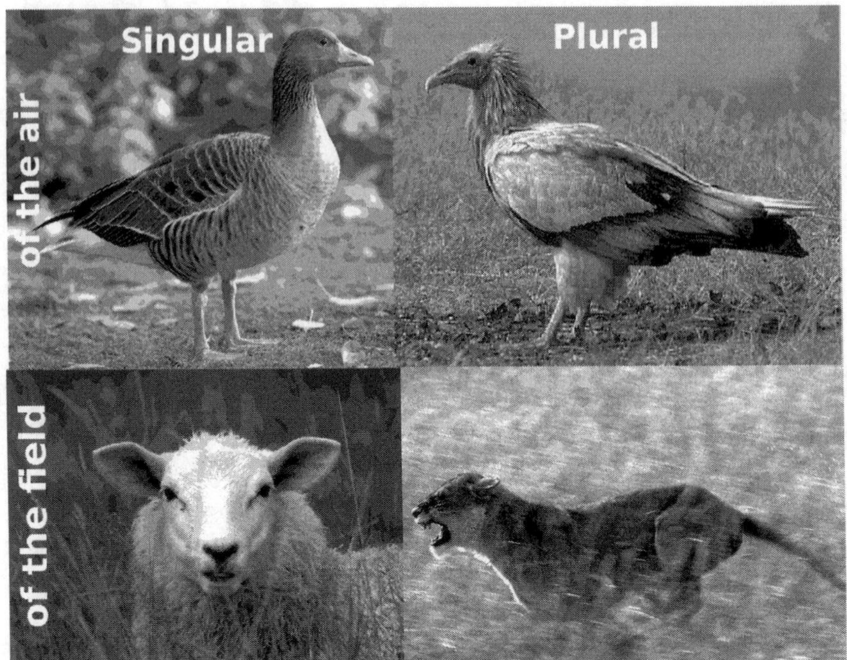

Figure 4.1: Bird/Beast of location, singular-domestic versus plural-wild. (Wiki Commons)

Is there external support for the use of these terms to refer to domesticated farm animals? We have a time line for the spread of Neolithic farming and its domestication of animals.[16] Swine and cattle domestication became widespread about 8000 BC, sheep and goats followed about 7000 BC, while chickens and dairy cows came a little later, about 6000 BC. Although chickens showed up perhaps as early as 6000 BC in China, the first report of European chickens was about 3000 BC, which is well after the NR. So chickens were probably not denizens of the "first farm."[17] Are there any other domesticated birds? Well, geese and ducks were domesticated by the Egyptians by at least 4000 BC, which is a full 1000 years before chickens. There does not seem to be much research on the origins of goose breeds, perhaps because geese were not as economically important as chickens. To complicate matters, archaeological evidence (from middens) is ambiguous because wild geese travel great distances, and it is difficult to distinguish between wild and domesticated remains found in archaeological sites. Thus, I surmise that it is possible for Gen 2:19 to refer to domesticated geese, but impossible for it to refer to carrion birds.

16. Pringle. "Neolithic Agriculture" 1448; Larson et al. "Ancient DNA" 15276–15281.
17. Westal and Zhou. "Did chickens go north?" 205–218.

> Gen 2:20a *The man gave names to all the cattle, and to the bird[s] of the sky, and to every beast of the field . . .*

The image is very striking: God brings the animals to the man one by one to discover what their names should be. For the first time we find man doing something that God himself could, but would not, do.

Why is that?

Not only was Adam capable of naming, but he was commanded to name; indeed, his first task was naming. The word *qara*, to call, is duplicated for emphasis. It is not the abstract concept of a name but the act of naming that is highlighted. The emphasis is on the ability to name rather than the existence of names. It suggests that naming implies differentiation, ranking, and control.

Aristotle is often credited with being the father of biology because he started naming or categorizing living things.[18] Egorov (with Luzin) was the father of the Moscow school of mathematics because he established set theory on the ability to name, the Axiom of Choice.[19] Gödel used the power of naming to halt the atheist agenda of Russell and the positivists, demonstrating that he could name an infinity of unprovable truths.[20] All sciences, like all endeavors, begin by naming, so it is in this very concrete sense that Adam is the father of farming, the NR, and civilization as we know it today. It is because he mastered the power of names which, as I discuss in later chapters, has an even deeper significance to mankind.

Now we understand why God did not do the naming of creatures for Adam: He wanted Adam to learn how to farm for himself. Once again, Adam's "aloneness" was not simply emotional isolation; it was also physical isolation. Adam needed a farm with farm animals to survive off the land. It was not enough for him to pick wild fruit and grow some beans; he needed the additional calories supplied by domesticated animals and birds. (We address the "vegetarian" verse of Genesis 1 in the next chapter.) This is not to say that Adam was not bored shelling beans by himself, but rather that God solved one of Adam's problems by bringing him domesticated animals.

For example, Switzerland was settled by French-speaking grape growers who lived in the valleys but could not survive in the snowy mountains. But when the German-speaking cattle herders arrived later, they settled in the mountains because they could use the unique ability of cows to digest grass to provide milk through the brutal winters. The humble cow had the magical ability to turn yellow hay into golden food, enabling an empty

18. Lennox. "Aristotle's Biology"

19. Graham and Kantor. *Naming Infinity*

20. Goldman. "The God of the Mathematicians"

ecological niche to be filled and forever changing the Swiss countryside. Farm animals make farming viable.

Why is it that Gen 2:19 features two items in the list of creatures whereas Gen 2:20 features three items—God brings beast and bird, while Adam names cattle, beast, and bird?

Some have argued that "cattle" is just another word for beast, but that makes Gen 2:20 unnecessarily redundant, a luxury unexpected in this compressed creation account. But if domestication results in cows being more important, say, than donkeys, we might be seeing the categories multiply as a result of Adam's breeding success with cows.

Gen 2:20b . . . *but for Adam there was not found a helper suitable for him.*

Recognizing what Adam was doing when he named (and bred) the domesticated animals brought to him by God, I can finally see why Adam lacked a helper. I have earlier argued that Cro-Magnon women pre-existed Adam by 40,000 years. If none of them were capable of sifting chaff, it was not because they lacked flesh and bones, rather they lacked the one thing needed to name, to rank, to control, and to farm: language. Therefore, the delay between Gen 2:18 and 2:21 is not incidental or a *non sequitur*. It explains not only the need for Eve's role, but Adam's response to Eve. She was not there just to make conversation on rainy days when he could not work in the pasture, she was not there just to give him encouraging hugs after a rough day mucking the stable, she was there to help him survive. Farming was and still is hard work. James Herriot writes about a Yorkshire farmer at his wife's funeral, wiping the tears out of his eyes and repeating "Aye, she was a grand worker."[21] For if she had not been, the farmer would likely have preceded her to the grave.

4.2.3 The Third Social Creation—Eve

> Gen 2:21–22 *So the LORD God caused a deep sleep to fall upon the man, and he slept; then He took one of his ribs and closed up the flesh at that place. The LORD God fashioned into a woman the rib, which He had taken from the man, and brought her to the man.*

Just as Adam was artistically formed from dust, so Eve is fashioned from Adam's rib. Both are made from pre-existing stuff, but Eve even more so, because she inherits the "God breath" first given to Adam.

21. Herriot. *All Creatures Great and Small* 395.

Why from a rib?

Matthew Henry's commentary is priceless, "Not made out of his head to top him, not out of his feet to be trampled upon by him, but out of his side to be equal with him, under his arm to be protected, and near his heart to be beloved."[22] Today we know that the bone marrow of the rib is where the body makes new blood cells from pluripotent stem cells which were considered at one time to be ageless cells, optimal for cloning. Eve is not literally a clone, because she lacks Adam's Y-chromosome. In principle, however, one can "knock-out" the Y-chromosome in a male somatic cell to change the sex of a clone, so in practice Eve was Adam's clone.

This makes Eve's creation subtly different from the previous two creations. The first, impersonal creation of Gen 1:26 was the *ex nihilo* creation of the DNA of mankind, whereas the second, personal creation of Gen 2:7 involved an epigenetic "turning on" of the ability to speak. This third creation, while more intimate than that of Gen 2:7, was not accomplished by *ex nihilo* information production, or even by the tuning of pre-loaded information. Rather, it was accomplished by the suppression of a Y-chromosome, an information loss. It is truly astonishing that addition can result from subtraction.

How can something new come from an irrecoverable loss of a Y-chromosome? The text goes on to give two explanations: Adam's and God's.

> Gen 2:23 *The man said, "This is now bone of my bones, and flesh of my flesh; she shall be called Woman, because she was taken out of Man."*

Finally, we see the point of this third creation. By contrasting it with the previous two creations, I can identify what makes it special. It is rather too glib to quote the French Revolution "*Vive la différence!*" as if women are a different species from men because Gen 1:26 has already recorded the creation of female humans. Nor is this creation "the creation of the other," or "the complement to Adam" because language has already enabled Adam to talk with another being, God, who certainly has everything that Adam lacks.

What exactly is it that Gen 2:22 has accomplished?

Adam says Eve is made of the same flesh as himself. For she shares not only his genetics but also his epigenetics, being made of the same substance. Only the removal of the Y-chromosome can be said to be the creation of something other, something not-me, something Adam must treat personally, as equal but separate.

22. Henry. *Commentary on the Whole Bible* 20.

How can removing a piece of information create information?

It is because the Y-chromosome suppresses or controls the genes on the X-chromosome. So powerful are the male hormones produced by the Y-chromosome that administering testosterone to a woman early in her pregnancy with a genetic female will produce an anatomic male.[23] The removal of hormones produces information that would not otherwise be expressed because the X-chromosome tool kit is cryptic, hidden, waiting for an opportunity to be expressed. Eve is then the expression of the plans hidden in Adam's chromosomes and her cryptic existence now revealed is something other than Adam, someone else that Adam can talk to. It is the same personal relationship that Adam has with God but it is now with a person made of the same stuff as himself. Because there are now precisely three persons in the entire world, it can be described as the creation of an Edenic trinity.

As Vladimir Lossky argues, the significance of a trinity is that it permits mutual support without dualistic tension; it can be defined equivalently as three relationships or three persons; its relationships are symmetric and non-hierarchical; and, it is fully recursive and yet finite.[24] So much of the "egalitarian" versus "complementarian" debate vanishes when the properties of a trinity are examined, because the relationship of a man and woman necessarily includes God. (Many twentieth-century dilemmas are a consequence of this desire for "objectivity" by the exclusion of self, recursion, and person.) But this is only Adam's view, more is revealed in the chapter when we consider God's view.

> Gen 2:24 *For this reason a man shall leave his father and his mother, and be joined to his wife; and they shall become one flesh.*

God sees the situation differently. Man is separated from woman (the mother) and is reunited with woman (his wife) to become one again. Adam sees the motion as moving from one to many, God sees it as moving from many to one. Sometimes we call this "the circle of life" but once again the analogy is too glib, for Gen 1:26 describes that same biological circle.

What is unique about the Gen 2:24 circle?

Any answer must build upon both genetic and epigenetic foundations, it must include both the one and the many, it must involve both brains and language. I conclude that "one flesh" is not a mere euphemism for sex. Even St Paul agrees when he condemns prostitution on the basis of this verse (1 Cor 6:16) adding the commentary (1 Cor 6:17), "*But he who is joined to the Lord becomes one spirit with him.*" There is something more in Gen 2:24

23. Chapelle. "Analytic review" 71–105.

24. Lossky. *The Image and Likeness of God.*

than is included in Gen 1:26. It must be more than material, more even than epigenetic. It must be spiritual.

My conclusion is that the purpose of this third creation is a spiritual entity we call society, whose science is sociology. If sociology is based on speech, on "agreed upon conventions" of communication, then Adam and God already had a society in Gen 2:7. But a society requires more than two persons, just as worship requires more than one person. The dynamics change completely when three are in the room. Notice how in Genesis 3 the serpent undermines this society by questioning Eve's understanding of Adam's retelling of God's Prohibition. It was an attack on language and remembered texts. That could not have occurred between only one person and God because Adam would not have misquoted something he heard directly. Therefore, the Fall is not caused by a genetic defect (a mistake in the design), nor caused by an epigenetic failure (a mistake in the programming) but by a spiritual or societal breakdown (a broken relationship).

What exactly was the spiritual defect that led to the Fall?

Look again at Gen 2:24. Society is characterized by "joining," by "one flesh," by its unity. A trinity is more than simply three persons, it is more than multiplicity, or otherwise Greek pantheism also would be trinitarian. A trinity requires unity, not just in purpose, but in essence. In just such a way, the Edenic societal trinity required a perfect unity of God, Adam, and Eve, which the serpent subverted. But when St John explains in his first epistle how to detect the Gnostic infiltrators in the Church, he talks about the defining characteristic of the Church as "love for the brothers" (1 John 3:14). The Church is the New Testament solution to the Fall, finding a unity in the Holy Spirit. This unity, constructed out of many persons, has a sociological existence that Dietrich Bonhoeffer called "body life."[25] So its deficiency, its defect was disunity, dissension, or selfishness. Therefore, before the Fall, God intended for Man to communicate: the first creation by hearing Him; the second creation by answering Him; and, the third creation by worshiping Him together.

Could the Cro-Magnons have worshiped Him?

I do not think so, or at least, not fully worship, because it seems that worship is communal and linguistic. It is an offering of the self, a self-referencing gift only possible with language. If the Cro-Magnons did not have language, then they did not have the self-abstraction to offer themselves in worship. But look at what happened when Adam was given language: He was excluded from the entire world of speechless ones; he was alone. The same gifts that empowered him to name, to differentiate, and to rank, have

25. Bonhoeffer. "*Sanctorum Communio*; Bonhoeffer. *Gemeinsames Leben*.

now isolated him. So, in the third creation, as planned all along by God, Adam is given the wife that language binds tightly to him. And through procreation (not a new capability because it is the key aspect of the first creation), language becomes the glue of family, the foundation of society, and the basis of worship. Out of one, many come; out of many, come but one.

I have fleshed out the Biblical underpinnings of the Neolithic Revolution, showing the relationship between language and the breath of God. Language gives power to separate cattle from beasts of the field, but only within the God-given community does it bring about unity, support, and worship. Now let us consider the meaning of the Prohibition of Gen 2:16–17.

4.2.3.1 The Prohibition, Gen 2:16–17

We can apply our grasp of this second creation to understand the Prohibition. The concept of the *Imago Dei* should refer to the first, bodily creation of man, as seen in the Cro-Magnons: his genes, his musculature, his posture, his artistic sense, yes, even his musical sense. It is the second, Adamic creation that gives man the intellect, the language, the ability to grasp abstract principles. The language that gives him power to differentiate, to domesticate, to subdue God's creation in obedience to His commands is also divisive, leaving him alone and without equal. The third social creation, however, provides community, enables worship, introduces joy over duty, and promotes love over obligation. It is the spiritual fulfillment of man.

The first creation, the *Imago Dei*, was a genetic, bodily creation (which, incidentally, excludes racism because we all possess the Imago). But the *Imago Dei* is not the element that separates Adam from Cro-Magnons. Rather, what separated Adam was the epigenetic changes signified by the breath of God. If the second creation of animals is taken to be domestication, we can apply the same interpretation to Adam: He was a domesticated Cro-Magnon. Domestication reshapes the existing genome, eliminating some alleles while emphasizing others. That is what epigenetics does; it made Adam epigenetically distinct from the preceding Cro-Magnons. He had the same genes but they were differently expressed.

The form of this second, epigenetic creation is highly significant because the method of its formation also reveals the method of its deformation: sin. Because the first creation genes were extremely hardy, surviving millennia without change, there was little danger that humans could deform their genes (unless they engaged in artificial breeding experiments)[26]. The second creation epigenetic effects are less robust, however. They change in

26. Etkind. "Beyond eugenics" 205–210.

three or four generations, as mentioned four times by Moses: (Ex 20:5, 34:7, Num 14:18, Deut 5:9) visiting the iniquity of the fathers on the children to the third and fourth generation. And if sin is perniciously heritable, then one would expect, and indeed finds, many Biblical prohibitions of behaviors that can affect the offspring epigenetically (e.g., idolatry, drunkenness, sorcery).

Finally, the third, social creation is extremely fragile, affected in less than one generation by upbringing. Broken relationships are a constant plague so the majority of Biblical commands concern this type of societal deformation. Therefore, the three types of creation turn out to be the key to understanding the three types of sin or corruption: genetic, epigenetic, and societal sin.

> Gen 2:16–17 *The LORD God commanded the man saying, "From any tree of the garden you may eat freely; but from the tree of the knowledge of good and evil you shall not eat, for in the day you eat of it you will surely die.*

The placement of this Prohibition after the second creation and before the third tells us the nature of the infraction (not "sin," as such, because the word is first used in Genesis 4) and the type of death introduced by disobedience.

If the first creation already introduced death, as many Cro-Magnon bones attest, what does God mean by "surely die"?

Given the serpent's interpretation of the Prohibition and the actual consequences of eating the fruit, commentators are divided about the strength of the consequences of violating the Prohibition. Nothing in the text gives any indication that it means anything less than the ingestion of a fast-acting poison that would kill within twenty-four hours. If the second creation concerns the immaterial epigenetic aspects of language and soul, however, the Prohibition might refer to a less material or non-genetic mortality, an epigenetic death rather than a genetic (physical) one. I say "less material" because epigenetic information has a material base in genetics in the same way that sentences rely on words and speech relies on phonemes. For just as there are more ways to mangle a sentence than to kill the words that make it up, there are many ways to destroy epigenetics without eliminating the genes. Because the Prohibition in Gen 2:17 is followed by the domestication of cattle, Adam would understand an epigenetic interpretation.

So, what then is the nature of epigenetic death as opposed to physical death?

Many conservative commentators account for the immateriality of God's warning about death as the destruction of relationships, a third creation type of death. But the third creation, that of Eve, comes after the

Prohibition whereas Adam's second creation comes beforehand. It would seem then that an epigenetic (second) death is being described in the Prohibition, rather than simply a dead relationship, which would more naturally follow the third creation. Of course, later creations build upon earlier ones, so it would be impossible for an epigenetic sin to avoid a spiritual failure. But the consequences of this epigenetic sin are much greater than simply broken relationships, because the repair takes so many more generations. Then my paraphrase of the Prohibition becomes: *On the day you eat of the fruit, you will find yourself unable to talk or think clearly, plagued by temptation, fear, vice, and degenerate children, your special holiness will be dead.*

How could a poisonous fruit, made of material things, have such an effect on immaterial passions and vice?

It can happen through the brain connection, via the (epi)genome. Just as the twentieth century discovered many brain chemicals that alter behavior, (cocaine permanently effects the addict), so the twenty-first century found that these effects are hereditary, affecting Adam's offspring. Epigenetics describes the environmental impact on the genome and in the twenty-first century we are only just beginning to appreciate its significance. The expression of genes can encode as much or more information as the genes themselves. Then what the poisonous fruit corrupted was the epigenetic formation of Adam, God's second creation, leaving behind damaged goods that have plagued mankind ever since.

4.3 Genetics

In previous chapters, I have discussed the new discoveries in geology and genetics that result in a whole new understanding of human origins. In the last section, I looked at some of the hidden gems of Genesis 2, showing that most misinterpretation comes from conflating it with Genesis 1. But when Genesis 2 is freed from the need to harmonize with "ex nihilo," *it can be located in geography, in history, and in anthropology, teaching us a great deal about the Biblical view of man. Now let us look at how science teaches us about the three-fold composition of Adam: genetics, epigenetics, and spiritual nature.*

The view offered is neither the dualistic separation of our nature into hardware and software, nor the Greek distinction between matter and non-matter. It is not even the more recent tripartite division that separates the non-matter part of ourselves into conscious and self-conscious, or into soul and spirit. Rather it is a unique separation resolving the paradoxes that result from false dichotomies while suggesting solutions to some social afflictions. In the first section, we look at genetics, then epigenetics, and finally the social makeup of man.

4.3.1 Genetic Creation

So far, the discussion in this chapter has been about Adam and Eve exclusively. They came after the creation of the world including the genetic creation of mankind, "male and female," in Genesis 1. In the next chapter I will devote more attention to that genetic creation, as distinct and separate from the epigenetic creation in Genesis 2. Not too surprisingly, the major disagreements about Adam's putative existence relate to his genetic makeup, because genetics was the first tool that biologists had. Genes are also the most permanent features of Adam; they last for millions of years, carefully transcribing their information generation after generation. So reliable is this copying process that random errors creep into the human genome of three billion letters at a rate of one letter in ten billion per generation. As a result, we can trace the lineage of humans back through hundreds and perhaps thousands of generations to reconstruct our heritage.

The conflict between Genesis and genetics arose when several scientists and theologians argued that our genetic history is not consistent with the Genesis story of a single father of all mankind, but rather with humans descended from a population of several thousand individuals at a minimum. The argument is based on the number of variations of a Mendelian inherited trait, an allele.[27] For example, eye color can be blue, brown, dark brown, hazel, or gray. But because everyone has paired chromosomes, a person can inherit, say, the allele for blue from his mother and the allele for brown from his father. Brown is a dominant allele or trait, so that will be the color of his eyes but he can still pass the recessive blue allele down to his children. Now if Adam were the father of all mankind, the argument goes, there can only be two alleles for any trait because that is all that he could carry. If we consider Eve as a potentially different human (though Genesis says she was cloned, with the same alleles), we get a maximum of four alleles. Conversely, if we find a trait with 2000 alleles, then we know the human race has never consisted of fewer than 1000 individuals. This has been Francisco Ayala's argument and many have found it persuasive,[28] though not all, because

27. Mendel. "Versuche über Pflanzenhybriden." In: Druery, "Experiments in plant hybridization" 3–47.

28. Ayala et al. "Molecular Genetics" 6787.

Ayala injudiciously chose a hyper-variable site, assuming that it contained non-variable alleles.[29]

Did Adam exist as a historical person?

Vern Poythress considers Ayala's argument and describes the hidden assumptions that can color geneticists' conclusions. Given the past history of failed scientific predictions, he argues, we know that empirical science is too uncertain to make the absolute judgments needed for faith.[30]

Now, just as science, the product of fallible scientists, is not infallible but changes with every new discovery and theory, so also our interpretation of Scripture, the product of fallible theologians, is not infallible but changes with every new discovery and philosophy. Theologians, like scientists, are often in disagreement, making theology as uncertain a foundation for faith as science. Therefore, this book takes a different tack than arbitrating between competing authorities.

I suggest that, given our limited understanding of Hebrew and ancient texts, which can also be colored by hidden assumptions, our faith should rest on neither science nor texts alone. Nor does one trump the other.[31] For if Genesis 2 is not Genesis 1, then Adam is the epigenetic father of mankind, who need not be the genetic father of all mankind, as described in Genesis 1. Just as St Paul argues in Romans 5 that Christ is the spiritual head of all mankind, separating the physical and spiritual headship, so I would also say Adam is mankind's epigenetic head, and assign the genetic headship to the unnamed humans of Genesis 1. And it is right that they remain unnamed because speech was reserved for Adam, for his epigenetic headship.

In this view, it is nearly irrelevant whether 1000 genetic alleles exist in the human lineage or not. They neither contradict Genesis nor undermine St Paul. Granted, many who draw scientific conclusions from the theology of Romans 5 find it difficult to split the concepts of moral headship and biological fatherhood to find a third way. Consider however, that many of our supposedly purely metaphysical concepts rely on a physical analogy. As a result, when our analogy to the scientific world changes, so does our theology. The discoveries in epigenetics during the past twenty years are as important to theology as the discovery of atoms, cells, or quantum mechanics. And because the analogies change over time, so does the metaphysics, the theology, and the interpretation of Genesis. Once again, we rediscover the significance of *midrash*, that the interpretations may vary but the text remains the same. By analogy, Adam is a biological *midrash*: His genetic text

29. Gauger. *Science and Human Origins.*

30. Poythress. *Did Adam Exist?*

31. Collins. *Did Adam and Eve really exist?*

remains the same as that of the Cro-Magnons but his epigenetic interpretation matures with time.

4.3.2 Epigenetic Creation

To summarize the second creation, described in Genesis 2, of this personal, specific, Adamic, and Neolithic being, I note all the differences from what we see in the first creation described in Genesis 1, the general, bodily, and Paleolithic creation. This second creation was a personal, artistic formation from pre-existing bodily material, imbued with divine breath, not just life in general but an immaterial, self-aware spirit. Likewise, the first command given was his appointment as cultivator of a garden, with plants specially chosen for food. Then the second command given was to name places, rivers (implied), and especially, animals. Because all of the animals brought to Adam were domesticated animals, this act of naming included the science of animal husbandry. These properties are exactly those that define the Neolithic Revolution—the spread of a special people group that did not melt into the Paleolithic genetic landscape—bringing farming technology with a specific language.

The relationship between Gen 1:26 and Gen 2:7 needs further examination. How could the "divine breath" of Gen 2:7 be the first language? Did not Cro-Magnon peoples have beautiful stories painted on caves? Why is this not language?

Language goes beyond the visual, beyond the logographic to the purely phonemic. A brain capable of language is also capable of abstraction, of science and technology. The difference between the two could be material. When God formed Adam, He may have added to the Paleolithic genes a "talking gene," such as the famous FOXP2 gene. Or it could be a semi-material difference, an epigenetic factor that operates on the genes. For example, perhaps babies in the womb that are exposed to certain "language hormones" develop into talking babies, the way bee larvae exposed to royal jelly develop into queens. Or it could be an immaterial process, a patterning of the brain, a nurture factor, such that babies growing up in a talking home learn to talk, while those growing up in a speechless Paleolithic home do not.

Why ask for scientific precision from a Biblical text?

Each of the three reasons have far-reaching ethical consequences for the doctrine of Man. If I were to argue that Adam's genes were different, then the Cro-Magnon race would appear sub-human by design, and racism is an expected outcome. If I were to argue that Eve's womb was different, then I would be arguing for superiority via development, and racism is unfortunate but potentially reversible after some generations. But if I were to argue for nurture, for upbringing, then racism is a societal evil, which can be actively transformed by education in less than a generation.

What information can we glean that might help us decide how to proceed?

In Gen 9:6 we read that killing Cro-Magnons was forbidden because "*they were made in the image of God*," which speaks against a material difference between Adam and the Paleolithic humans. More precisely, whatever material differences exist between the two are not great enough to erase the essential humanity of the Cro-Magnon, a humanity which is expressed in the *Imago Dei*. Now there are shelves of books written on the Imago, identifying a near infinity of properties. These properties may be part of the Imago, but for the purposes of this book, I take the minimalist view that an image is of material and not of immaterial construction. Thus the Cro-Magnon is at the very least a physical replica of Adam. Among other things, this interpretation means that God makes no genetic distinctions between races, nor has a preference for one "genetically pure" race over another. Neither National Socialism nor claims about the "curse of Ham" are defensible—all possess the *Imago Dei*.

But what about the view that all differences are societal; that only customs separate Adam from the Cro-Magnons?

As we discussed earlier, Gen 6:3 supports a category distinction between the "sons of God" and the "daughters of men," which cannot easily be reduced to a cultural difference. While we called this difference "genetic" when we first discussed it, it is now clear that the difference is not primarily genetic but epigenetic. Therefore, differences between races are not simply immaterial, cultural, or societal differences but have a material component as well. Just as it is wrong to think material differences justify moral distinctions (Gen 9:6), so it is wrong to think that epigenetic differences can be addressed simply by changing laws and societal expectations. Eve's womb made a difference, and if we do not understand this, we will not be able to address the multi-generational changes that separated the daughters of men from the sons of God.

Does not the conclusion that Adam is materially identical to Cro-Magnons contradict science? If the difference was not material, why do we find in the Neolithic Revolution that dark hair alleles or short stature gene variants followed the Neolithic migration of Indo-European speakers northward?

A distribution of allele frequencies between Neolithic and Paleolithic man is best seen as a statistical, or an informational, difference between them. Information is neither completely material nor completely immaterial; it is a "third thing," intermediate between the two. I will discuss this point in more detail later, but that is why earlier Bible scholars enamored of Greek body/spirit dualism, did not see this second creation as distinct from both the first and the third creations. Thus it is correct to attribute this non-material, non-societal, statistical difference as an epigenetic difference in which the reorganization of identical material resulted in a qualitative difference.

I cannot emphasize this point strongly enough. Epigenetics is a twenty-first-century discovery that radically changes how we view people, how we view ourselves, how we view Scripture. It was not known to previous generations, who confused it with either genes or upbringing. It solves the 200-year-old riddle of "nature versus nurture" by positing a third category, a *tertium quid*, between these two extremes. It explains the nature of Moses's warning (Exod 20:5, 34:7, Num 14:18, Deut 5:9) that the sins of the fathers pass down to the third and fourth generation. It is a multi-generational switch that can be easily set but not so easily reset. It explains why Man is a tripartite being just as God is, not trapped in the binary Greek categories of "body or soul." Philosophically, it provides an escape from the dualism, inherited from ancient Greek thought, that has caused so much heresy over the ages: A tripartite nature, like a three-legged stool, is stable on any surface due to the way each of the parts contribute to the whole.

What exactly is this epigenetic inheritance that I think it is so important for us to consider?

I first began to consider this approach as a result of watching a science video describing the life cycle of the Monarch butterfly.[32] All Eastern Monarchs winter over in a few square kilometers of Mexican mountain forest, leaving in the early spring to fly north and lay their eggs on milkweed plants, their sole food source. When the caterpillars hatch, they eat their fill and metamorphize into butterflies that set out on the return migration northward in the spring. Three generations later, in mid-summer we find Monarchs far up in Canada. Their eggs are laid on mature milkweed plants getting ready for fall. That fourth generation of Monarchs is unlike the previous three. It is equipped to fly 3000 miles and live for nine months without food—it is the "methuselah" generation. These methuselahs fly south, joining an ever growing stream of migrating Monarchs, down the east coast of the United States, around the Gulf of Mexico, and toward their wintering home—that few square kilometers out of a million. How do they do it?

Just this year, a paper reported that they had isolated a special protein from the Monarch genome that points in the direction of the magnetic field, a magnetometer better than the ones found on NASA space probes.[33] How do they know where to go?

32. Urquhart. "Flight of the butterflies in 3D."

33. Qin et al. "A magnetic protein biocompass" 217–226.

Somehow, the pinhead brain of the insect has a Google map in it, which specifies the global magnetic field and indicates the next rest stop.

Where did the map come from?

Clearly it had to be inherited through four generations at a minimum, an inheritance formerly thought to be genetic but now known to be epigenetic. For, as the Monarchs flew their long journey down the East coast of the US, they could save almost 500 miles if they took a shortcut over the Gulf of Mexico instead of flying around it. Unfortunately, the stamina and the speed of Monarchs cannot match that of migrating geese, and having no way to cross the Gulf in a single day, would drown in the cold nights. As the oil industry followed oil out into the Gulf of Mexico, it built giant platforms to extract the oil from a mile below the surface. And today, for several days in the fall, the rigs are densely covered with Monarchs. Somehow, a Monarch found this refuge, and four generations later, his great-great-grandchild returned. The map in the Monarch's head is not based on landmarks, which the Gulf of Mexico lacks. Nor is it written in genes, which would then be unchangeable. Nor is it taught, because caterpillars never meet their parents. Therefore, present knowledge suggests that the map must be epigenetic.

What does this say about us—do we likewise have epigenetic maps in our head, premonitions of danger, unexplained desires?

The history of mankind is littered with examples of epigenetic memories: fear of spiders; proclivity to drink; musical talent; dedication to detail. Freud called them the unconscious. Jung thought they were due to cultural memories. Following Jung, Myers and Briggs called them personality types. Comedians called them cultural stereotypes. And the Bible called the best sort, "holiness," warning us against its loss. This epigenetics is what Adam received, and it was a fragile gift, less durable than the gift of genes. Genes endure a thousand generations, whereas holiness could be lost in four generations. But there was another gift, more delicate even than epigenetics, more ephemeral than a generation, the one which Genesis 2 describes last.

4.3.3 Spiritual Creation

The story of Eve as the third, spiritual creation is at the same time less obvious and more important than the genetic first or the epigenetic second creations. As we see later, in the New Testament, Eve is not just the mother of all living, but the prototype for the Virgin Mary and the Church. This traditional view is supported, among other sources, by St John's first epistle, which appears to be a commentary or a *midrash* on Genesis, and in particular, on Eve. (A detailed discussion of this point is beyond the scope of this book's emphasis on science and Hebrew.) Compounding the confusion is the negative impression of Eve over the millennia, not least from Milton who suggested that Adam ate the apple when he decided he could not spend eternity without her.[34] If, following up Milton's claim, one replaces "Eve" with "the Church," one can see how tangled the metaphor becomes. Eve has lost her rightful place as the pinnacle of Creation, the prototype for the Heavenly Jerusalem, becoming simply the irresistible temptation, the handmaiden of Satan.

But Eve need not be so maligned. Playing Devil's Advocate, could not Eve's fall be simply a case of bad education? If Adam learned to talk from God, and Eve learned to talk from Adam, then perhaps her inability to quote God correctly may be due to Adam's paraphrase of the Prohibition? In which case, the miscommunication that provided an entry for the insidious serpent could be Adam's fault, not Eve's. That is one of many ways to parse this story that partially absolves Eve, so how can we confidently assign the blame to one alone?

This is one of those situations in which *midrash* is crucial for understanding the text. If different interpretations can move the blame around, then no one is innocent. It may seem strange to Western ears, but simply being a member of society carries guilt by association. This is why Isaiah cries out (Isa 6:5) "*Woe is me! for I am undone; because I am a man of unclean lips, and I dwell in the midst of a people of unclean lips.*" The idea that neither Adam nor Eve can be morally isolated is one of the defining characteristics of a trinity, of the third spiritual creation. It also explains the peculiar curse on Eve, Gen 3:16, *"your desire shall be for your husband, but he will rule over you,"* because the curse describes a breakdown of the Edenic trinity.

The subsequent history of the world—the spread of language, the spread of technology, the specialization of civilization, the equality of human beings, the globalization of society—all are consequences of this third creation, this pinnacle of Creation Week, the formation of Eve. If the first genetic Paleolithic Revolution lasted 40,000 years until the creation of the Garden, and the second epigenetic Neolithic Revolution lasted 8000 years until the creation of cities, then this third historical Social Revolution is a 5000-year accelerating ascent toward a finale that all began with Eve (though it was interrupted by the Flood). Everything that has been written, from the hieroglyphs of Egypt and pictographs of Harappan to the tomes of the Congressional Record, are a testimony to her influence. The topics of Civilization, Culture, and Arts are dedicated to her, perhaps accounting for why the Greek Muses are all female. Even if I would try, I could not do justice to all the aspects of life that are a direct result of this third creation. So in frustration, I leave it to the classicists to describe the importance of nurture, of socialization, of proper upbringing. The remaining forty chapters of Genesis are the unfolding story of her special contribution but since I have

34. Milton. *Paradise Lost*. IX.908.

proposed to cover only the first eleven chapters, it is with great reluctance I leave Eve to the theologians and return to the text.

4.3.4 The Tripartite Creation

Genesis tells us that we humans have a tripartite construction but it does not indicate that our nature is divided in the way envisioned by the Greek philosophers or subsequent theologians.[35] When Jesus was asked about marriage (Matt 19:4–5), he went back to Genesis 1 & 2, so likewise, when we try to understand human nature, we must return to Genesis 1 & 2. Table 4.4 shows the comparison. Now if there be three separate creations in the formation of man, then there are at least three separate destructions in the fall of man: a destruction of his genetics; a destruction of his epigenetics; and, a destruction of his society. The genetic damage undermines what separates man from beast. The epigenetic damage undermines rationality, what separates talking, reasoning man from mute Cro-Magnons. And the societal damage undermines community, tribes, and families. Later destructions build upon the earlier ones, so that genetic damage, like HeLa cells, live mutely in a petri dish, with barely even a bestial existence. Or epigenetic damage, like autism, leads to a solitary and isolated existence.

Category Reference	Creation 1 Gen 1:26	Creation 2 Gen 2:7	Creation 3 Gen 2:18
Functional purpose	male & female = reproduce	breathed in Adam = talk	bone of my bone =share
3-fold Nature	Body	Mind	Spirit
Relationship w/God	Walk	Talk	Worship
Attribute of God	Image	Breath	Trinity
Material unit	DNA	Person	Community
Science field	Genetics/Biology	Math/Linguistics	Sociology/Politics
Biology info	Genetic	Epigenetic	Developmental
Anthropology	Cro-Magnon	Modern	Cultural
History	Paleolithic	Neolithic/Mythical	Historical
Rate of Change	Ten Millennia	Century	Year
Sin, Destruction	Dead	Dumb	Dysfunctional
Restoration	Resurrection	Regeneration	Righteousness
Functional unit	Pair	Individual	More than two

Table 4.4: Attributes of Tripartite Creation

35. Laidlaw. *The Bible Doctrine of Man.*

Therefore, despite the many similarities among these three creations, they are not equivalent, nor are they arbitrarily divided. For example, attempting to use a dualistic Greek division into material and immaterial results in a peculiar split through the middle of the second creation that renders it incoherent: Regeneration is partly physical and partly mental; sins must be cured both instantly and over many generations. This last confusion is widely recognized in the oft-asked question: "What makes sexual sins seem worse to Christians than other kinds of sin?" Part of the answer must be, "Because it is epigenetic, persisting over many generations." And that answer will be repeated many times throughout this book because in our time, there is a confused attempt to solve second creation problems with third creation fixes. But no amount of "acting nice" can remove a methyl-tagged epigenetic problem, just as no amount of epigenetic breeding will produce a blue rose or a talking chimpanzee. Some sins have more material consequences than others, more *chatta'ath*, and thus they require more effort to right.

With this new understanding of the severity of genetic and epigenetic sin, I can finally explain why the sin of Noah's generation was so pernicious. In their breeding experiments intended to remove the curse of Adam (Gen 6:3), a (quasi)genetic sin,[36] they introduced the sin of Cain, an epigenetic one. For any society that begins to "improve" its genes by killing the weak, by culling the daughters, by destroying the misfits, is epigenetically changing itself into a race without empathy. A society without the Down's syndrome children is without the innocent. And that generation will grow up with even less empathy for their children until it becomes a nation of the strong, the cruel, and the selfish. This is the explosive, uncontrollable power of positive feedback. Nor does the fault remain epigenetic; the evil rapidly expands its horizons to both genetic and societal change. There is only one cure for positive feedback: to pull the plug, to cut the connection, to insist that nothing destructive be done to "improve" one's progeny.

Why such absolute condemnation; surely some self-improvement is warranted?

Because one nation's "improvement" is another's impoverishment. Because every well-meaning intention has unforeseen consequences. Because the medium is the message.[37] Because the only certain inheritance it bestows on the next generation is the license to meddle with their inheritors.

36. Some epigenetics, such as allele distributions for height or intelligence, move together and behave as pseudo-genes. This is especially true for bottlenecks and "founders effects," hence "quasi-genetic."

37. McLuhan, *Understanding Media*.

The Rabbinic tradition of the *Lamed Vav Tzekikim* says that every generation must have thirty-six hidden righteous ones for whose sake God does not destroy the world. In like manner, the world must have cleft-palate babies, Down's syndrome children, cystic fibrosis friends, and Alzheimer's parents or we will lose our ability to care, to nurture, and to cherish. For without them, our society will lose its third creation distinctives, our crucial differences from the animals.

Therefore, the most important scientific lesson from Genesis 2 is not its location of Eden nor even its revelation of origins, but rather its anthropology, the construction of man via three creations. For if man is made of three parts, then we must reject all materialist descriptions of man as a talking ape, and all dualist descriptions of man as an ensouled machine. For all such dualistic conceptions incorporate a tension between the two parts, which invariably degenerates into the extremes seen in denominations, in religions, and in political philosophies. But the Biblical partition of anthropology is like a balanced load or a tri-cameral government, directing without dominance, liberating without license, simultaneously self-correcting and self-respecting.

4.3.5 Genesis 2 Timeline

> *In this chapter I have argued that the order of events matters. I identify three parts to man because three creations happened in sequence. In this section I attempt to put all those events into a time line that is matched to scientific data on prehistoric man. And there we notice some peculiar recurring events.*

About two millennia of pre-history is given in Genesis 2, followed by two more antediluvian millennia up to the Flood of Genesis 6–9, and then six millennia up to the time of Abraham. While myth and human memory cover the latter eight millennia, we have only Genesis (and interpretive science) recording the pre-Edenic history. Therefore, the first few verses of Genesis 2 are important because they alone cover these critical two or three millennia before Adam. They describe the complete control God has over the climate and the extensive preparations required for the appearance of Adam's race. This exquisite planning may also mark a philosophical divide. As shown in Table 4.5, note how creation and fall are spread over time, progressively developed and progressively destroyed.

Does this evolutionary time line undermine the power of God, who could obviously have collapsed many such steps into one massive miracle? Does it not give too much power and authority to intermediate (secondary) causes that compete with the direct will of God? Perhaps I am unduly influenced by a scientific reading of history that assumes the past must follow the same set of developmental rules as the present?

#	Ch	Event	Action	BC Date
1.	1	The Big Visit	Establish earth and heavens	13,700,000,000
2.	1	Many Messengers	Genetic: populating the earth	50,000–12,000
3.	2	Messenger #1	Watering the Reservoirs	~11,000
4.	2	Messenger #2	Closing the Gates	10,900
5.	2		Eden dried out, Garden est.	10,700
6.	2	Visit #2	Epi: the breathing	~10,700?
7.	2	Job #1	Trees, farming, genetics	10,600–9590
8.	2	Job #2	Names, science, teaching	"
9.	2	Visit #3	Molding from the rib	"
10.	2	Job #3	Delegate job #1&2 to sons	"
11.	3	Fall #1	Job 1 lost, transformed	"
12.	3	Messenger #3	The guard at gate	"
13.	4	Fall #2	Job 2 lost, the mark	~10,600
14.	6	Messenger #4?	Destroying the gates?	9590
15.	7	Fall #3	Job 3 lost, the flood	9590–now

Table 4.5: Time line of Eden's creation

Some have argued that the difference between "theistic evolution" (TE) (e.g., Biologos) and "progressive creation" (PC) (e.g., Bernard Ramm) is the degree to which Aristotle's secondary causes are thought to operate autonomously.[38] For example, if God created the law of gravity, then He need not directly cause dead trees to fall to the ground to be recycled, but could let the secondary cause of gravity do the job for Him. The TE argues that God need only have set up the general parameters for the climate, and everything in Genesis 2 would have unfolded as predictably as an acorn becomes an oak. In contrast, the PC would argue that autonomy of secondary causes is not sufficient for the effect. An entire series of unlikely events was necessary to create Adam, and the sheer improbability is evidence for the hand of God. Some critics refer to the PC position as if it were medieval occasionalism (OC), a view according to which no event can take place without direct intervention by God because secondary causes have no autonomy.

I note that "unlikeliness" is a continuous variable. The TE and OC viewpoints are simply extreme positions on both ends of the spectrum of PC. We tend to gloss over probable events, but notice improbable ones. Therefore, the PC position on the continuum depends upon the knowledge

38. "BioLogos, Forum" *Biologos*; Ramm. *Christian View of Science and Scripture*.

zoom scale: The further away we stand, the more TE it appears, and the closer we look, the more OC it appears. The time line of Genesis 2 is full of very intriguing, very improbable events all unfolding in a pattern that reveals a distinct purpose. And the more we learn about its history, the more excitingly improbable and purposeful it becomes.

In the next volume I argue that there is both a temporal coincidence between the fireball event that scorched North America and the closing of the Gates. Textual references combine these two events in various mythologies, so it would seem that a comet sent by God initiated the events of Gen 2:4. Mythology also implicates a meteor in the opening of the Gates some 1500 years later. As I will discuss in a later chapter, comets and meteors play an important role in Genesis 1, and though I will not analyze Genesis 19, an ancient meteor impact is generally invoked as the cause of the destruction of Sodom.

Table 4.5 shows just how many of the chain of events recorded in Genesis were associated with meteors and comets. When Ps 104:4 says (KJV) "*Who maketh his angels spirits; his ministers a flaming fire*," or (ESV) "*he makes his messengers winds, his ministers a flaming fire*" it is reasonable to think that these meteor impacts are directly attributed to God. And if these fiery messengers are indeed sent by God, then we have abundant evidence of God's direct action in the world, secondary causes notwithstanding.

The number of times that a fiery messenger arrives is rather astonishing–are there really that many comets bombarding the Earth? Or was it happening at a specific time for a specific purpose?

In the next chapter I argue that these same comets supply the dark matter that holds the galaxy together, as well as helping fulfill Gen 1:2, where the Spirit of God—Mind, Logos, Purpose, Plan—hovers over the face of the waters. If "the heavens and the earth" are translated "spacetime and matter," then "the face of the waters" consists of the first astronomical objects God makes, comets.[39] The astronomical proof of this hypothesis will have to be the subject of a future book, but there is much evidence in the remainder of Genesis 1. The next section shows us just how scientifically accurate the first chapter of Genesis really is.

39. Sheldon. "Comets, Water, and Big Bang Nucleosynthesis."

PART 5

Day to day pours out speech, and night to night reveals knowledge.
There is no speech, nor are there words, whose voice is not heard.
Their voice goes out through all the earth, and their words to the end of the world.

Psalm 19:2–3 (ESV)

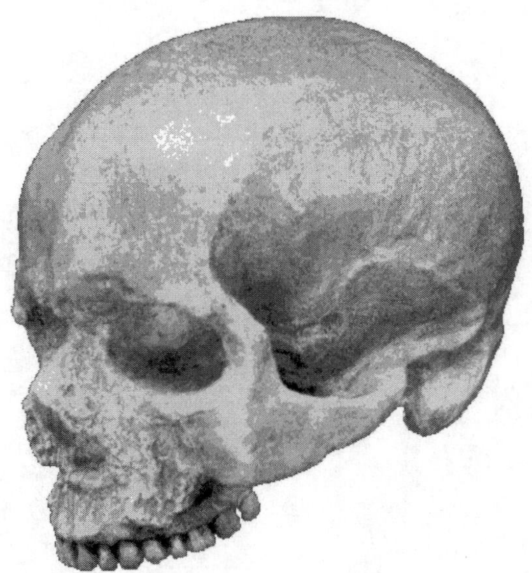

Figure 5.0: Cro-Magnon 1 holotype found 1868 at Les Eyzies, France. (Courtesy Smithsonian)

CHAPTER 5

Wordless Ones

5.1 Wordless Ones

THE LIGHT REACHED HIM before the sound did, a brilliant blue-white searing light that he had never seen before. He instinctively crouched on the path, turning his back to the burning heat and covering his face with his hands. Through his fingers he could see the silhouette of his head casting a shadow on the ground even in the full sunlight of a clear afternoon. His shadow grew darker even as the heat grew greater, scorching his neck until the brown grass beside him burst into flame. A sonic boom hit, lifting him from his heels and rolling him off the path and down the burnt hillside. Then everything went black.

The cool water flowing over his head and back revived him. He slowly realized that he had rolled into a creek at the bottom of the ravine. His body burned and throbbed, especially his back. The sun now hung lower in the smoky sky, a hazy ball of orange fire. All around him was blackened grass, looking oddly like an eye-dazzled afterimage, revealing patchy color only where the dark shadows of trees and boulders had been, minutes before. It was a world he had never seen, a world of black ground and white sky, a world of ash and cinders, a world of rising gray smoke lit by an angry red sun.

He stood up in the creek, his hands feeling over his arms and legs. They were all intact and unbroken, though heavily bruised and scraped from the tumble down the ten meter deep ravine. His back felt as if it were still on fire, and it was painful to touch. Perhaps the women could clean and cover it. The wind blew the smoke into his face, stinging his eyes. He coughed, and then could not stop coughing. Red spittle appeared on his lips, and then it became hard to breathe.

He knelt down in the brook and put his face as close to the water as he could. The air seemed less smoky near the water, and finally the coughing produced blood-flecked phlegm staining the water as it rushed down the hill. Though his body seemed unbroken, his breath came in deep, bubbling gasps. He knelt in the water for a long time, gasping for air, feeling his heart pound, and his back throb. He was faintly aware of the heat of the sun, the heat of the earth, and the sting of the smoke. He still as a statue, with the water splashing over his knees and calves, washing away the crimson stains that dropped, in a slowing rhythm, from his parted lips.

A loud sound awoke him from his stupor, and he lifted his head. An enormous elk was crashing through the smoke and scrub oak, eyes rolling, antlers tossing. Its coat was mottled with frizzled stripes and white ash. It would fall and then get up to stagger a few more steps through the ash before falling again. Its muzzle was stained with pink froth. It lurched toward the creek but fell, then came tumbling down the ravine amid a small avalanche of stones, landing half in, half out of the water. Its great head strained forward as if it were going to stand, and then after thirty trembling seconds, the antlers dropped, and it did not move again.

The sight of the elk terrified him. Clearly it had died the same way that he was dying— falling, gasping, bleeding. Would this be the end for him as well? The thought of dying gave him new strength. He listened to his breath—it was no longer bubbling. Nor was his heart pounding so badly. Breathing was painful but no longer uncertain. Even the stream ran clear. Now that living was not so difficult, he became aware of his back and its raw nerve endings. He tried to stand but his thighs had cramped in the kneeling position, and it took him several minutes to straighten his legs. Bit by bit, his head cleared, and his heart-beat slowed.

The grass fires had all gone out but in the hazy distance a stand of fir trees was wafting a blue column of smoke into the smoldering sky. Perhaps he could walk again. He focused attention on his legs. They did not respond, so he reached down to lift his knees with his hands, carefully placing his ankles below him. But when he tried to stand, his treacherous legs gave out and he went splashing headlong into the creek. He pushed himself up to a sitting position and looked around. A sun-bleached branch wedged among the boulders caught his attention, and he leaned over to grip it and pull himself up. But it broke in his hand. The piece he was holding was over a meter long, with two broken stubs of branches forking out about two-thirds of the way up. It made a nice hand hold, so he gripped it near the top and placed it on the ground to keep his balance. With much trembling, he managed to stand up. Like an old man, he hobbled out of the water, with pounding heart and gasping breath.

He stopped, waiting for his body to recover, and saw the elk again, laying in the water. It seemed such a waste to leave it there; the women could have made a week's worth of provisions from it, as well as providing valuable antlers and hide. Now he was torn as to whether he should return to the camp empty-handed, or at least bring home a leg or two. He reached for the knife at his waist, but the knife and its leather thong were gone. He looked back at the creek where he had knelt for so long, but could see no knife among the black pebbles and rippling water. Without a knife, there was very little he could do. He turned his back on the elk and the creek, and looked up at the smoking hill. It would be a steep climb. Placing his branch in the rising ground in front of him, he put one foot down, waited for his breath, and then the other. He lifted the branch and placed it on the hill further up. It was going to be a long journey in a foreign land.

She was in the cave when she heard the yell. Looking up from her work on the deer hide, she saw a bright object moving across the sky from the west, leaving a trail of smoke behind it. The object grew brighter as it came, and everything grew dark in the light of that new sun. She averted her face until the bright thing mercifully passed beyond the entrance and out of direct view. As she watched, the sky turned white with light. The hearth and the arch of stone that framed the entrance grew brighter and bluer, while sharp shadows split the cave into inky darkness so black she could not see her hands or the baby at her feet. And then the sky exploded in a wave of heat, and everything went dark. Somewhere she heard screaming.

Her eyes adjusted to broad daylight as if the dawn were coming again, and she realized it was herself screaming. Not until her eyes rested on the baby—mouth wide open, eyes clenched shut, its face a purple panic—did she stop yelling, clutching the baby to her breast. Then she sat motionless for a long while, staring at the sky and the hillside that ran sloping down toward the river.

The grass was burning, lifting streamers of white smoke into the windless air. In the east, the sky was darkening; it looked like rain. She noticed that the river was rising, rising fast, with dark water rushing in the wrong direction, upstream. The pemmican that was drying in the sun by the river was inundated by the muddy current. But she could not move.

A wind arose from the west, toward the shore, bringing the smell of burning grass and ash and fanning the flames. The pines on the opposite ridge suddenly burst into flame, the fire racing across the tops of the trees. She saw flocks of birds—seagulls, shorebirds—flying against the wind high above the growing rumble of the storm. Their great masses of beating wings darkened the smoke-filled sky; their shrill cries were muted by distance. But still she did not move.

The eastern sky grew black and in the distance strangely colored lights danced among the clouds. Brilliant orange and purple lights flashed in the darkness, bringing deep growls of thunder. Soon the lightning was reaching down through the clouds, shivering the earth with spectacular bolts of every shade. The first rain came down in huge drops, the size of pebbles, splashing even into the cave where she sat as still as a statue. The drops were salty, like tears.

The river was a roiling tumult overflowing its banks. Huge waves came crashing up from the east, with foaming crests and tangled branches. Each wave raised the water—greenish-black under the heavy clouds—so that half the valley was now under the waves. The rain from out of the east now was larger than any she had ever seen—a great watery hail that stripped the leaves from the trees. Rivulets ran down from the hill above her into the foaming river below; gullies formed in the packed earth around the cave. She glimpsed something dark, the body of a dog or a child washing down the hill. The baby in her lap whimpered, he had become detached from her breast. She did not move. The baby grew still.

For a second time this day, the night came upon her. The water fell in great sheets that were more felt than seen in the dim twilight. Thunder boomed incessantly. As the storm moved westward, complete darkness fell. But, now and again, a lightning flash would light up the cave and she could see the spreading water below, not many meters away. The changing winds had driven the rain deep into the cave. Her face was soaked in spray, her brown hair plastered against her broad forehead and high cheekbones. She could have retreated into the cave, but she did not. Rather, she waited, peering into the darkness for the flashes that lit up the curtain of rain and the approaching waves of black water. The flood was less than a meter from the cave entrance now. Soon the cave would be one with the river.

Suddenly the rain stopped completely, as quickly as it had begun. All was silent outside. The booming retreated into the distance. It was still dark, but perhaps just a little brighter than it had been a few moments before. She could see the river again; it was two meters below the cave and retreating fast. Huge trees were sucked along in its retreat, a waterfall of limbs that rushed down the stream. Even boulders were loosened by the rushing water, rolling and tumbling in the eastward current. For the third time this day, the dawn came, this time in a gray and featureless sky.

The sky brightened very gradually, without shaking off its covering of clouds. The river continued its retreat, until once again it flowed within its banks. In the silence she heard water dripping. At last she moved. Wearily she stood up, lifted the baby to her hip, and stepped to the entrance of the cave. Pools of water splashed under her bare feet. It was a world she had never known, a ravaged brown landscape with no speck of green, scattered with black spikes that had once been trees. Below her the ground was smooth, coated in a shining layer of mud. Above her the hillsides were rough, a five-o'clock shadow of black stubble revealing a denuded land. Above that were the gray billowing clouds, still moving toward the west, hiding the setting sun.

Very briefly, in the tiny gap between the horizon and the western mountains, a ray of red sun slipped through. The sunlight lit up the air as if it were a solid beam, and she saw it tracing a path toward her. For an instant, her upturned face was lit by a warm glow of light, but then the light was gone. Still in that moment, she knew. She knew that the world had not perished, that she would live, that the baby would live. She looked back into the cave. Water had soaked everything. The baby whimpered again. It needed attention, the cave needed attention, there was a lot of work to do.

It was morning. She had eaten the last of the cereal grains, stored on a bowl-shaped rock in the inner part of the cave. There was no likelihood of finding more, for when she had gone to pick the fields by the salt-flats where the grasses grew thick and lush, she found them barren for as far as she could see. New islands had formed, and the tributaries between them were now strange to her. She returned to the cave late in the afternoon and fed the baby, but her milk was drying up, and the baby was already feeling light. If she did not find food soon, the baby would not live. It was time to move. Laying the sleeping baby by the hearth, she turned to the deer hide that had been left unfinished and felt the leather for where it needed scraping.

Hearing a noise outside, she picked up the hide scraper and turned. The outline of a man filled the entrance, dark against the bright afternoon sun. He was tall and thin, and looked quite hungry as well. They looked at each other for a long moment, she and the baby, he and the walking stick.

Then he bent down and picked up a flint laying among the knives that needed resharpening. He found a short stub of deer antler nearby and, laying his walking stick down carefully, began to press the antler against the flint. Small flakes of stone came off, and after a while, he rubbed the sharp blade with his thumb, seemingly satisfied. She had been scraping one side of the hide, and now she carefully cut a strip about a centimeter wide and perhaps a meter long, curving from the foreleg to the back. When she was finished, she lifted it up and he walked over, looping it about his waist and then around the haft of the flint. It was then that she saw his back, crusted with dirt and scabs.

She reached out a hand to touch his back, and he made a sound, but did not jump. She drew back her hand, and then more slowly brushed her fingers across it. The skin was peeling in strips and the oozing flesh had crusted over with layers of dirt. Leaning over, she reached for the drinking gourd, motioning for him to sit. He squatted on his heels and wrapped his arms around his knees. She poured some water over his back. He flinched but did not move away from her. Her fingers began to work the crust loose as she continued to pour water on his back. Slowly his back grew clean, and she folded the flaps of skin back down over the pink flesh.

Reaching over the hide, she gripped the scraper and cut an X into the hide. Pulling it over his head like a cape, she sat back on her heels and looked at him. He stood up and looked down at the cape, then at her. She made an explosive sound, blowing air between her lips, and finally drummed her fingers on the ground. He repeated the sound and then went over to the flint pile and picked up his walking stick.

She lifted the baby to her hip, and slipped a soft leather skin around its stomach. Gathering the corners, she swung the baby onto her back, and knotted them over her shoulders and waist. Then, picking up the gourd and the scraper, she walked out of the cave. He, meanwhile, found a hand ax and some arrow heads among the flints. While he was fitting a flint to his walking stick, she went down to the river to refill the water gourd.

Looking up at the mountains, she located the exact spot the sun had appeared after the storm. Setting her face in that direction, she began to climb along the now dusty banks of the river. He stepped out of the cave and called, but she did not turn her head. He took his new knife and cut another strip of leather off the cape. Placing a fist-full of flints in a fold of the cape, he wrapped the strip around it making a purse-pocket. Picking up his new spear, he took her path down to the river where he stooped and drank. Then, using his spear as a walking stick, he caught up with her in long strides, burdened as she was with a baby. When he was abreast of her, she turned and for the first time in a week, she smiled.

It would be a year like no other, a miraculous year, a year of thunder and rain followed by balmy blue skies and unusual warmth. The rains kept them supplied with water, no matter how dry the terrain they crossed. On some days, it would be a brook running down from a hill, while on other days, it would be puddle that hardly lasted the noon. But every day there was water, and she drank and the baby drank, and the man silently filled the gourds. She never forgot the position of that setting sun, but with fixed determination, traveled westward by day and by night. Several times the thunderstorms arrived in the evening and each time, as if to remind her, the setting sun would pierce the clouds and pave a golden path across the glistening rain-washed earth. She called out to the man, and they stood there together, watching the light, the shining road that drew them westward. In this way they walked with the sun and waited with the clouds, covering twenty or thirty kilometers a day.

The food was no less miraculous than the water, for every day brought something new. One day it was a flooded bog with wild rice in grassy clumps that practically harvested themselves as they brushed by. Another day it might be a deer, struck in mid-leap by the lightning of the passing storm, hooves pointing the direction they should follow. At first the man would load himself down with provisions for a week and then sheepishly drop them when the next meal arrived. Soon he became accustomed to the routine, and burdened himself only with enough food and water for the day's travel.

When the rains came, they huddled back to back, and the deerskin cape that provided both of them shelter seemed hardly the worse for wear. The baby slept peacefully on her lap through even the loudest noises. Once, she wondered if the child had been deafened that day in the cave, but was relieved the next day to hear it burbling to itself in the papoose. When the baby grew restless on long travel days, she would entertain it by imitating bird sounds or animal calls, which seemed to have infinite ability to keep it occupied. Soon she found that the baby would announce its thirst or hunger or bowel condition with different sounds, and despite not seeing its face for hours at a time, she knew exactly what it needed.

One afternoon they came upon another group of humans. Three dark-eyed men, each carrying a stout spear, were standing on a ridge some distance away. They watched the little family making their way across the pebbly stream bed below. She drew closer to her man and together they picked their way carefully over the stones under the silent gaze of the onlookers. It was only when she heard a child's cry that she looked up to see the cave opening below the ridge, shielded by small willows. Although she did not see any movement, she felt several more pairs of eyes watching her party through the leaves.

For some reason, the baby chose this moment to announce its thirst, making the meadowlark sound. She did not want to stop in view of this cave, it did not feel safe. She made the bear sound. But the baby was not appeased. It made the lark sound again, followed by the dog sound. She made a long bear sound and tried hard not to look in the direction of the cave. The baby wailed.

Finding a flat rock on the far side of the stream, she stopped, undoing the knot at her neck and swinging the papoose around. The man turned back from his advance to the bluff above, and handed her the gourd. Leaning over she rinsed it in the stream and then brought it to the baby. It made the meadowlark sound and laughed. Reaching with two tiny hands it pulled the gourd up and then poured it over its head. It laughed again. She had never heard the baby make that noise, and so she held it on her lap, waiting to see what it meant.

She heard the sound of a pebble rolling behind her and she saw the man stiffen, but she did not turn around. The baby made several new sounds, and presently she saw a shadow on the ground. First a hand, and then an elbow, and then a little girl, not more than 7 or 8, standing shyly by the rock, looking at the baby. The baby burbled at the newcomer. She had long black hair, matted into several locks that framed a round brown face and brown eyes. She reached out her hand and the baby gripped her index finger and laughed.

Soon there were two women and three children around the rock. They all took turns touching its cheeks, offering a finger. The baby seemed to be enjoying the attention. It went through its entire repertoire of sounds: bird calls, animal cries, even thunderstorm noises. The people were enraptured. Just then a cloud rolled over the sun; it looked as if the usual afternoon rain was coming. The people seemed frightened by that, and melted away. The baby was quiet, its eyes looking up at the clouds. Then it made the meadowlark sound, and she remembered the gourd. Turning around to pick it up, she saw that the flat rock had been decorated with presents: a bit of pemmican, a flower, and a smooth stone roughly shaped like a person.

Filling the gourd, she brought it to the baby's lips, but it took only a brief sip, and closed its eyes. Swinging the baby onto her back, she knotted the papoose around her neck again. Collecting the presents, she dropped them in the papoose with the baby, and stood up. She looked up at the cave but only the little girl could be seen, standing in front of the willows. The group of men had not moved from their station on the ridge. The sun peeked out from the clouds, and bid them come. Turning her back on the cave and the people, she climbed up the stream bank and the man joined her. They had several more hours of travel before sunset.

The weather became chillier as fall arrived. The sun called them southward where the land was more desolate. The food changed from rice and game to tubers and succulents. Sometimes they had to try many different plants until they found one they could eat. Here the baby was invaluable. A potential plant or root would be broken to expose the sap, and then presented to the baby. If the baby reached for it, they would taste it; if the baby pushed it away, they would rinse it off their hands.

As they journeyed, they came to a desert with scraggly bushes. Even tubers could not be found here. But in the morning, a brown sap appeared on the thorny bushes. The baby, toddling forward from her lap that first day, reached out to eat it. They tasted it too, and it was sweet. They were able to collect a goodly amount before it disappeared around noon, melting away in the heat. But the next morning, the sap seemed to be just as abundant as the day before. If they arose early enough, they could collect enough for a day's journey before it got too hot. The baby also seemed to thrive on this sap, his first real solid food. His eyes grew bright and he laughed more often. In this way they were able to travel for many weeks through the most desolate of lands.

Sometimes their path turned northward because the afternoon thunderstorm tracked away from their southwesterly direction; no water could be found except where the clouds had dropped their precious cargo. It was after just such a diversion that they found themselves coming down from the hills into a hidden river valley. The bushes they had come to depend on disappeared, and green vegetation grew thickly upon the banks. The river gushed and chattered in a green line surrounded on both sides by brown desert hills, running northward and perpendicular to their path.

Descending to the river, they filled up their water gourds and dangled their feet in the water. They waited for the thunder clouds to clear away, so that their sun might break through and show the way again. Then a strange thing happened. The clouds cleared away, but there was something wrong with the sun. The eastern edge was gone, as if a bite had been taken out of it. As they watched, the sun grew dimmer, and more and more of it vanished. With great dismay, they saw the last bit of the sun, glowing like a spark, disappear. They were surrounded by a strange twilight. The baby crept into her arms, and the man stood close beside her, his spear in his hand.

But an evening bird began a beautiful song and the river gurgled on unabated. A wind came up, bringing clouds from the west and lifted her hair. For a brief moment it seemed like dawn. But this time the clouds did not part, and the long twilight gave way to night. The baby was fast asleep. The man sat down and spread his cape around them both. The bird with the beautiful voice sang again. The baby sighed in its sleep, a sigh that sounded remarkably like the nightingale's song.

They followed the river northward for several days. It meandered through a lush valley while the mountains grew taller on both sides. At one point the mountains closed in on each other, squeezing the river through a narrow gorge of black, water-drenched cliffs and white rapids. Forced off the shore, they waded through the shallows along one bank of the river. The shallows became pebbles, and the pebbles became boulders as the river churned into rapids. When it looked like they could go no further, suddenly the valley opened into a marsh and on the far side, into a salt lake of deep blue overlooked by tall red cliffs. Grasses with full bunches of seeds grew thickly in the flats. Dark openings on the cliffs foretold cool relief from the weather. A herd of deer, surprised by their arrival, fled, leaping and bounding over the pasture, flashes of brown over the verdant grass. Even the air seemed fresher here, both deeper and more invigorating.

The woman went to explore the cliffs. When she stepped inside a dark, cool cave, the baby laughed. With a practiced eye she looked over the stones and found a flat place to rest. The man followed her in and she motioned for the cape. She laid it on the floor, and with a swift motion of her flint, she cut off the frayed edges and made a new papoose. The baby really was too big for the old one, and she was finding less and less leather to knot around her waist. But the new papoose did not wrap around her back, it hung diagonally off her shoulder so that the baby could rest on her hip. She swung the baby up onto her hip in the new sling, picked up the gourd and headed down to the flats to harvest grain.

The man watched her go, and then reached down to the remnant of the cape where he kept his pouch. He took out the bit of antler that was all that remained of his stash, and flaked the flint on his spear. When it was sharp, he picked it up and headed out to the flats as well, but upstream from the woman and baby. It was time for another deerskin cape. And a cape for the baby as well.

5.2 The Creation Week in Hebrew

In the previous chapter, I proposed that Eden was a real location during a researchable era in the history of man. Understanding the development of Eden and of man explains both the nature and the magnitude of its loss. In this chapter, I take the final step backward to the origin of the universe and Earth, to show that this development of Eden and man is simply the culmination of ten millennia of millennia of millennia of planning. In this chapter I will discuss how, point-by-point, Genesis builds up a "Big Bang" story of the universe dominated by comets—the "dark matter" of modern science, but the fiery messengers of God. Along the way, I will exegete rare Hebrew words, finding scientific meanings for many of them. When we graph the Genesis day against the scientific time, I find a remarkable correlation, demonstrating that Genesis always was scientific. However, there is one event I cannot plot on that graph, and it becomes the final section of this chapter, the ex nihilo *creation of man.*

5.2.1 The Mnemonic

In the ANE as well in many animist cultures, the creation event is thought of as a marriage between Earth and Sky.[1] The exposure of the West to the ancient mythologies of Egypt or Babylon has caused us to assume that all mythologies evolve with this image as the norm.[2] That was the received wisdom of twentieth-century scholars, as epitomized in James Frazer's *The Golden Bough* or Joseph Campbell's *The Hero with a Thousand Faces*.[3]

This twentieth-century romanticism of pre-history has held up about as well as the nineteenth-century romanticism of Indo-European linguists. For not only the MT, but also Norse skalds demonstrate that myth was instead composed of sophisticated linguistic constructions, using error-correcting media, to transcribe specific historical events for posterity, as discussed in Volume 2 & 3.

As a result, rather than accreting meaning and content as it evolved through time, myth was instead losing meaning and content as it was passed down. Many of the peculiarities that Frazer or Campbell identified as common to myth are in fact error correction codes to prevent degradation of the data! Mistaking the error correction code for the meaning is a category error. It is like "explaining" the origin of the Bible as a sacralization of manuscripts in codex form. To use C. S. Lewis's term, the chronological snobbery exhibited by twentieth-century materialists such as Frazer and Campbell is misplaced. They thought that the primitive mind was somehow incorrigibly myth-making, when instead the ancients knew more about science and technology than they, as twenty-first-century scholars are now finding out.

So, despite the last two centuries of debate, the exegesis of Genesis 1 does not lie somewhere on a line between "literal" and "allegorical," as if the authors had only two modes of communication. Nor do we need to learn "nuance" as we assign greater or lesser amounts of truth to "figurative" communication, "frameworks," or non-chronological literary-analysis techniques. Rather, we need to recognize that not just Moses, but the authors before him knew a great deal more about the world and its creation than did we in the twenty-first century. The difficulty for Moses was not accommodation or "telling a simplified lie because the truth is too difficult," as some accuse John Calvin of suggesting, nor was it explaining the Creation "selfies" that God showed him on the mountain, in the way some suppose a text should be interpreted visually. No, Moses's difficulty was finding a way

1. Stackert et al. *Heaven and Earth*, 293–326.
2. Weeks. "The Bible and the 'universal' ancient world" 1–28.
3. Frazer. *The Golden Bough*; Campbell. *The Hero with a Thousand Faces*.

to convey important data that would not get corrupted by generations of fallible human beings retelling and copying a story they did not understand. The greatest challenge in writing about Genesis is the certainty displayed by both "literalists" and "accommodationists" alike. Moses's first and foremost difficulty was and remains us.

If even cosmologists disagree about the origins of the universe, how can we be certain of what Genesis describes about its formation? Do the words in our modern dictionaries have the same definitions as they did when Moses wrote Genesis, back through the mists of time? Are we sure that *tohu wabohu* does not mean for Moses "a gravitationally bound weakly ionized dusty plasma cloud"?

And if not, then we must show the greatest humility, and display the greatest diligence to discover what exactly Genesis is recording for us. We may never find all its secrets—nay, I am certain of it—we *will* never find all its secrets. We must make allowances for our incorrigible ignorance because there will always remain truths that only future generations will discover, as intended by the author himself.

If we cannot uncover the whole story, if we cannot fully understand Genesis, what should our strategy be? Must we answer every question with an "I don't know" and speak only of passages we think we do understand?

Our strategy remains the same—the scientific method. We must hold our interpretation as hypothesis, or multiple hypotheses that we sometimes compare and contrast, and sometimes complement and converge. But at all times, *midrash* respects the text as something holy, as one would respect a father. That is, we may question that our faulty ears have heard it correctly, that our trembling hands have transcribed it correctly, that our limited minds translated it correctly, but we never question the text, its motives, its potency, or its authority, just as a scientist does not question the data once it is properly received. To do otherwise, to invent data, rewrite the text, or disrespect a father, is a moral failing regardless of our scholarly acumen or scientific education. Our goal, as has been the goal of scholars in previous centuries, is to sift the good from the bad, to recover from the tangled skein the golden thread of the divine plan that placed us here and now, and for this purpose.

Therefore Frazer and Campbell, in thinking they were locating the source of all myth in human aspirations, have done us a great service. They have shown us what happens to most stories that are often retold, so that we can recognize what makes Genesis 1 unique. We can identify the techniques that Genesis used to avoid the loss of information found in most other creation accounts. And the first and most obvious of these error-correction techniques is the numbering scheme: six days in which a progressively more complex event is described.

Because no human nor astronomical timepieces existed on Day 1, Day 2, or even on Day 3, these first three days could not have been primarily significant as durations of time. The first mention of a timepiece—(Gen 1:14) "*and let them be for signs and for seasons, and for days and years*"—comes on Day 4. Therefore "evening," "morning," and "day" were not principally demarcations of time. Further complicating an interpretation of "day" as a 24-hour duration is the discovery that tidal friction has doubled or tripled the length of a day over the history of the Earth. In addition, the sidereal day, as seen by an outside-the-earth observer, is shorter by four minutes than the solar day of an on-the-earth observer. As a result, defining day as "nothing but" a duration of time is anachronistic reductionism. That is because words are not pictures, nor can they simply be mapped onto sense impressions or discrete objects, as Wittgenstein once attempted in his youth. The solution is really quite simple—the word "day" can mean several things at once, just as it does when we say to our spouse, "I had a rough day" or to the children, "In my day, life was simpler." And if words can be ambiguous when everyone speaks the same language, how much more so when written in an ancient language that has not been spoken for 2500 years!

If "day" is not a literal term, how will we know what this passage is saying?

The same way that we carry on a conversation in a noisy restaurant or rock concert venue— making sense of a sentence by inferring missed words from the context of the words we do hear. Language is a redundant medium with much error correction, so we are rarely left completely in the dark. The scientific method has simply imported our innate linguistic ability to form hypotheses about fragments of speech while checking and revising our inferences in the light of new data. I once had a surreal five-minute conversation with a friend in Boston about green tea. We each thought the other unusually dense until I finally realized that she was referring to the subway line known as the "Green-T" and the meaning snapped into focus to the merriment of all. So there may be an aspect of Genesis 1 that is concerned with duration of time, but I think it does not play a central role in the story, especially not in the first three days.

What then is the point of the numbering of the Days?

So that we will not forget one of them, nor get them in the wrong order. It is a common pedagogical technique. The staff of the treble clef is taught with a mnemonic like, "Every Good Boy Does Fine"; the order of the planets is taught with "My Very Excellent Mother Just Served Us Nine Pizza-pies"; and rainbows have a color scheme, "Roy G Biv." In all these cases, the mnemonic prevents us from dropping or adding a term, as well as enabling us to keep them in the correct order.

What is so important about keeping all six Days?

Now we are getting to the crux of Genesis 1—its intention and purpose. At every step, Genesis 1 tells what needs to precede and what needs to follow. Every Creation Day is numbered so that we will not forget a single one, just as Moses admonishes us (Ps 90:12) "*to number our days that we may gain a heart of wisdom.*" And perhaps the most important characteristic of numbers is that, like the British, they stand in a queue.

How do we know that the order is linear, and not, say, two sets of three with the last three fitting into the first "framework"? What do we lose if we place them in a different order?[4]

We need the order because we are re-creating worlds. We recreate worlds in fiction, trivially enough. We do it on the farm less trivially when we raise corn or pigs, or at our house when we plant azaleas or daffodils. We do it in the government, when we legislate for or against certain type of land usage. We do it in foreign policy, when we open borders or send Marines. In all these examples, we are changing the environment so as to benefit some inhabitants. This is what sets humans apart as "sub-creators" of God's world, the ability to plan ahead and make decisions about the future and our role in it. At every step and at every act of sub-creation, Genesis 1 tells what needs to precede and what needs to follow.

Is this some sort of "God-talk," an effort to make an obscure chapter relevant?

No, because when Jesus was asked a rather technical question about divorce law involving Moses, he quoted Genesis 1 and 2 as the final word (Matt 19:4–5). In our modern world, which is busy deconstructing marriage, Genesis remains as powerful and as relevant as ever. Without the mnemonic of Genesis 1, we are like Moses mediating spats, forced into pragmatic lose-lose situations. Because nothing in the Bible makes any sense except in the light of Genesis 1.

For if God did not create light, then Stephen Hawking is right about replacing God's "blue touch paper" with gravity.[5] If God did not create life, then Stanley Miller is right about his bottle full of methane and electric sparks.[6] If God did not create plants, then Charles Darwin is right about his "warm little pond."[7] If God did not create animals, then Alfred Tennyson

4. Kline. *Kingdom Prologue.*

5. Hawking and Mlodinow. *The Grand Design.*

6. Miller. "Production of Amino Acids" 528–529.

7. Darwin. *On the Origin of Species.*

is right about his "nature red in tooth and claw."[8] If God did not create humans, then Friedrich Nietzsche is right about the superman's "might makes right."[9] And if God did not create society, then Karl Marx is right to say "the point, however, is to change it."[10]

Alone among creation stories, the order of Genesis describes the chronology rediscovered in the twentieth century to the discomfort of scientists and materialists alike, as Robert Jastrow records in *God and the Astronomers*.[11] Since this unique ordering is central to both Genesis and twentieth-century science, it provides the key to understanding the remarkable Genesis 1 passage, and why it presents a different paradigm from undirected materialism (a.k.a. naturalism).

Analysis of Genesis 1 must respect the ordering of the Days and therefore the organization of this chapter follows that natural division. In Day 1 I discuss the character and history of spacetime, showing its remarkable fit to the text. Once the lexicon is modernized and the science updated, it is apparent that Genesis belongs to a technical genre. In the same way, Day 2 addresses the formation of planets and the properties of water. In Day 3 the origin of plant life and its development on planets is considered, paying close attention to the details of the technical Hebrew. In Day 4 I address the bane of Creationists, the apparently non-chronological creation of the Sun. In Day 5 and Day 6 a look at animal life once again turns up new categories in the Hebrew. Finally, I look back over the entire Creation Week to tabulate the Biblical and scientific origins of all the entities discussed. We will see a breathtaking concordance between the two, which suggests that the first eleven chapters of Genesis are indeed technical, demanding a technical exegesis.

5.2.2 Day 1: Cosmology

> *1:1 In the beginning, God created the heavens (*shamayim*) and the earth (ʾ*erets*).*

Every creation myth offers a beginning for matter, none offers a beginning for time. In that way Genesis is unique. The opening words of Genesis describe the first Day but it starts without even an acknowledgment of time. Augustinus Aurelius responds to the question "what was God doing before

8. Tennyson. *In Memoriam A. H. H.*
9. Nietzsche. "*Also sprach zarathustra.*"
10. Marx and Engels. *Ludwig Feuerbach.*
11. Jastrow. *God and the Astronomers.*

He created the world?" by explaining that time was created with space, so that there was no "before" before, no "there" there.[12] That was 1500 years before Albert Einstein explained in his Special Theory that space and time were convertible, so that the creation of one is the creation of the other.[13] The lack of temporal markers in Gen 1:1 perhaps indicates this unusual origin or perhaps Stephen Hawking's creative "imaginary time," which eliminates temporal causation altogether, is meant.[14] Even Hawking, however, cannot fathom non-causal beginnings, so he attributes the Creation to gravity, something Einstein never did. For Einstein's General Theory requires that spacetime and matter be equal partners in gravity, neither dominating the other. Therefore it is significant that we find that the opening verse, Gen 1:1, describes these three components of Einstein's model with the simple phrase, "*In the beginning* (atemporal "in")*, God created the heavens* (spacetime) *and the earth* (matter)."

As we will see below, if we update Gesenius's dictionary for the twenty-first century, by connecting *shamayim* with spacetime and *'erets* with matter, the entire text opens up. It makes the agreement of Gen 1:1 with the "Big Bang" (BB) model of modern cosmology truly astonishing. That agreement has been the topic of many books in the decades since Belgian priest, Georges Lemaître,[15] first described it in 1927, Pope Pius XII recognized it in 1951,[16] and evangelicals embraced it, as in, for example, the books of astronomer Hugh Ross.[17]

Because Gen 1:1 has been interpreted as the creation of two locations—the sky above and the land below—our expanded context reveals some important features of the exegesis of Genesis. First, early exegesis is often only approximately correct; acquired knowledge enables a comprehension unknown to previous generations. So what Augustine regarded as fact we should consider tentative, pending future discoveries. Which is to say, the sacred text remains constant but its many translations will vary, so treating Genesis as simply a collection of elementary facts diminishes its power and its message.

Second, words do not always have the simplest or the most "literal" meaning. Because the dictionary is constantly under revision, we gain

12. St Augustine. *Confessions.*

13. Einstein. "Zur Elektrodynamik bewegter Körper" 891–921, transl. Jeffrey and Perrett. "On the Electrodynamics of Moving Bodies."

14. Hawking. *A brief history of time.*

15. Heller. "Lemaître, Big Bang and the Quantum Universe."

16. Pius XII. "The Proofs for the Existence of God"

17. Ross. *The Creator and the Cosmos.*

little security from the literal dictionary meaning. Our ignorance, however, should not excuse the mistranslation of Gen 1:1 *'erets*, as "earth" because we are given ample reason to doubt that it refers to solid land. The next verse (Gen 1:2) describes it as "formless and void." Not until Gen 1:8 and 1:10 are "earth" and "heaven" defined, counter-intuitively as "firmaments." Something other than solid land must be intended by Gen 1:1; otherwise, the (mnemonically exact) ordering of Genesis is lost. If the order is important, one cannot redefine a word retroactively without producing circular logic puzzles.

Finally, if Genesis is a polemic against paganism, as many commentators suggest, the cultural tendency to project a pagan reading into Gen 1:1 is a good indication that it should not mean "sky" and "land." Its non-intuitive, counter-cultural didactic lesson would be unnecessary if it were in agreement with ANE mythology.[18] The point of mnemonics is to teach something new, not to mimic culture. In that case, by using intentionally ambiguous language, the writer is misleading all those who expect Genesis to be derivative of local mythologies; he is punishing those students who arrogantly are not paying attention. In this sense, Genesis is a self-aware text. It not only carries information, but it carries disinformation for those who do not respect it. Literary criticism refers to this self-awareness as "irony," a characteristic of all great drama from Sophocles to Shakespeare. For example, there is no question that, in the final chapters of Genesis, the story of Joseph demonstrates irony. We will encounter this self-awareness often in Genesis, which we summarize as the grammar school lesson: "Show respect to the text."

> 1:2 *And the earth was without form, and void; and darkness was upon the face of the deep. And the Spirit* (ruwach) *of God moved upon [ESV hovered over] the face of the waters* (mayim).

If the interpretation of *'erets* as matter is not mistaken, then to be "without form and void" would be one of the four states of matter: solid, liquid, gas, or plasma. Neither liquids nor gasses have a form; they take the shape of their container. But only gasses or possibly plasmas, could be considered "void." Because we are discussing the beginnings of astronomical objects, we can use the astronomical term for a dilute gaseous blob of matter, "nebula."

Then what is the meaning of the terms "face of the deep" and "face of the waters"? Is "the deep" (*tehowm*) synonymous with waters (*mayim*)? And why do we get the poetic phrase "face of" (*paniym*) appearing twice in a text that may not be intended as poetic at all? Why does the English Standard

18. Weeks. "The ambiguity of Biblical background" 219–236.

Version (ESV), along with the Jewish Publication Society (JPS), translate the verb *(rachaph)* as "hovering over"? And finally, why is "waters" (*mayim*) neither singular nor plural, but dual (as in the English phrases "pair of scissors" or "pair of pants")?

It may seem that we now have more questions than answers about Gen 1:2, but answering them will be time well spent. First, the invention of a context for arriving at a strained meaning is pseudo-mythologizing, and is to be avoided. One such attempt is the idea that the Hebrews believed in a three-story universe with exactly two kinds of water, one below and one above, separated by a crystalline "firmament," as Younker and Davidson document.[19] On that view, the use of the dual for "waters" is said to derive from this bizarre worldview. If it sounds unconvincing to us, it would sound less convincing to Moses—a man who outlived all of us and probably knew a great deal more about the ancient world. Any "explanation" that invokes an unsupported mythology to create a unique definition has simply replaced one hypothesis by two more, violating Occam's Razor as well as the respect due the text.

Rejecting all invented contexts that modify the lexicon, what can we learn from science? If we take the phrase "over the face of" to mean "surface of," then Gen 1:2 is telling us something about the visible layer. If we assume that formless matter refers to a nebula, then astronomers divide nebulae into two sorts—those that have a surface and those that do not. A transparent nebula has no surface and we can see right through it, whereas an opaque nebula presents us only its surface, which can be bright in the reflected light of a nearby star. If "*the surface of the nebula was dark,*" it implies an opaque nebula without a nearby light source.

Yet Gen 1:2 says more than that. It says that, not just the nebula, but the "*surface of the deep*" was dark. If we take Gen 1:1 to refer to "matter and spacetime," then Gen 1:2 is about nebulae and inter-nebular (or intergalactic) space.

Why would intergalactic space be dark?

Cosmologists tell us that after the BB, which marked the beginning of spacetime and matter (Gen 1:1), the universe was hot, consisting mostly of ionized hydrogen (protons) that were transparent to light. But as the universe expanded and cooled, the protons recombined with electrons, forming atomic or molecular hydrogen that was opaque to light (dark nebula). Not until later, when the first stars ignite, does the resulting ultraviolet (UV) light re-ionize the hydrogen gas (by stripping off the electron), making the night sky transparent again—as recorded for Day 4. The amazing correspondence

19. Younker and Davidson. "The Myth of The Solid Heavenly Dome."

between Gen 1:1–2 and the BB model is what convinced astronomers that the Genesis account was scientific.[20] So the translation now reads: "*The matter was gaseous and dilute, and the surface of the nebulae were opaque.*"

What does the last sentence mean, "The Spirit of God hovered over the surface of the two-waters *mayim*"?

The statement appears odd because the standard cosmological model has no water until at least 100 million years later, when the stars ignite and burn hydrogen into oxygen. Coincidentally, over the last twenty years, cosmologists have become increasingly perplexed by the nature of the "dark matter" that was made in the Big Bang. The first two candidates— MACHOs and WIMPs—have not worked out.[21] But small, black comets have all the right properties to function as dark matter.[22]

Could Genesis be telling us that the dark matter is water?

Yes, I believe it may be. If so, then the BB created seven times more water than all the stars in the universe, a major revision of the standard model. The "magnetic Big Bang model,"[23] demonstrates that the overlooked magnetic fields of the Big Bang may be responsible for superabundant carbon and oxygen production. So I will continue this exegesis assuming large quantities of water and ice were created in the BB, to discover whether it has explanatory power for the Hebrew text.

Using the older (and literal) 1611 King James Version (KJV), the "spirit of God" is a translation of the Masoretic Hebrew text (MT) *ruwach*. King David uses this word in Ps 51:11 for "Holy Spirit," which also appears in Gen 6:3, where God's Spirit is disturbed by man's violence. So *ruwach* is creative, enlivening, intelligent, and personal but it is not equivalent to what the KJV translates as "soul," in contrast to "body." It would be wrong to simply reduce this movement of the *ruwach* to an "enlivening spirit" because the Hebrew does not support "substance dualism," whereby the body is a lump of lifeless material until a ghostly soul is added like Dr˙Frankenstein's electricity. Electricity is neither intelligent nor personal. Rather, as many commentators have argued, this *ruwach* is much closer to John the Evangelist's *logos*— a mind or a purpose. For lack of a better word, let us use the phrase "creative intelligence" to translate the word.

That brings us to the very odd choice of verb that follows. The KJV translates *rachaph* (appearing 3x in the MT) as "moving upon" while the ESV/JPS translates it "hovering over" because the Deut 32:11 reference and

20. Ross. *The Creator and the Cosmos*

21. Silk. "Will we ever know what dark matter is?"

22. Sheldon. "The Wet Comet Model," 9606–27.

23. Sheldon. "Comets, Water, and Big Bang Nucleosynthesis."

the Syriac cognate are usually associated with a bird hatching or brooding its eggs. Because the Holy Spirit is sometimes described in the Psalms as a dove, the verb choice almost works. But we do not usually associate a dove with *logos* or "personal" characteristics and certainly not with "intelligence." The reason for this verb lies not in the subject but in the object—"*over the surface of the two waters.*"

It would seem that God's "creative intelligence" is doing something with water, yet nothing in this object invokes images of birds, hatching or otherwise. What are we missing?

The answer came unexpectedly. In 2011, the online publication of the discovery of cyanobacterial fossils on extinct comets nearly took down its server with over 40 million hits.[24] Some of these fossils are so very old that they may predate the most ancient fossils on Earth (stromatolites).[25] The possibility of a comet-based biosphere spreading life through the galaxy becomes even more compelling if comets make up the majority of matter in the universe, the "dark matter." To scientists raised on the concept that life is but a 10-meter thick infection on the outer skin of a 6370-km-radius Earth, which is itself a "tiny blue speck" in the vastness of the cosmos, that is a radical idea. It means that life outweighs the planets and outnumbers the stars but it is implied by Genesis because comets are made of water.

One objection is that comets are made of dusty ice, not liquid water, as required for life. How can dirty snowballs carry life through the vast reaches of inhospitable space?

In 1986 an "armada" of satellites met the returning Halley's comet. One foolhardy satellite braved the sandblasting dust to take a picture of the central core, the nucleus of ice responsible for the enormous shining tail of the comet. The core was not the expected white or off-white snowball, but coal black, with the sunny side surface a sizzling 130C/266F, above the temperature of boiling water. Out of that ice-cooled black core erupted gigantic geysers, spewing water and steam into space and thus producing the tail.[26] Subsequent missions to comets Borrelly, Wild-2, and Tempel-1 confirmed that Halley was no exception, but that all comets are jet black, with rigid, cratered surfaces and water geysers full of organic molecules. Evidently, the dust in a dirty snowball mixes with melting ice to form a cemented outer coat that turns jet black. It is cracks in this outer coat that permit the trapped steam to erupt in geysers. As a comet ages it loses more and more ice and water, but the rigid outer coat cannot shrink, so that the

24. Hoover. "Fossils of Cyanobacteria in CI1 Carbonaceous Meteorites."

25. Nutman et al. "Rapid emergence of life," 535–538.

26. Huebner, ed. *Physics and Chemistry of Comets*.

comet gradually hollows out like a giant eggshell. The shells of these galactic eggs protect the watery interior from the damaging cosmic rays that would sterilize all life. Indeed, when infected with life, as most appear, they become ideal incubators.[27]

Now comets, for all their bio-engineered design features that absorb sunlight and circulate hot water, have only a brief week or two of summer as they approach a star. Then they endure millennia of winter as they recede into the cold void of space. That makes them inhospitable for all but the most patient of microbes, who do not mind this Rip Van Winkle existence. For life to develop or mature, it must find another sea where it is always summer, where the sun always shines, and the water is always wet. Life needs comets to spread, but planets to thrive: two kinds of surfaces, two kinds of sea, two kinds of water.

Therefore the dove of creative intelligence broods over its cosmic clutch, awaiting the day when the "eggs" will hatch on a planet that is being formed for them. The preparation of that second sea then becomes the topic of the rest of the chapter. And this may be why the word "water" is in the dual, which is a more satisfying explanation than a narrative about "crystalline firmaments." Then our loose paraphrase of Gen 1:2 is as follows: *The matter of the universe was in dusty ices, and the opaque nebula were dark, but God's creative intelligence brooded over [the clutch of life-bearing comets making the journey to] a second sea.*

Can Creation be about spacetime, if tradition has never supported this interpretation?

If the definition of "heavens and earth" as "spacetime and matter" in Gen 1:1 was not intuitive to previous generations, so also the first three Days of Genesis 1 remain counter-intuitive. When we describe an object or a location, we often have a visual image in our minds so that we work from outside to inside, or from left to right, or clockwise from north to south. But Gen 1:1 seemingly starts out with heaven, then describes earth, then water which obviously needs the earth to hold it, but then it goes up to stars, then back to water, before finally redefining earth again! There seems to be no clear direction to the mental picture; it appears to be completely disorganized. It is this hodge-podge of locations that may have generated so many creative attempts to reorganize this chapter into some hidden mental framework.

But when we begin to understand Gen 1:1–2 from a scientific perspective, both the temporal and spatial order emerges like the three dimensional

27. Sheldon and Hoover. "Evidence for liquid water on comets" 127–145; Sheldon and Hoover. "Implications of cometary water" 6309–0L.

objects hidden in a Magic Eye image.[28] It is not just that the Big Bang is a time-sequence that explains the ordering in Genesis, but that the spatial particularities emerge after the generalities, the planets form after the stars, which form after the galaxies, which form out of the dark matter. Then because Gen 1:2 discusses dark matter, it is entirely appropriate for Gen 1:3 to discuss the "re-ionization" era that followed the formation of galaxies and the ignition of the first ice stars that emitted a great deal of ultraviolet light.

When we are no longer confined to the surface of the Earth by ancient exegesis, the spatial progression logically proceeds from the large to the small. We move from a consideration of cosmology to a consideration of stars, the topic of astronomy.

Gen 1:3 *And God said, Let there be light: and there was light.*

This is another of those simple statements that disguise a princely sum of information. We begin with the trivial observation that this is Gen 1:3 and not Gen 1:1. It comes after, not before, the creation of matter and spacetime, as if the immaterial depends on the material. In most retellings of Genesis, the creation of light comes first, yet strangely in Genesis the darkness was created before the light.

Is this not counter-intuitive? Did not Plotinus (and later Augustine) tell us that bad things have negative existence in the way a shadow is defined as the absence of light? So how could darkness come first?[29]

Cosmology may provide an answer to this riddle. The first three minutes of the Big Bang were dominated by energy, by heat, and by light. But eons of expansion reduced the temperature until ordinary matter condensed out of this unimaginable brightness, at which point the light was absorbed by this newly reconstituted matter.[30] All this cosmic evolution is hidden between Gen 1:1 and 1:2, so that when we are introduced to the universe in Gen 1:2, the skies are now black.

That may be why Gen 1:3 seems to repeat itself. The implied light of Gen 1:1 was extinguished by the nebulae of Gen 1:2. Cold, dark matter has filled the universe like squid ink, ready to extinguish whatever flame or star might try to light the darkness. So Gen 1:3 is telling us about the transformation of our universe from the opaque nebula created by the cooling Big Bang to the crystalline expanse we take for granted in Hubble Space Telescope photographs (Figure 5.1). According to standard Big Bang theory, this "dark age" of the universe existed from about 1 million to about 150 million years after the beginning, at which point the universe became transparent again.

28. MagicEye. *Magic Eye.com*

29. Calder. "The Concept of Evil"

30. Weinberg. *The First Three Minutes.*

What made the light reappear and how did this transformation come about?

After the glowing plasma from the Big Bang cooled into a dark nebula, the warm atoms combined into simple molecules—hydrogen combining with oxygen to make water, carbon combining with oxygen to make carbon monoxide. All these newly-formed molecules absorbed light, even as the universe continued to cool (panel 1 of 5.1). Eventually this "chemical" era of the universe passed because the temperature dropped too low for any more reactions. After this, the only change possible was a change in state from free gas to trapped ice, as happened when gas molecules encountered a cold surface and froze into ice crystals. The condensation point for water vapor is the "frost point" which, in absolute temperature or the Kelvin scale, is 273K. The condensation point for oxygen is 56K and for hydrogen 20K. These conventional "freezing points" all assume high atmospheric pressure, however in the vacuum of space, hydrogen (H) and helium (He) exist only as gasses. After 13.7 billion years of expansion and cooling, the temperature of the universe today, as measured in the voids between galaxies, is about 3K. As a result, the only gaseous clouds are those of H and He, with trace amounts of heavier molecules. This means that over half the nebular gas was removed by freezing, and the continual expansion of the universe has made the remaining gas very dilute. Despite the near vacuum, the astronomical distances meant that light was still absorbed by traces of gas, so the sky remained black.

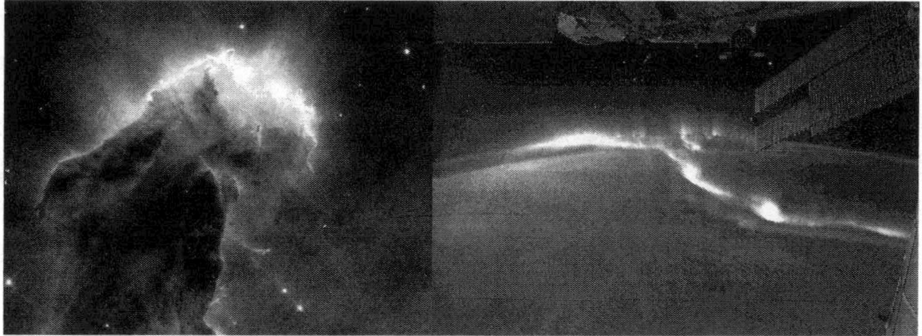

Figure 5.1: Dark nebula in the Eagle Nebula; Aurora Borealis from Space Station.(NASA)

As the grains of ice clumped together to make comets, the comets were soon big enough to exert a gravitational tug on neighboring clumps and grow larger. Faster and faster, the positive feedback or "gravitational instability" caused growing clumps to form stars. When the pressure from the weight of ice exceeded the repulsive nuclear force of the atoms, the stars ignited and burned with nuclear energy. Unlike most of the stars we see around us today, those first stars were full of oxygen from the ice. That made them hard to ignite but once lit, they burned much hotter than our Sun. Instead of radiating a warm yellow sunlight, those first stars were as hot as a welder's torch, giving off harsh blue and UV light guaranteed to peel the skin off an alligator were any created.

This UV light did two things. It heated the outer layers of nearby icy comets, making geysers that, like miniature rocket engines, scattered the clumps and prevented more icy stars from forming. It also stripped the electrons from the hydrogen and helium gas, making them a transparent, ionized plasma. (It is only when these energetic ions are guided by the magnetic field into collisions with the atmospheric atoms that they excite electrons to produce the glowing light of the aurora, as in panel 2 of Figure 5.1.) The UV light from those first stars spread wider and wider as more and more space became transparent. These islands of transparency merged together and after about 150 million years (according to the standard model), the night sky was washed clean of dark nebula and gleamed with the pinprick light of a thousand million suns.

> Gen 1:4 *And God saw the light, that it was good: and God divided the light from the darkness.*

This period, when the universe transitioned from opaque to transparent, is known as the "re-ionization" era.[31] But the era did more than turn on the lights. It also energized the comets, heating their ice into jets of steam. That gave them the velocity they needed to reach nearby dusty ice clouds to precipitate star formation there by seeding another gravitational instability. This process may account for the speed with which the earliest galaxies formed soon after re-ionization (birth<300 My), long before gravity alone would pull enough hydrogen together to make the stars. As the stars formed and their heat expelled the comets, the comets traveled to pristine dust clouds, starting condensation anew.

In such a way galactic formation was seeded and spread by comets, clumping matter into galaxies along comet trails. This caused the structure of our universe to appear like a web of connections eerily reminiscent of neurons in the brain.[32] Or if we take the negative of this statement, we might say that these trails of light divided up the dark and empty expanses of the universe. Perhaps this is why the discovery of dark matter is so difficult. These excited coal black comets are so very skittish that they can only be

31. Robertson et al. "Early star-forming galaxies" 49–55.
32. Wang et al. "Modelling galaxy clustering" 537–547.

identified by their collective gravitational tug on the galactic stars, which keeps the outermost stars from flying away from the spinning galaxy. The light scatters the dark, and the dark corrals the light.

I am not certain if this new model of dark matter comets properly predicts the expansion of the universe but it is certain that current, comet-free cosmology models do not predict it. One problem with the Standard Model of cosmology is that if the clumping of matter takes too long, the expansion of the universe will produce galaxies very slowly, if at all. But if we crank up the model's density dial to produce galaxies more quickly, the universe collapses into black holes or creates enormous galaxies of very hot stars, which is not what we in fact see. Somehow, the rate of star formation in the standard model must be fine-tuned but the problem is that the standard model cannot be tuned at all without destroying the agreement of the model with reality concerning the proportions of primordial Lithium, Helium, and Deuterium!

To solve this problem, two extra dials have been added: a "dark matter" dial of invisible gravitating matter to speed up stellar collapse (as well as hold galaxies together) and a "dark energy" dial of anti-gravity to repel galactic collapse (and distribute galaxies like a lacy curtain). This "Standard Model" goes by the acronym ΛCDM (pronounced "lambda-cee-dee-em"), where the Λ refers to the dark energy dial,[33] and the CDM refers to the cold dark matter dial. Astronomers are in two camps concerning CDM. Some support "massive compact halo objects," (MACHOs) which look like miniature black holes while others support "weakly interacting massive particles" (WIMPs), which are thought to be undiscovered atomic particles looking like overweight neutrinos.[34] No setting of the dials, however, can explain the formation of dwarf galaxies, "dark matter galaxies," or smooth (non-cuspy) galaxy cores, which are problems mooted by the presence of the comets described in Gen 1:2.

> Gen 1:5a *And God called the light Day, and the darkness he called Night.*

What does it mean for God to name light and darkness?

It would seem that Day and Night are delineated, so we guess that this definition is about durations of time. Yet, as we argued earlier, there are no timepieces yet, no sundials, no lunar months, and no stellar zodiacs. So if it is about duration it must be a coarse determination.

33. Davis. "Cosmological constraints on dark energy" 1731.

34. Cui. "A Review of WIMP"; Danninger and Rott. "Solar WIMPs unravelled."

Alternatively, the separation could be in space rather than in time, in which case this definition involves a material property, a distinction between light matter and dark matter, between stars and comets, between galaxies and inter-galactic space. This fits better with the previous passage, Gen 1:4. As noted earlier, this separation of the cosmos permits galaxy formation within the large scale structure of the universe. Then our rough paraphrase becomes "*God called the bright matter day but the dark comets night.*" Or one might offer a poetic version, "*God ignited matter into light, but hid the comets in the night.*"

> Gen 1.5b *And the evening and the morning were the first day (*yom*).*

Finally, we come to the repeated phrase "evening and morning were the *n*th day." Readers may recall that this repeated phrase is the critical mnemonic device for keeping the creation items in order. But the device starts with evening and ends with morning. This is not the way days are described in most languages; rather, it is the way the night is described. Because night has just been defined, this narrative device is drawing attention to itself; it is self-referential. And as we remarked earlier, self-referential texts are like sudden quizzes; they are tests to determine if the student has been paying attention.

Why is the first night called the first day?

We look back and see that the day/night distinction separates the universe into galaxies and voids, into stars and comets, or possibly even earlier when in Gen 1:1, we were given a matter versus spacetime distinction. So evening and morning are not to be distinguished principally as durations but as separators between two dissimilar eras, between two different phases of matter, or between two nonidentical information states which mark "days." Therefore, "day" in this context is not to be associated with the presence of sunlight, but as a duration between two time markers.

If so, the phrase "evening and morning" indicates this transition. If we understand what was changing during in this textual day, if we understand the dependent variable, we can place the separator at the right spot, the space-time location where the transition occurred. The location is important because, as the story unfolds, the six night/day separators of this transition, the dependent variable, is becoming increasingly refined and subtle even as it gets closer to home.

5.2.3 Day 2: Planetology

> 1:6 *And God said, Let there be a firmament* (raqiya') *in the midst of the waters* (mayim)*, and let it divide the waters from the waters.*

With Day 2, we have moved out of cosmology toward the *raqiya'*, which the KJV/JPS translated "firmament," from the Latin Vulgate *firmamentum* ("a strengthening support" Lewis-Short).[35] The choice of a transliterated Latin word suggests that the KJV translators did not have an English cognate word. The Vulgate also simply transported the Greek LXX *stereoma* ("a solid body, foundation" Liddell-Scott)[36] into Latin which suggests they did not have a better Latin word either. Brown-Driver-Briggs (BDB) use an analogous Syriac word root (i.e., an educated guess) to derive "expanse," as well as to give their second definition, the LXX/Vulgate "solid bowl."[37] BDB also mentions a related adjective in Num 17:3 where metal is to be beaten into "broad" plates. All this leads the modern ESV/NAS translators to use the word "expanse" as Younker and Davidson document.[38]

What is this firmament? Is it just a primitive view of the sky as a crystalline bowl that separates clouds from ocean, as some have suggested?[39]

Verse	Meaning	Verse	Meaning
Gn1:6	decl. r. divide waters	Ps 19:1	demonstrates design
Gn1:7a	made r. and divided	Ps 150:1	demonstrates power
Gn1:7b,c	loc.,water above/below	Ez 1:22	loc.overhead, gleams crystal
Gn1:8	called r. *shamayim*	Ez 1:23	location above cherubim
Gn1:14	location. r. of s.	Ez 1:25	location above cherubim
Gn1:15	location. r. of s.	Ez 1:26	location below throne
Gn1:17	star location, r. of s.	Ez 10:1	location above cherubim
Gn1:20	bird location, r. of s.	Da 12:3	shines bright

Table 5.1: The meaning of רָקִיעַ (*raqiya'*).

No, I argue that this is a sophisticated presentation of Einstein's General Theory that could not be fully appreciated until now. For it is a consequence of the theory that an expanding universe cools while converting energy into

35. Lewis and Short. *A Latin Dictionary.*
36. Liddell, Scott, and Jones. *A Greek-English Lexicon.*
37. Brown, Driver, and Briggs. *Hebrew and English Lexicon.*
38. Younker and Davidson. "The Myth of The Solid Heavenly Dome."
39. Walton. *The Lost World of Genesis One.*

gravitational energy, and gravitational energy into curved spacetime. That is why the *raqiya'* is declared to be heaven.

As we see from Table 5.1, the word *raqiya'*, appears most frequently, 9/17x, in Genesis 1 describing heaven, 2/17x in Psalms describing attributes of God, 5/17x in Ezekiel describing locations in heaven, and 1/17x in Daniel describing saints. In Ezek 1:22 it is likened to clear shining crystal. Possibly in Ezek 1:26 and 10:1, it separates the throne from the cherubim, which may imply a rigid material substance. In Dan 12:3, we are told that it is bright. From our earlier discussion of nebulae, that suggests opacity. It is not surprising that, historically, scholars have found the word difficult to pin down!

But notice that none of these later uses of the word require rigidity or even solidity of the substance, which in any case does not match the Gen 1:20 description of birds flying through it. In Gen 1:14, 15, and 17, it can support the presence of heavenly bodies, and in Gen 1:8 provides the space for the definition of Heaven, but the image of it as a rigid solid support appears to be a projection of the LXX translators forcing Hebrew words into Hellenistic Greek categories. Trying our best to put all these meanings into one word, we might translate this *raqiya'* as a "force field" that emits light—a favorite of science-fiction movies—so that it simultaneously is transparent, supports heavy bodies, and allows motion through it. But we do not need Star Wars to explain the Hebrew word. We already have a perfectly good word from science: "gravity" or a "gravity field." (Gravity fields glow when they compress and heat matter, such as meteorites that fall into them, converting gravitational into thermal and then into light energy.)

It is gravity that invisibly suspends the stars in the heavens, and gravity that birds seem to effortlessly violate. It is gravity that demonstrates God's power and design, and gravity that brightens meteors as they blaze across the sky. It is gravity that Albert Einstein explains in his General Theory, and gravity that Stephen Hawking invokes to create the universe.[40]

Does this word really work for other verses in Genesis 1?

We could translate Gen 1:6 as, *Let there be gravity between these comets, and let it separate the comets from the planets.* That's the process, described earlier, by which a gravitational instability clumps the comets together.

So far so good, what about the next verse?

> Gen 1:7 *And God made the firmament, and divided the waters which were under the firmament from the waters which were above the firmament: and it was so.*

40. Hawking and Mlodinow, *The Grand Design*.

After substituting for firmament, we get: *And God made the gravity strong, so that it divided the free comets from the trapped planetary ocean (*melted comets*) below*. Cometary water appears only in the brief moments when a comet passes near a sun and melts. On a planet, the gravity field provides the container that holds the atmosphere, which permits liquid water to exist year round. Comets can then be seen as the transportation system while planets are the hydroponics farm for a galactic agricultural economy, which is because cyanobacteria, the fossils discovered on comets, are the quintessential pioneering plant.[41]

> Gen 1:8 *And God called the firmament Heaven. And the evening and the morning were the second day.*

Why does God define *raqiya'*, this gravity, as Heaven, as if gravity describes His home? First, the MT word for heaven, *shamayim* appears 38/420x in Genesis, either describing a contrasting location from earth, or describing God's habitation. The KJV capitalizes the word here in Gen 1:8, but does not capitalize it in the remainder of 37/38x it appears in Genesis, even when, as in Jacob's dream, it describes the abode of angels. So it would seem that the definition in Gen 1:8 does not represent God's habitation (big H) but rather a location (small h) that is not on the surface of the Earth.

Secondly, definitions usually move from the general to the specific, with the left (subject) side of the definition more general than the right (predicate) side. But if "heaven" means anywhere other than the surface of the Earth, then it looks as if this definition is backward because gravitational fields are more local than outer space! The KJV solved this by capitalizing "Heaven" to particularize it. But perhaps that was not so much a definition as a declaration, not an assignment but an equivalence meant to indicate that now, outside the Earth, "gravity = space." If so, this declaration is perhaps the earliest statement of Einstein's equation for gravity.

What does this equivalence mean?

From the Big Bang until this period, matter dominated spacetime because its heat and explosive power expanded the universe. But the declaration suggests that a transition has occurred: Gravity has somehow become more important than matter (or heat or pressure) in shaping spacetime. The difference is the temperature. For example, the sun's atmosphere is so hot it is continually escaping the sun's gravity, generating the solar wind. Our atmosphere, by contrast, is too cold to escape the Earth's gravity, to our great relief.

41. Sheldon and Hoover. "The Cometary Biosphere" 6694–0H; Sheldon and Hoover. "Cosmological Evolution" 7097–41.

Why heaven? Would not the gravity field be stronger down in the planetary ocean than in heaven? And (with apologies to George MacDonald's *Light Princess*)[42] is not Heaven a place without gravity?

The key to understanding Gen 1:8 and Day 2 is to understand the dependent variable, the day/night transition involving gravity. The transition is from a hot, pressure and matter-dominated Big Bang to a cool, gravity-dominated spacetime. The continuing expansion of the universe changes the ratios of gravitational, kinetic, and thermal energies. Gravitational energy is contained in massive objects, pictured as a rubber sheet drumhead with a lead ball sinking into a "gravity well." Kinetic energy is contained in fast moving objects with shallow gravity wells. And thermal energy is contained in hot objects where all the atoms are jostling about violently trying to escape—the opposite of a gravity well. Energy, like money, can be converted from one form to another, as long as the total amount is conserved. The power of the BB model lies in this dance of convertible energy transformations. As the universe expanded and cooled, the kinetic and thermal energy transformed into gravitational energy, where the fire (heat and light) cooled faster than the smoke (matter). Eventually the pressure due to hot photons was less than the pressure due to hot matter, with the result that spacetime transitioned to matter-dominated universe about 1000 years after the BB. This transition might be the subject of God's declaration, but unfortunately it would lie between Gen 1:1 and 1:2, which is too early for Gen 1:8.

Fortunately, there is a second matter transition better positioned to be the one referenced by Gen 1:8. Even after 1000 years, the Big Bang was still very hot. It was no longer hot enough to initiate nuclear reactions because much of the heat was transformed into the kinetic energy of an expanding gas. The expansion was occurring inside an enormous gravitational well, which meant it was all uphill, that is, converting the kinetic into gravitational potential energy. As if it were hitting a pop fly ball, the kinetic energy all went into altitude. The matter cooled from plasma into gas, the gas (excepting H and He) cooled into ice grains, and the sticky ice grains clumped into comets. The comets clumped gravitationally into ice planets, which then vacuumed up the remaining gas until they became so massive they ignited into short-lived ultra-violet (UV) stars. Finally, the UV radiation from these stars re-ionized the gas and heated the comets, stopping the clumping cascade. This brings us from Gen 1:2 to Gen 1:6, preparing us for the second matter transition.

For a long while, the universe had only UV stars but the H and He that would not condense eventually clumped, helped along by supernova

42. MacDonald. *The Light Princess*.

shock waves from exploding UV stars, so that "ordinary" sun-like stars began to form. At this point, the magnetic Big Bang model smoothly returns to the Standard Model. It solves the "early galaxy" problem, where a frenzy of forming ice-star galaxies produced the structures we now observe: A hundred billion H/He stars and a few remnant white-dwarf ice-stars,[43] all swimming in an extended sea of skittish comets (providing the dark matter or gravitational glue that holds the galaxy together).[44] Because the hydrogen-burning stars were like our Sun, their light was also like that of our Sun, warm and gentle. It allowed comets to approach closer than did the harsh UV stars of the first generation. Under these tranquil conditions (large gravitational field, weak radiation field), comets again could orbit the central star, collecting and merging to form icy, Jupiter-like gas giants. It is not coincidental that the search for extraterrestrial planets has found 1000 Jupiter-like planets for every Earth-like one, though the ratio has greatly surprised planetologists.[45] This second matter transition may be the one referenced by Gen 1:8.

The unique property of these new Jupiter-like objects is their gravitational effect on primordial comets, which now attract, unlike the previous UV stars which repelled them. So if we assign the independent variable of Day 2 to this ratio of gravity to radiation energy, then the evening-morning transition in Gen 1:8 marked by the declaration, is a transition from a hot, repulsive UV star to a cool, attractive Jupiter-like planet.

Much has been written about the special astronomical conditions needed for life to survive on Earth, all pointing to the crucial role played by Jupiter.[46] It is Jupiter that deflects galactic comets into solar orbits, transforming them into short-period comets that can bring water to Earth. It is Jupiter that protects Earth from asteroidal debris that might destroy it. Jupiter also raises a tidal bulge on the Sun that circularizes the Earth's orbit, thereby making the winters warmer and the summers cooler. Once the Jupiters are in place, we can have a solar system, and once a solar system is in place, we can collect the raw materials to build an Earth-like planet—dividing the waters below from the waters above. Therefore our paraphrase becomes, *And God declared the gravity field a Solar System.*

43. Kepler et al. "A white dwarf with an oxygen atmosphere" 67–69.

44. Brandenberger. "Introduction to Early Universe."

45. Boley, et al. "The In Situ Formation of Giant Planets."

46. Ward and Brownlee. *Rare earth*; Gonzalez and Richards. *The Privileged Planet*

5.2.4 Day 3: Plate Tectonics and Botany

> Gen 1:9 *And God said, Let the waters under the heaven be gathered together unto one place, and let the dry land appear: and it was so.*

Now that the solar system is built and the Earth established, God gathers the watery comets into one place, for it takes many comets to fill Earth's oceans. If we assume a comet is about half water and has a diameter of about 5 km, then it would take some 50 million comets. During the Late Heavy Bombardment from 4.1–3.8 billion years ago (Gya), that would be about one comet impact every six years.[47] The oceans could not have been filled much earlier or much faster than this, because the Earth would have been too hot and boiled off all the water. Nor could they have been filled too much later because we have fossilized algae, stromatolites that date from 3.65 Gya. And if we can use carbon isotopes as tracers of life (because photosynthesis changes the C-12/C-13 ratio in precise ways), then significant hydroponics was taking place some 4.1 Gya.[48]

A comet impact every six years is much more frequent than we experience at the present, so where did all the comets come from?

The formation of Jupiter would deflect many galactic comets into solar orbits that could supply the necessary rate. Others argue that Jupiter would also deflect asteroids from the asteroid belt. From counting craters on the Moon and bringing back samples to date the craters, the Apollo astronauts concluded that the Late Heavy Bombardment impact rate about 3.85 Gya was much greater than at present. But then it had to be a big change to get mentioned in Gen 1:9.

Why is the dry land mentioned?

There is enough water on Earth, presumably from comets, to cover the planet with a blanket three kilometers deep, as is observed on the watery moons of Jupiter. So the real question is why the Earth's oceans do not cover the globe as evenly. That is the significance of dry land. Strangely enough, Earth did not always have dry land. Immediately after the molten Earth cooled during the Hadean, it formed a smooth crust like a billiard ball, which would have been evenly immersed in a cometary ocean like Jupiter's moon Europa. But something cracked that surface shell into tectonic plates, and then the plates started to move. Depending on chemical composition, the Earth's plates are made of two kinds of rock, buoyant continental rock and heavy oceanic rock. Both types float upon the deeper molten mantle.

47. Gomes et al. "Origin of the cataclysmic Late Heavy Bombardment" 466–469.
48. Bell et al. "Potentially biogenic carbon."

The oceanic plates are constantly being formed at undersea volcanic ocean ridges and consumed at ocean trenches, where they dive under the continental plates floating higher on the mantle. When water from comets is poured evenly around the Earth, the deep oceanic trenches fill first. The continental plates rose out of the water, making dry land. So Gen 1:9 may be discussing the creation of continental plates and plate tectonics, as well as the formation of the cometary ocean. And, as it turned out, they happened at the same time, when the molten rock on the Earth cooled enough to allow oceans to form.[49]

> 1:10 *And God called the dry land Earth; and the gathering together of the waters called he Seas: and God saw that it was good.*

For the last time in this chapter, God gives a definition. But as we argued in Gen 1:8, it could better be called a declaration. Unlike Gen 1:8 (but like Gen 1:5), this declaration refers to two categories that are opposites, making it easy to find the dependent variable—the day/night transition of Day 3—because it is the same transition that caused oceans and continents to form.

What is that dry land/wet ocean transition?

The transition came in two, nearly simultaneous parts: the cometary bombardment that filled the oceans, and the initiation of plate tectonics. They are probably more closely linked than they might appear, because one of the effects of cometary impacts is to crack the crust, with major impacts fracturing the crust down to the molten mantle below. If we imagine a continental plate shaped like an inverted bowl floating in the molten mantle, then a crack across the dome of the bowl would release magma and split the plate in half. The two halves would move apart, and the cooling magma would form a basaltic oceanic plate. This process is what produces the Jordan River valley that extends all the way down to East Africa's Great Rift valley. Perhaps plate tectonics would have started without impacts anyway, but it is circumstantially coincidental that the two happened at the same time. And once the process was begun, the convective churning of the mantle kept it going to this day.

And a very necessary process it is, for plate tectonics are absolutely essential for higher forms of life. Without plate tectonics, the sedimentary rock would have remained on the ocean floor, trapping oxygen and carbon in the carbonates. That would remove the oxygen from the atmosphere and lock the trace minerals away from the leached rocks on the surface. But with plate tectonics, the sedimentary rocks are sucked under at the oceanic trenches, melted, and recycled into carbon dioxide driven lava eruptions in

49. Gråe Jørgensen et al. "The Earth-Moon system" 368–380.

the "ring of fire" volcanoes. That way the atmosphere does not get old and stale, and fresh mountain building is always bringing more minerals to the surface. But plate tectonics does even more than that.

It has long been argued that cyanobacteria living in Earth's oceans began the process of turning the carbon dioxide atmosphere into oxygen. It took them 3 billion years, or from 3.85–0.55 Gya to create an oxygen atmosphere.[50] Then, during the Cambrian Explosion at 0.55 Gya, twenty-three new phyla of animals appeared that could breathe the oxygen to populate the Earth, as discussed by Stephen Meyer.[51] But cyanobacteria need the rare elements Molybdenum and Vanadium to make the enzymes that "fix" nitrogen (convert nitrogen gas into proteins). Usually the ocean lacks these elements, but during the "snowball earth" 0.8–0.6 Gya, glaciers eroded the mountains that in turn were the product of plate tectonics.[52] So, without plate tectonics, there would have been no nitrogen fixation, and without nitrogen fixation, there would be no oxygen, and without oxygen there would be no Cambrian Explosion, and without a Cambrian Explosion there would be no habitat, no place for Adam or us.

No wonder God said plate tectonics was good!

> Gen 1:11 *And God said, Let the earth bring forth grass (*deshe*), the herb (*'eseb*) yielding (*zara*) seed, and the fruit tree (*periy 'ets*) yielding (*'asah*) fruit after his kind (*miyn*), whose (*'asher*) seed is in itself, upon the earth (*zer'o-bo al-ha'erets*): and it was so.*
>
> Gen 1:12 *And the earth brought forth grass, and herb yielding seed after his kind, and the tree yielding fruit, whose seed was in itself, after his kind: and God saw that it was good.*
>
> Gen 1:13 *And the evening and the morning were the third day.*

If we turn to the fossil record, we find that the events mentioned in Gen 1:11 are much, much more recent than the beginning of plate tectonics. The seed-bearing plants (angiosperms) appeared about 100 million years ago (Mya), which is a jump of 3500 million years from the events of Gen 1:10. But the next day, Day 4, seems to be discussing the creation of the Sun and Moon, which occurred at 5 Gya and 4 Gya, respectively, or long before the rise of angiosperms!

Should this jump bother us? Does it not indicate that something has been left out of the account?

50. Holland. "The oxygenation of the atmosphere and oceans" 903–915.
51. Meyer. *Darwin's Doubt*
52. Glass et al. "Coevolution of metal availability" 100–123.

Yes, it should bother us. If conventional interpretations are correct, it would ruin our identification of the Genesis mnemonic with the scientific chronology, and the whole point of Genesis 1. If I am correct that Genesis is a technical account of creation, then a failed chronology is a major problem, revealing that either my interpretation or the translation is incorrect. On the other hand, if the traditional translation of the text is incorrect, then the responsibility for the chronology lies with the first translators: the Greek LXX scholars. In Day 1 & 2, we used the surprising results of modern cosmology without impugning the understandable ignorance of the LXX translators. But Day 3, Day 4, and Day 5 are based on astronomy and biology, well known to the rabbis, which the LXX translators forced through a Hellenistic science filter, imposing Greek metaphysical categories on the descriptions. That imposition has left Biblical scholars in the Greek and Latin traditions with a faulty translation extending all the way back to the first century BC. Reversing that damage will not be easy, but it must be done to repair the mnemonic and the tragic dismissal of Genesis as an inaccurate chronology. And so I urge you to gird up your loins and embark with me on an extensive journey through the MT.

With correct understanding as our motivation, let us have a look at the MT words for angiosperms: "grass," "seed," and "fruit tree" in this passage. As we saw with *stereoma*, a single mistranslated word can be responsible for many difficulties. This one resulted in a memorable scene in the movie *Inherit the Wind*. If I cannot repair the career of William Jennings Bryan, I can at least restore his reputation,[53] as well as our confidence in the Genesis mnemonic.

Let us begin with the MT word translated by KJV as "grass," *deshe*, appearing 15x as listed in Table 5.2. When *deshe* appears in parallel with *'eseb* or *chatsiyr*, the KJV translates it "green herb" or "tender grass," to distinguish it from the more mature blade. As those who pick greens for a salad will know, the young shoots are tender, high in protein, and not so full of cellulose. For example, ruminants such as cattle and sheep that chew the cud can handle the high cellulose diet but horses need more tender shoots to survive. So when contrasted with grass, this word indicates young shoots with relatively little cellulose which are in the vicinity of grass.

53. Lawrence and Lee. *Inherit the Wind.*

Verse	Meaning	Verse	Meaning
	+'eseb		
Gn1:11,12	*TBD*		alone
Dt 32:2	Small/large rain	2Sa 23:4	Out of earth, clear shining
	+'eseb+chatsiyr	Jb 6:5	Non- vs ruminant food
2Ki 19:26	Blasted like grass	Jb 38:27	Out of wasteland-life
Pr 27:25	Grow like grass	Ps 23:2	All good
Is 37:27	Blasted like grass	Is 66:14	Flourish like herb
	+chatsiyr	Je 14:5	Lactating doe food
Ps 37:2	Wither, cut w/grass	Je 50:11	Heifer fattening food
Is 15:6	Withers like grass		

Table 5.2: The meaning of דֶּשֶׁא (*deshe*).

What does the word signify when it appears alone?

From Table 5.2, *deshe* refers to food 4/7x: Job 6:5 contrasts it with ruminants, Jer 14:5 to a lactating doe, and Jer 50:11 to heifer fattening, or rich ruminant food. If we interpret Ps 23:2 as referring to sheep, then it means rich ruminant food again. The other 3/7x it is used, it appears to be a transition from life to non-life, from bare earth to green herb. The constant factor in both usages relates to high protein, or as the feed industry calls it, nitrogen content. Ruminants, with their symbiotic bacteria, need less nitrogen than horses and donkeys, so the feed companies list the amount of nitrogen in the horse feed. But nitrogen is not free; it must either be put in the field as fertilizer or, more commonly, produced by growing leguminous plants that host nitrogen fixing bacteria in their root nodules.

Nitrogen fixation is significant if Day 3 is discussing an event that long precedes the formation of Earth. It may refer to the blooming of cyanobacteria, the pioneering first organism that appears when there is water, sunshine, and atmosphere. No other organism can both photosynthesize and fix nitrogen, which enables them to be the first lifeforms capable of colonizing a sterile comet or planet. In both 2 Sam 23:4 and Job 38:27, this green herb appears overnight from bare earth. The rapid spread accurately depicts the rapid spread of cyanobacteria, blue-green algae or "pond-scum," which can turn the mud at the edge of a pond green.

Does this interpretation fit the Gen 1:11 passage?

The ESV translates this passage, And God said, "*Let the land produce vegetation: plants yielding seeds according to their kinds, and trees bearing fruit with seed in it according to their kinds*" where *deshe* is translated "vegetation" recognizing that "green herb" is not grass, and that it is contrasted with a word that is more general than grass, "plants yielding seeds."

But this interpretation still seems to require the creation of angiosperms at 100 Mya. How does this resolve the problem of the plants being created before the Sun?

In Table 5.3, we tabulate all uses of the MT word *'eseb* that JPS/KJV translates "grass," and ESV translates "plants." It appears 21/37x as plants humans can eat (where we take the modifier "of the X" to mean domesticated for human consumption). Another 8/37x are ambiguous, so the ESV is a better translation. Several of the references are to plants that are susceptible to easy withering, so it would appear that the term often refers to broad leaf plants. Putting this together, the passage refers to garden plants like spinach, kale, and broccoli, and (less likely) to wheat or cereals.

Why then does Gen 1:11, 12, and 29 alone add the phrase "yielding seeds," as if only a cereal grain were meant?

In Gen 1:12, "herb yielding seed after his kind" the verb *mezria'* (*hiphil* participial stem of *zara'*) is translated "yielding" 3/56x, Gen 1:11–12, 29, but elsewhere translated "sowing" 47/56x, which is active compared with the more passive "yielding."

What made the Genesis 1 usage so different from the others?

In my view, it was translator's bias. A human generally does the sowing of wheat. But here in Gen 1:11 the plant "sows" as if it could stride up and down the rows scattering its own seed. So, for the sake of logic, the term was given a more passive translation. Yet an active form makes perfect sense. The *hiphil* verb stem is "causative," so the translation could read "herb caused to sow its own seed." At Day 3 in the Creation we have no animals, so plants must disperse their own seeds, as maple trees, for example, disperse "helicopter" samara seeds on the wind.

Now if a plant is going to use the elements for dispersal, it must structure its seeds accordingly. But if Day 3 has just separated the seas from the land and there is yet no soil to take root, then all the continents are still bare rock.

So what sort of dispersal might that be?

Verse	Meaning	Verse	Meaning	Verse	Meaning
+yielding seed		**+of the land**		**alone**	
Gn1:11,12	*TBD*	Ex10:12	domesticated	Dt 29:23	cultivated
Gn1:29	human-edible	Ex10:15	domesticated	Dt 32:2	cultivated?
+of the field		Jb5:25	domesticated	Ps 92:7	cultivated?
Gn 2:5	domesticated	Ps72:16	domesticated	Ps 102:4	edible?
Gn 3:18	domesticated	Am 7:2	domesticated	Ps 102:11	cultivated?
Ex 9:22	domesticated	**+in the field**		Ps 106:20	cattle feed
Ex 9:25	domesticated	Dt 11:15	cattle feed	Pr 19:12	cultivated?
2Ki19:26	domesticated	Zc 10:1	cultivated	Pr 27:25	edible
Is 37:27	domesticated	**alone**		Is 42:15	cultivated?
+in the land		Gn1:30	human edible	Je 12:4	cultivated
Ps 105:35	cultivated?	Gn 9:3	human edible	Je 14:6	donkey food
				Mi 5:7	cultivated?

Table 5.3: The meaning of עֵשֶׂב (*'eseb*).

Pine trees have flaky seeds that can blow into corners of the cliff and find enough soil to grow, but there is an even more ubiquitous rock plant, one that covers almost every square inch of bare rock above the tree line. It is called lichen, and looks like a gray-green scale upon the rock.

What kind of seeds do lichen have?

Microscopic spores carried for miles and miles upon even the gentlest breeze. So Gen 1:11 might be talking about spore-forming plants, or wind-dispersed edible broad leaf plants as distinct from non-seed-producing cyanobacteria.

What then does "*fruit tree yielding fruit after its kind whose seed is in itself*" mean? To begin with, is there a fruit that is not "after its kind," and do not most fruits have seeds? So why these unnecessary phrases, as if the author of Genesis is suddenly trying to fill column inches?

Answering this question will require more analysis because the sentence has a rather strange syntax (see Table 5.4). The word *periy*, which appears 119x in MT, clearly means "fruit." But it also applies to cereal grains as well as productive humans, as in "fruit of your labors." Rather than divide the meaning into literal and metaphorical senses, it might be more accurate to define it as the "good product" of a living thing. That is, a seed is defined as its ability to grow into a plant. It is a "fruit" if it is a good and useful product as well. A poisonous seed is not a fruit nor is a banana a seed.

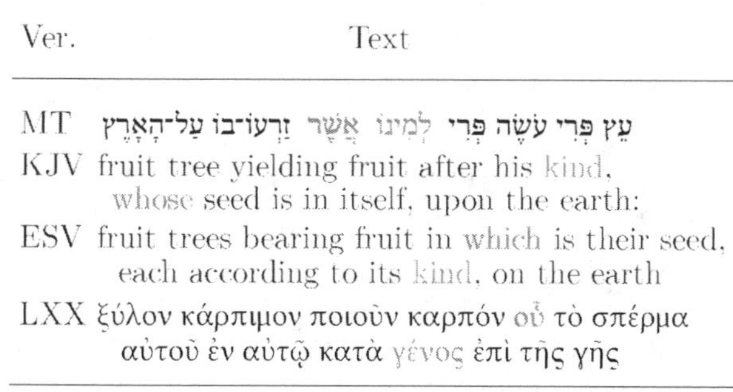

Ver.	Text
MT	עֵץ פְּרִי עֹשֶׂה פְּרִי לְמִינוֹ אֲשֶׁר זַרְעוֹ־בוֹ עַל־הָאָרֶץ
KJV	fruit tree yielding fruit after his kind, whose seed is in itself, upon the earth:
ESV	fruit trees bearing fruit in which is their seed, each according to its kind, on the earth
LXX	ξύλον κάρπιμον ποιοῦν καρπόν οὗ τὸ σπέρμα αὐτοῦ ἐν αὐτῷ κατὰ γένος ἐπὶ τῆς γῆς

Table 5.4: Fruit whose seed is in itself (Gen 1:11) in translation.

The MT *'ets* is translated "tree" 162/328x or "wood" 107/328x and most of the other uses denote objects made from wood. So the combination *periy 'ets* translated "fruit tree" reappears in Genesis 3, where the fruit of these Garden trees provides sustenance for Adam and Eve. Because fruit means anything good (edible), the definition could be paraphrased "woody plant with good-to-eat parts."

The MT *'asah*, which KJV translates "yielding," is translated 1333/2633x as "to do," and 653/2633x as "to make," but only 4/2633x, here in Genesis 1, as "yielding" or "bearing." A better translation that does not leave Genesis 1 as an exception would render the fruit tree as "doing/making fruit." So, just as we saw earlier with the reference to vegetables, the MT word is far more active than either the KJV or the ESV translation suggests.

How could a tree do/make something when it has no motile abilities?

The rest of the sentence clues us in. The fruit tree makes fruit "of its kind," (MT root word *miyn*) "Kind" is a technical term that appears 30/31x in the Pentateuch, in connection with the Creation Week, Noah's ark, or kosher laws. Only 1/31x (Ezek 47:10) does it mean something like "diversity." But if it is a technical term, it must exclude something. Technical terms are particularizing; they distinguish from other, similar things.

What could possibly be excluded from the list of fruit from fruit trees?

From Table 5.4, we see that the MT follows the technical word with a relative clause begun with *'asher*. Relative clauses are long explanations modifying a word in a way that cannot be summarized by a simple adjective. It is analogous to an in-line definition in software code. And in this case, it follows the technical word *miyn*, as if to define it.

What does the clause define *miyn* as?

The MT has the phrase *zer'o-bo al-ha'erets*, "seed of itself [is] upon the ground," which the KJV translates "whose seed is in itself upon the ground," the ESV translates, "in which is their seed, each according to their kind, on the ground" and the LXX translates (into Greek of course) as "the seed of it in itself according to its kind upon the ground." Tackling the thorny syntax, the relative clause has two prepositions, "in itself" and "upon" as well as two nouns, "seed" and "ground." Table 5.4 shows the various solutions by the ordering of the two words: The KJV leaves the words in the same order as the MT (read right-to-left), while the ESV and the LXX place the *miyn* after the seed, taking the relative clause to be about *periy* rather than *miyn*.

To distinguish between these options, we have one more tool, which we used in Chapter 2, a Hebrew syntax parser that is not based on an Indo-European translation, but on the Semitic language of the MT itself.[54] The Emdros3.4 parser with the 2011 WTS ruleset claimed that the hyphenated MT *zer'o-bo*, is a verbless clause meaning "the seed is in itself," and that the preposition that follows is not part of the relative clause at all; it goes all the way back to "fruit tree . . .upon the ground." This also appears to be the JPS/ESV translator's choice. It would mean that the tree that grew on the ground also made fruit (after its kind) which had seeds in it.

There are two niggling problems that this syntax does not resolve. Most fruit has seeds, for the simple reason that animals disperse the seeds when they eat the fruit. But there are no animals on Day 3, so we have, in microcosm, the same non-chronological problem as on Day 4 which talks about the creation of the sun after the mention of green herbs!

The second problem is that the MT uses a hyphen for a verbless clause. Whatever that modifier *-bo* on "seed" is doing, it is not acting as a predicate—though 200 years before the Masoretes, the LXX translators treated it exactly that way! Reluctantly siding with the LXX, the ESV and the 2011 Hebrew parser against the MT and the KJV assuming the hyphen was a later addition (as were the MT *matres lectionis*), let's put the sentence parts back together. We have the creation of a nitrogen fixing plant, a second spore-forming lichen (or a broad leaf plant with wind-dispersed seeds), and a third, woody plant on the ground whose edible part has seeds in it.

What is this third plant?

We can answer this question working backwards by first saying what it is not (following Ferdinand de Saussure). This woody plant must be contrasted with the first two plants, so let us consider their differences. Nitrogen fixation is accomplished by only two organisms: symbiotic rhizobacteria found in nodules in the roots of legumes; and by cyanobacteria. Because cyanobacteria used to be considered a plant known as "blue-green algae," I will assume that Gen 1:11 describes it. The reason blue-green algae is not called a plant today is that all plants have cells with nuclei (eukaryotic),

54. Lowery, "Review of Emdros."

while cyanobacteria lack a nucleus (prokaryotic), which is characteristic of bacteria. And this provides the first clue—one way that trees are different is that they are eukaryotic cells with nuclei.

Now bacteria grow enormously quickly. But without a nucleus, they have a limited tool set so they are not very adaptable. Likewise cyanobacteria are amazingly good at what they do—pioneering the sterile seas by converting sunlight, CO_2, and molecular nitrogen, N_2 into body mass—but their success is their downfall. More sophisticated organisms quickly arrive to feed off the cyanobacteria. The earliest of these communities are called "bacterial mats," they produce the oldest fossils found on Earth, stromatolites dated at 3.65 Gya.[55]

What organisms follow cyanobacteria into the otherwise sterile world?

Such life forms would look to the unpracticed eye very similar to the cyanobacterial pond scum, except that they have nuclei. They consist of algae and fungi, and show rudimentary specialization. The most interesting of these second wave lifeforms are the spore-forming lichens, the symbiotic mixtures of algae and fungi. They can exploit the dry land of sterile rock far away from the tidal pools needed by stromatolites. The algae photosynthesize while the fungi dissolve the rock for minerals, and together they slowly break the rock down to make soil. But neither cyanobacteria nor lichens have any vascular or woody tissue that transports sap. So this is the second clue; unlike pond-scum or lichens, a tree has vascular tissue.

Let us take these two negative comparisons and see if they can be made to work with the three positive characteristics that Gen 1:11 ascribes to this fruit tree: (a) It exists "upon the ground"; (b) it makes fruit; and, (c) the seeds are in itself. Addressing (a), growing "upon the ground" is different from bacterial mats, which have no internal structure, floating at the bottom of tidal pools and ponds. Likewise, lichens coat the surface of a rock but cannot lift themselves up "upon" the ground. In fact, you will find lichens on tree trunks, but not on soil or ground because they would too quickly get drowned in dirt. So this positive characteristic would be the presence of a vascular stem or support structure consistent with the negative properties deduced.

The second property, (b) to "make fruit," would appear to be a specialized operation of some part of the plant. No one would accuse pond-scum or lichens of "making fruit," even if the entire plant were eaten in soup (as has been done). Rather, fruit is a specialized subset of the entire plant. So this positive characteristic refers to a multicellular plant with specialized

55. Nutman et al., "Rapid emergence of life"

subcomponents, and that is consistent with our negation of the first two plants.

Finally, the third property, (c) "the seed in itself" will take a bit of finagling. Because there are no animals to spread the seeds, "fruit with seed in it" suggests that the "seed" is not really the seed kernel that we took it to be a few words earlier. One hint is that the word "kernel" comes from a German root whose Latin cognate is "nucleus" (from the Latin word *nucula* for "little nut"). Then the "seed in itself" might be translated "ennucleated" or, in biological terms, "eukaryotic." Yes, it is a stretch but it might work. Both algae and fungi are eukaryotic, so they can be grouped with the previously mentioned plant. However, if we translate it as "chloroplast" (about the same size as a nucleus), then we can distinguish this plant from fungi, which is one half of a lichen. Putting all of this together, the meaning of this "fruit tree" is something like "autonomous multicellular, eukaryotic, chloroplast-possessing, vascular plant."

Why is this suggestion an improvement over "apple tree"?

Because fruit trees do not appear on Earth until some 100 Mya, whereas cyanobacteria, lichens, and vascular plants are far more ancient. They may be more ancient than even biologists realize because, according to Richard Hoover, the extinct comets that occasionally impact the Earth, "carbonaceous chondrites," possess microscopic fossils of cyanobacteria, diatoms, amoeba (eukaryotes), and acritarchs (spores of extinct vascular plants) older than 450 Mya, and potentially older than the Earth at 4 Gya.[56] In other words, Day 3 might be describing primitive plant life on comets that predated life on Earth.

Even if this wild speculation proves correct, comets do not have land or seas, so why then does Day 3 begin with God separating the dry land into land and seas?

It is a puzzle but, if I am permitted to continue the argument, I would also include other planets and moons, such as Mars, Europa, and Enceladus which, NASA tells us, have (or once have had) land and seas. If Mars qualifies as a location mentioned in Day 3, then perhaps the Earth-like planets discovered by the Kepler mission in other solar systems should be included as well. Many of these other planets might have played a key role in the "staging" of life for future transport to Earth.

Is all this irrational exuberance about other worlds necessary? Did not William of Ockham say "Do not multiply hypotheses unnecessarily?"

It is necessary because Day 4 is next. That Day alone has been the death of many a Creationist model of the origin of life. If my understanding

56. Hoover, "Fossils of Cyanobacteria "; Hoover. "Private communication."

of Genesis 1 is correct and the numbered days are a mnemonic device to make sure we keep them in order and do not lose track of any, then Day 4 is my nemesis. Day 4 suggests that the Sun and Moon were created after the vascular plant discussed in Day 3—a plant which could not grow without sunlight! Rather than move Day 4 backward, as most Creationists do, I have redefined the herbs of Day 3 as the pioneering plants of an ancient galactic biosphere spread by comets and illuminated by alien suns.[57]

5.2.5 Day 4: Solar System

> Gen 1:14 *And God said, Let there be lights (*ma'owr*) in the firmament of the heaven to divide the day from the night; and let them be for signs, and for seasons, and for days, and years:*
>
> Gen 1:15 *And let them be for lights in the firmament of the heaven to give light (*'owr*) upon the earth: and it was so.*

If the sudden appearance 100 Mya of the angiosperms was Darwin's abominable mystery,[58] then the lights of Day 4 are the Creationist's abominable mystery. Because the Sun is about 5 Gya, and the Moon about 4 Gya, it looks like Day 4 has gone backward in time. But if we insist on chronological order, then the Sun is created after the plants that depend on sunlight for life. Numerous suggestions have been offered to solve the chronological conundrum: The Sun was already there but a cloud deck meant that it was invisible until Day 4; that the Days of creation are not chronological; or that the order in which God speaks is not necessarily the order in which the events unfold. All of these solutions turn out to be non-chronological reordering, which is forbidden if the Days are a mnemonic device.

Can we make sense of Day 4 without non-chronological nuance?

We have shown how reinterpreting Day 3 as a galactic biosphere can predate the Sun and the Moon, but it is also possible that something other than the Sun and Moon are described in Day 4. Looking at the words usually translated "Sun" and "Moon" in Gen 1:14, we can use the understandings from Days 1–3 as follows: *And God said, let there be stars in the gravity fields of spacetime to separate matter from vacuum. And let these stars be for signs, for seasons, for days, and years. And let these stars in the gravity fields of spacetime shine light on the solid planets. And it was so.*

Is it fair to translate "lights" as "stars" here, when the context is different from later MT usage? Should we not demand consistency in translation?

57. Sheldon. "The Cometary Biosphere" 8152–42.

58. Friedman. "The meaning of Darwin's `Abominable Mystery'" 1–18.

We discussed this problem in Gen 1:1, where "heavens and earth" were taken to mean "spacetime and matter." The problem is not just that context is critical in any translation but that dictionary definitions are created in the same way we make translations—as hypotheses checked to see if they work. If we find that "stars" makes more sense in Gen 1:14, we are following the same prescription as the lexicographer when he provides separate meanings in the dictionary for Genesis 1.

Is this not a highly dangerous approach? If everyone makes their own private dictionary, as post-modernists tend to do, how will communication remain possible?

There are two glimmers of light in this post-modern dungeon: The first is that God himself defines words, especially in this chapter. And the second is a curious property that words share with people, with God (and with nothing else). Words are recursive and "self-aware." That is, we define words with words. If this were math, we would be in deep trouble because this "circular logic" approach is considered invalid. But language is not software and people are not computers, or as they say in logic-drenched France, *Vive la différence*! If people or words or God were like computers, there would be no beauty, no poetry, no personality to them. So in some very deep and mysterious way, we must spend a lifetime getting to know others, getting to know God, and getting to know words.

So then, let us not complain about ancient Hebrew or run to commentaries. We must do our own spade work. But cheer up, He has buried the treasure just deep enough to frustrate the faint-hearted but shallow enough to reward the courageous.

As we work through our translation of Day 4, we discover a certain ambiguity in the English word "light." Sometimes it means photons, at other times stars, Sun, or Moon. The MT word translated "light" appears in two forms, *'owr* and *ma'owr*: The word *'owr* is used 43x as a verb or 123x as a participle, which 114/123x KJV translates "light," meaning "photons" or "light-beam," often contrasted with darkness or lack of photons. But *ma'owr* is a concrete instance of a photon factory or lightmaker. It is a masculine noun that appears in Exodus, Leviticus, and Numbers 10/19x and another 4/19x outside the Pentateuch, to mean "oil lamplight" (Prov 15:30 manages to imply both). But it is the 5/19 translations in Genesis 1 that need refining.

Notice the repetitive phrase "firmament of the heavens." It is reminiscent of "bird of the heavens," discussed in the previous chapter, where the singular meant domestication and the plural meant domination. Here, it would seem, the firmament is clearly domestic.

Our modified translation now reads: Gen 1:14 *And God said, Let there be lightmakers in the tamed gravity-field to divide the day from the night; and let them be for signs, and for seasons, and for days, and years:* 15 *And let them be for lightmakers in the tamed gravity-field to shine photons upon the earth: and it was so.* 16 *And God made two great lightmakers; the greater lightmaker to rule the day, and the lesser lightmaker to rule the night: he made the stars also.* 17 *And God set them in the tamed gravity-field to shine photons upon the earth,* 18 *And to rule over the day and over the night, and to divide the photons from the darkness: and God saw that it was good.* 19 *And the evening and the morning were the fourth day.*

What is this "firmament of the heavens," this "tamed gravity-field"?

If it were plural, it would refer to Gen 1:8, where gravity dominates spacetime. But in the singular, it is dominated by spacetime. It might refer to satellites, such as the Moon, that control the Earth's spin axis and "tame" the otherwise random tumbling that would result in climate disasters.[59] Or it may even refer to the orderly plane of the planets, where Jupiter has "cleared out" asteroids that may otherwise hit the Earth. In any case, it conveys the message that the solar system is somehow domesticated, prohibited from wild perturbations, an ordered state which Isaac Newton attributed to "the Effect of [God's] Choice."[60]

Now we come to the crux of Day 4: Why does God not simply say "Sun" and "Moon," why does He use the poetic metaphor "lesser light" and "greater light"? And why does Gen 1:15 simply summarize Gen 1:14 without telling us anything new? As we have said before, Genesis is far too compressed a story to waste a whole verse on repetitive and redundant information. So why the repetition?

14a And God said:	וַיֹּאמֶר אֱלֹהִים
Be lightmakers in the firmament of the heavens	יְהִי מְאֹרֹת בִּרְקִיעַ הַשָּׁמַיִם
15a And there were for lightmakers i.t.f.o.t.h.	וְהָיוּ לִמְאוֹרֹת בִּרְקִיעַ הַשָּׁמַיִם

Table 5.5: Significance of MT parallels between Gen 1:14 and 15.

Starting with the difference between Gen 1:14 and 15, we can line up the MT in Table 5.5. The two phrases, excepting the variant spelling of *ma'owr*, are exactly the same: "l*ightmakers in the firmament of the heavens.*" In Gen 1:14, we encounter a direct quote, "*And Elohim said, 'Let there be . . .'*" But Gen 1:15 is not a quote; it is a statement of fact, "*And there were for . . .*" where the verb is now finite and the lightmakers are the object of a preposition

59. Laskar et al. "Stabilization of the earth's obliquity" 615–617; Spradley. "Ten lunar legacies" 267–275.

60. Newton *Opticks* 402.

lamedh, here translated "for." Earlier, when God says "Let there be X," the response is "And there was X." But here the response is "And there was for X."

What is the "for" for? Is it not completely unnecessary?

The NAS/KJV/JPS solve this problem by using the ambiguity of the English word "light" to mean both a producer (lightmaker) and a product (photons), so that the creation of the producer in Gen 1:14 is for the purpose of the product in Gen 1:15. Unfortunately, Hebrew is not as ambiguous as English. Then the translation becomes "The creation of the producer is for the purpose of the producer," which does not make much sense.

However, "for" is a translation of the *lamedh* preposition, and prepositions are notoriously hard to translate, so we look for other meanings. The Hebrew-English lexicon, Brown-Driver-Briggs[61] (BDB), has fifteen pages on the meaning of the *lamedh* preposition. Here are the top meanings: 1) denote direction to, for, in regard to, towards (not motion), reference to, (and least likely) addition; 2) denote locality at, near; 3) denote object of an intransitive verb (an Aramaicism considered to be late Hebrew); 4) denote a transition to a new state, into; 5) with reference to, belonging to, of, on account of, dative of feeling, etc.; 6) denote time, expressing concurrence, at, towards, against, during; and, 7) denote purpose when used with an infinitive. While BDB uses Gen 1:16,17 as examples in its fifteen pages, it expresses no opinion about the *lamedh* in Gen 1:15.

Meaning (1) makes no sense unless it has the rare sense of addition. "*And there were added to the lightmakers . . .*" Likewise (2), the lightmakers have been already localized in the firmament, so unless the "shining photons" exist only in their vicinity, there does not seem to be any new information here. I'm not sure what to make of (3), because "to be" is a special verb of existence that might be considered intransitive, but Genesis 1 is not likely to be "late Hebrew." Once again, all of Genesis is a transition so (4) would be superfluous. I can almost make (5) work with the translation "*From the lightmakers of the firmament were photons shining*," as long as there are other photons not due to lightmakers, possibly due to the cosmic microwave background radiation (CMBR). But (6) is intriguing, because it translates "*At the time of the lightmakers there were photons shining*" which is reminiscent of Hugh Ross's interpretive Big Bang model.[62] Finally, (7) does not apply because the verb is finite.

What have we learned about Gen 1:15?

The KJV choice of (1) does not work, but (2), (5), or (6) seem possible. Gen 1:15 either specifies a locality where photons were made or a

61. Brown, Driver, and Briggs. *A Hebrew and English Lexicon of the Old Testament.*

62. Ross. *More Than a Theory.*

time when photons were made. Then the remainder of Day 4 should discuss the particulars of either that locality or that time. It does discuss them but we are not sure whether Day/Night is a division of time or of space. For a farmer it is time, but for an astronaut it is space. And because we think this passage has astronomical overtones, probably both are meant. The key piece of information in Gen 1:15 is that we are no longer concerned with a general rule about photons shining but with the particularities of space and time.

Does this explain whether "greater and lesser lightmaker" refers to the Sun and Moon? Perhaps it does. If we had assumed that our vantage point for Day 4 was the surface of the Earth, then the greater and lesser could be nothing but the Sun and Moon. But this viewpoint also causes the firmament to shrink down to the Earth's atmosphere, makes Gen 1:14, 15, and 17 highly redundant, and creates problems with Day 3. But if we allow for an astronaut's perspective, if Gen 1:15 is particularizing, then suddenly we are being told that these greater and lesser lights are simply particular versions of lightmakers introduced earlier. The stars of Gen 1:14 have become suns of Gen 1:15. Paraphrasing, *And let it be the star in the galaxy that provides light for this planet*—would make our Sun simply one of the stars, as all modern astronomy textbooks begin by explaining.

It is astonishing that an approach suggested a mere 300 years ago was known by Moses 3000 years earlier. It is also worrisome that translations and interpretations of Genesis in the intervening 2700 years might not have understood the need to take that into account. Even more worrisome is the possibility that our present limited understanding of science may disguise and obscure other important truths of Genesis 1. So we are relieved that the text is organized that it makes sense either way; though with more science comes more sense.

Did Moses really think that the Moon generated its own light? How can it be a lightmaker if it merely reflects the Sun's photons, a fact even the Greeks understood?

Either we assume Moses was dense (or poetic, or metaphorical, etc.) and enlarge the dictionary entry for *ma'owr* to include the meaning "light reflector" or we argue that this is not the Moon. It turns out that nothing later in the text requires the Moon, so we lose nothing further if we remove it. However, we must still explain Day 4, which has three tasks assigned to these entities individually and/or corporately: to shine photons on the earth; to govern/rule Day and Night; and, to separate light from darkness. The number of these entities and their respective tasks is unclear, so we should examine the syntax of Gen 1:16 again.

There is still an ambiguity in our paraphrase of Gen 1:16 *And God made two great lightmakers—the greater lightmaker to rule the day and the lesser lightmaker to rule the night— and the stars.* Are there three lightmakers (Sun, Moon, stars), or does the Moon rule over two objects (night/stars)?

The KJV/NAS translations assume three lightmakers, taking the final "and" as paired with the "and" between greater and lesser lights, while the ESV/LXX/Vulgate assume two lightmakers, taking the final "and" to link stars with night. You can see how a farmer would go with ESV, but an astronaut would go with KJV. We prefer the KJV because the next two verses give us three tasks (see below), which match numerically with three distinct entities.

The three tasks are numbered in our paraphrase of Gen 1:17–18 *And God set them in the firmament of the heavens (1) to shine photons upon the earth, and (2) to rule over the day and over the night, and (3) to divide the photons from the darkness.*

We can easily understand the first task. The second is poetically true, so if we anthropomorphize the Sun, it can be said to "rule the Day." But this last task is a bit hard to fathom. Photons banish darkness, but they do not "separate" it. The opacity of the Earth blocks the sunlight from the backside during a rotation, so it is the Earth itself that "separates" light and darkness. Yet it is the lightmakers that are given this role. If we had to give grades for these tasks, then Sun, Moon, Stars get grades of A, B, and F for the three tasks.

That "F" is troubling; are there other possible entities that might be substituted?

If lightmakers were light bulbs, then the greater might be an incandescent and the lesser a fluorescent bulb, a hot thermal light source and a cool line spectrum source, such as the Aurora Borealis, the Northern Lights. In astronomy, we have nebula as well that can either reflect incandescent sunlight or emit fluorescent line spectra. Nebulae would predate the origin of the Sun, making the chronology worse, whereas Northern Lights would move the origin from 4 Gya to about 3 Gya, an improvement, but not enough to solve the 100 Mya problem with Day 3.

If these three light bulbs are the lightmakers, how well do they fulfill the three tasks? Both kinds of light bulbs send photons, though only in Norway would we say that the aurora rules the night. But in what sense do they divide the photons from the darkness?

If we interpret "darkness" as we did in Gen 1:2–3, where it is gas and dust that absorb light, then both incandescent and fluorescent light can clear out the obscuring gas, thereby dividing the space into transparent and opaque regions with the emission nebulae doing the separating. I would grade this solution as an A, C, C for the three tasks.

On the other hand, if lightmakers were power transformers that convert stored energy into light, the way coal-fired, nuclear, and hydro-electric power plants convert chemical, nuclear, and gravitational power, then the greater lightmaker is nuclear like the Sun. The lesser is gravitational, like Jupiter and Saturn. They put out heat (infrared light, IR) due to gravity-driven compression of their atmospheres. We get almost no visible light from Jupiter and Saturn, so the grade for the first task is an F. But nuclear energy rules most of the galaxy, and gravity certainly rules the vacuum, so they get an A on the second task.

What about separation?

Again, gravity does a great job condensing the dust and gas into stars and planets, so I give them another A for task three, "separation," resulting in F, A, and A.

Finally, if we broaden our definition of photons to include the entire electromagnetic spectrum, then perhaps the greater lightmaker produces visible photons and the lesser lightmaker produces infrared (IR) or radio wave photons. The Sun is a prodigious producer of visible while the Moon does make IR, and filling everywhere else is the CMBR. Then both greater and lesser lightmakers bombard the earth with photons, the day is dominated by visible ones and the night by infrared ones, and this radiation field does sweep away dust and gas. That works nicely with our preposition meaning (5) because the lightmakers do a better job than the CMBR. So I would grade this an A, A, and C.

Examining these solutions, it appears that they all move the creation of the greater and lesser lightmakers closer to the present, and therefore closer to the scientific chronology. But they do not move the chronology all the way to 150 Mya when angiosperms appeared, so none of them solve the Day 3 non-chronology as efficiently as the cometary biosphere. But we do see that the purpose of the "poetic" language is not mythical, obscure, or even aesthetic but rather to multiply the possible meanings of the text. Some have argued that God accommodates language to our weakness, which when combined with a static view of meaning, implies that God was condescending in our ignorant past but we are too enlightened to accept those meanings now. Yet that "higher critical" view does not explain what we have just found, that meanings multiply according to our knowledge, which is a much more dynamic accommodation of the text. But it also means that if we expect mythology, then that is all we will find. To repeat, there are three ironic, recursive, and personal things that judge us even as we judge them—God, Man and words.

5.2.6 Day 5: Entomology

> Gen 1:20 *Then God said, "Let the waters* (mayim) *teem* (sharats) *with swarms of living creatures, and let birds* ('owph) *fly above* ('al) *the earth in* ('al) *the open expanse [face of] of the heavens* (shamayim)*."*
>
> *1:21 God created the great sea monsters and every living creature that moves, with which the waters swarmed after their kind, and every winged bird after its kind; and God saw that it was good.*
>
> *1:22 God blessed them, saying, "Be fruitful and multiply, and fill the waters in the seas, and let birds multiply on the earth."*
>
> *1:23 There was evening and there was morning, a fifth day.*

For Gen 1:20, the KJV/JPS offers "fly above the earth in the open firmament of heaven" while the ESV has "fly above the earth across the expanse of the heavens." As we saw in Day 4, the MT seems to employ more poetic language than the translation, which is a red flag. We examine the MT in Table 5.6. The translation difficulties begin with the double use of the preposition *'al* meaning "upon" in the complex clause "upon the earth upon the face of the firmament of the heavens." If "firmament" was hard to translate, "face of the firmament" is even harder. If one takes the term to mean a material object, then flying on its face seems comical. But if it means "gravitational field," then several interpretations can be considered: a "geodesic" that follows the field like a dropped rock; an "equipotential" such as the geoid that defines sea level around the globe; and, a "null gradient" where the force of gravity suddenly vanishes, such as inside a hollow spherical asteroid.

The geodesic direction is straight up, which is an unlikely direction for energy-conserving bird flights. And while the comet hypothesis from Day 1 does produce hollow spheres, we have no winged fossils from carbonaceous chondrites, which makes this solution tenuous. So it seems that flying over the sea level geoid, e.g., a "surface," is the best translation.

That leaves the question of what sort of life form is flying. BDB defines *'owph* as "flying creatures, fowl, insects," but does not give an opinion on this verse, Gen 1:20. The KJV translates *'owph* as "fowl/bird" 68/71x, "winged" 2/71x and "flying" 1/71x, but never as "insect." Earlier we argued *'owph shamayim* is either a domesticated bird or a carrion bird depending on plurality. Here we need only tabulate verses that lack this adjective, noting that in Gen 1:20, *'owph* is modified by *raqiya'* (firmament), not *shamayim* (heavens). We give the statistics in Table 5.7. We can now begin to understand the nuances of *'owph*. Its principal meaning comes from the verb "to fly," but depending on context, it can mean bird, insect or anything winged. When it appears in a list with 2 or 3 other terms, it generally means any of them. If it is paired with animals, it means bird. When used in context of kosher rules (and not paired with animals), it is 3/10 insect, 3/10 bird, and 4/10 any of them. We also have three none-of-the-above poetic uses where we find 2/3 birds, 1/3 any.

20 And let birds fly upon the earth	וְעוֹף יְעוֹפֵף עַל־ הָאָרֶץ
upon the face of the firmament of the heavens	עַל־ פְּנֵי רְקִיעַ הַשָּׁמָיִם
21 And God created the great sea monsters	וַיִּבְרָא אֱלֹהִים אֶת־הַתַּנִּינִם הַגְּדֹלִים
and every living creature that moves.	וְאֵת כָּל־נֶפֶשׁ הַחַיָּה הָרֹמֶשֶׂת
with which the waters swarmed after their kind.	אֲשֶׁר שָׁרְצוּ הַמַּיִם לְמִינֵהֶם
and every winged bird after its kind;	וְאֵת כָּל־ עוֹף כָּנָף לְמִינֵהוּ
and God saw that it was good.	וַיַּרְא אֱלֹהִים כִּי־טוֹב׃

Table 5.6: The problem of flying birds.

What is happening to *'owph* in Day 5?

The term is not poetic; it is not in a list; it is not paired with land animals (rather, with sea creatures); and it ushers in no kosher rules. And the only time *'owph* appears with a swimming creature, it can be anything winged. Likewise, swarming behavior is more often associated with insects than birds. But it is the syntax of Gen 1:20–22 that clinches the case for insects, which is best seen from the verbs that describe insect behavior.

Parsing the verbs "Let them abound" is *qal,* imperfect-3rd person-masculine-plural, where the *qal* is the normal "active" stem of the verb, neither reflexive nor passive nor causative. It is masculine-plural because the actor, *mayim* (waters), is masculine-plural. The second verb, "Let him fly" is *polel,* imperfect-3rd person-masculine-singular, where the *polel* stem, along with the *piel,* is an active verb that describes transitions to a new state. It is masculine-singular because the actor, *'owph* (flying creature), is masculine-singular. Then the quotation becomes two balanced finite verb clauses joined by the conjunction "and." The only differences in the verbs are action versus transition and plural versus singular. It is all neat and tidy but for one detail: "flying" is an action, while "teeming" is generally thought to be a state. So the *qal* and the *polel* are backwards! According to the syntax, it would seem that "teeming" or "swarming" is hard work, while "flying" is a transition, a breeze. The next verse begins to explain.

Verse	Meaning	T	Verse	Meaning	T
	Waters+*o.*+earth (loc.)			***'owph* triplets (motion)**	
Gn 1:20	o. on earth on face of f.	?	Gn 6:20	o./animal/creeper	A
Gn 1:21	Winged o. after its kind	?	Gn 7:8	Animal/o./creeper	A
Gn 1:22	o. multiply on the earth	?	Gn 7:14	Cattle/o./creeper	A
	Kosher or nearly (clean)		Gn 7:21	Flesh/o./cattle/beast/swarm	A
Lv11:20	All the o. insects	I	Gn 8:17	Living-thing/o./animal/creep	A
Lv11:21	All the o. insects	I	Gn 8:19	Beast/creeper/o.	A
Lv11:23	All the o. insects	I	Gn 9:10	Living-thing/o./cattle/beast	A
Ps78:27	winged o. rained on them	A	Lv11:46	Animal/o./water-living/swarm	A
Dt14:20	Clean o. eat	A	1Ki 4:33	Animals/o./creeper/fish	A
	Non-kosher obviously			***'owph* doublets (food)**	
Gn40:17	o. eating bread	B	Gn 8:20	Clean animal, clean o.	B
Gn40:19	o. eating flesh	B	Lv 1:14	Burnt offering of o.	B
Lv 11:13	Detest among o.,vulture	B	Lv 7:26	Blood of o. or animal	B
Dt14:19	Teeming life w/o.unclean	A	Lv 17:13	Animal or o., pour out blood	B
Je 5:27	Cage full of o.	A	Lv 20:25	Clean/unclean animal/o.	B
	Miscellaneous (flight)		Je 12:4	Animals and o.	B
Ps 50:11	o. of the mountains	B	Ez 44:81	Shall not eat o. or beast	B
Is 16:2	Flee o. scattered nestling	B			
Ho 9:11	Fly away like a o.	A	*B=bird,I=insect,A=anything with wings*		

Table 5.7: The meaning of עוף (*'owph*).

Gen 1:21 can be parsed two separate ways. The traditional parsing is for the first finite verb to take three direct objects. The latter two are introduced with a *waw+'et* conjunction, where the *waw* means "and" and the *'et* is a direct object marker, translated something like "and another thing . . . ." In this traditional translation, the second direct object has an *'asher* relative clause that operates as a miniature definition with a finite verb and direct object as well. Schematically, "*God created (sea monsters) and another (every living thing, which swarms in water) and another (winged birds).*"

Alternatively, the novel second parsing treats everything after the *'asher* as a separate clause. In this case, there are two finite verbs, each with two direct objects. Schematically, "*God created (sea monsters) and (every living thing), which teem (in the waters after their kind) and (in winged flight after their kind).*" The advantages of this second parsing are twofold: It makes the descriptive phrase "after their kind" a balanced double direct object of the verb "to teem," and it handles the *'et* marker more naturally by nesting rather than by a run-on sentence loosely linked with "and another." This new syntax shows that winged *'owph* are not notable for flying but for teeming because that is the finite verb in the clause.

Is this action, "teeming," a characteristic insect behavior?

Before we do our usual statistical table, we should look at the next verse, which may answer the question. Gen 1:22 has a direct quote using a compound imperative verb followed by the conjunction "and," and then a finite verb clause. The traditional parsing takes that final clause to be parallel with the verb. So schematically: "*be fruitful, be multiplying, be filling the waters, and let* 'owph *multiply on the earth.*" However, the last verb is not in the imperative; it is in the imperfect. So the "let multiply" is more accurately translated "*be fruitful, be multiplying, be filling the waters, and* 'owph *will multiply on the earth.*" It appears that "teeming" has something to do with reproduction, and from Gen 1:21–22, this reproduction seems to involve water for everyone and additionally flight for *'owph*.

Verse	Meaning	Verse	Meaning
Location that teems		**Creeping Life that teems**	
Gn1:20	Let waters t. w/living	Gn7:21	Creepers that t. on earth
Gn1:21	Waters t. after their kind	Gn8:17	Bring forth creepers that t.
Ex 8:3	River t. frogs t.	Lv11:29	Creepers that t.
Ps105:30	Land t. frogs t.	Lv11:41	Creepers that t.
Ez47:9	Everything, t., w/rivers	Lv11:42	Creepers that t.
Life teems in triplet		Lv11:43	Creepers that t.
Gn9:7	Be fruitful, multiply, t.	Lv11:46	Creature that t.
Ex1:7	Israel fruitful, t., multiply		

Table 5.8: The meaning of שָׁרַץ (*sharats*).

The verb *sharats* "to swarm, to teem" (BDB) or "to creep, to crawl, to abound, to multiply" (Gesenius) appears 14x in MT, always in the active *qal* stem. But strangely, sometimes animals are the subject and sometimes they are the object of the verb. From the statistics in Table 5.8, when an animal "teems," then it is associated with a triple verb involving reproduction or else it is a creeping/swarming thing to begin with. But when a location "teems," water is always involved. Ps 105:30 looks to be an exception but for two facts: It repeats an event described in Exod 8:3, replacing "river" with "land," so that may simply be a case where "land of Egypt" includes the "river of Egypt." But more importantly, the animal that is teeming is a frog, which is an amphibian requiring its young to be hatched in water. So it would appear that when the verb "to teem" takes a location for its subject, it is referring to a reproductive life cycle that needs immersion in water.

Putting all this together, Gen 1:20–22 seems to refer to a watery location that teems with living creatures that have wings, which will then transition to flying over the earth at sea level. Birds do not reproduce in water; even sea gulls and albatrosses must nest on land. On the other hand, insects such as mosquitoes, mayflies, and dragonflies all have a larval stage in water, which pupates (on the surface of the water) and releases a winged insect that does not fly far from the surface. Given the lack of animals for mosquitoes to feed on at this time, I would translate *'owph* in Genesis 1 as "mayflies/ dragonflies."

Such an interpretation has consequences, the most immediate of which is that many of these flying insects require pristine brooks and rivers, not salty oceans. So this definition also implies that the dual "waters" may be indicating fresh inland seas and salty ocean waters. We need continents for dragonflies, but not land animals. That will be the result of the last Day.

5.2.7 Day 6: Zoology

> Gen 1:24 *Then God said, "Let the earth bring forth living creatures after their kind: cattle (*behemah*) and creeping things (*remesh*) and beasts of the earth (*chayyah 'erets*) after their kind"; and it was so.*
>
> *1:25 God made the beasts of the earth after their kind, and the cattle after their kind, and everything that creeps on the ground after its kind; and God saw that it was good.*

With the land dried out and the seas filled with fish, we finally come to the creation of the land animals. Just as the waters teem with life, so also the earth brings forth living creatures— *nephesh chayyim*. "Living creatures" is very generic but the concept can be contrasted with Day 5, where reproduction required water. This life does not need the watery nursery that distinguishes amphibians from reptiles, frogs from lizards. With this distinction in mind, we can address the translation of the triplet: *behemah*, *remesh*, and *chayyah 'erets*, "cattle, creeping things, and beasts of the earth."

The word *behemah* is translated "cattle" by the KJV 53/189x, often when contrasted with "beasts of the earth" *chay 'erets*. But when it appears alone, the KJV translates it "beast" 136/189x. Only 9/189x does it appear in construct, *behemah 'erets* (Deut 28:26, Jb35:11, Is18:6, Jer7:33, 15:3, 16:4, 19:7, 34:20) where it follows the same rule as "birds of the heavens," with the plural signifying carnivores. Therefore BDB gives three definitions: 1) living creatures other than man, fish, birds, and reptiles; 2) non-wild beasts, which occasionally includes cattle or riding animals; and 3) wild carnivorous beasts. In that case, Gen 1:24 might be translated "four-footed," which in modern terms is the super-class tetrapoda.

Verse	Meaning	Verse	Meaning
	doubled		doubled
Gn 1:24	cattle.r.r..beast	1Ki 4:33	beast.bird.r.r..fish
Gn 1:25	beast.cattle.r.r.	Ps 148:10	beast.cattle.r.r..bird
Gn 1:26	fish.bird.cattle.r.r.	Ez 8:10	r.r..beast.idols
Gn 6:7	destroy man.beast.r.r..bird	Ez 38:20	fish.bird.beasts.r.r..men
Gn 6:20	keep bird. cattle. r.r.	Ho 2:18	beast.bird.r.r.
Gn 7:14	beast.cattle.r.r..bird	Ha 1:14	fish.r.r.
Gn 7:23	man.cattle.r.r..bird		single
Gn 8:17	bird.cattle.r.r.	Gn 9:3	moving r. shall be food
Gn 8:19	beast.r.r..bird	Ps 104:25	sea with r. innumerable

Table 5.9: The meaning of רֶמֶשׂ (*remesh*).

From Table 5.9, the MT *remesh* appears doubled 15/17x—"creeping creeper"—which KJV translates "creeping thing," while the other two uses refer to a single *remesh*: Ps 104:25 "sea in which are creeper"; and, Gen 9:3 "creepers that live." The doubled usage always appears in a list, which 14/15x includes "beast" (sometimes translated "cattle"), suggesting that *remesh* is a non-beast. The exception is Hab 1:14 where only fish are listed, suggesting that *remesh* is a non-fish, but apparently can live either on land or in water. BDB has three definitions, corresponding to these cases: 1) creeping things; 2) sea animal/gliding thing; and 3) moving thing. In all cases, the noun is not translated by its context (as is usually the case) but by its verbal root, which is to say—a wild guess. In Gen 1:24–26 where *behemah* is a contrasting type of life form, we take *remesh* to be "non-four-footed." Most lizards and reptiles have a low-slung body with legs protruding to the sides, as do amphibians. That distinction might also account for the difference noted between the other two gliding/moving BDB definitions of sea-animals.

Finally, we have *chayyah 'erets*, "living thing of the earth," which, as I argue in the previous chapter, means domesticated animals when in the singular, wild animals when in the plural. This is a peculiar distinction because no humans yet exist to domesticate them. So perhaps what is meant here is "domesticatable" animals—precursors of the cows and sheep that we encounter in Genesis 2. Or we can generalize and suggest that these are the types of animals that are usually domesticated for their milk (and meat and hide), so they correspond to mammals. With these changes we can translate,

> Gen 1:24 *Let the earth bring forth land animals after their kind, tetrapods, reptiles, and mammals.*

5.2.8 Creation Week

The lessons we have learned from this extensive Hebrew exegesis are more profound than the simple word changes we observed. If we are told about dragonflies instead of birds, then the account we have is incomplete and patchy, not intended to give us a comprehensive report. But we might have supposed that already because we are not told about dinosaurs either.

What does it mean to have something as profound as Creation Week reduced to a few animals here and a few plants there?

First, it means that we cannot draw any conclusions from the absence of life forms. We do not even know the reason for the presence of specific life forms rather than others. It also means that the purpose of Genesis 1 remains obscure, elevating pond scum and dragonflies above romantic oak forests filled with singing birds. For too long we have highlighted those things that we enjoy, evaluating Creation from the viewpoint of aesthetics rather than efficiency, autonomy, and purpose. This new translation forces us to consider not just the beauty of our world, but the driving purpose behind every sacrificial cell, every ephemeral species, every transitory ecosystem. For the one thing conveyed by this gritty report is that there is a reason, a development, a plot behind these eccentric characters that the rest of the Bible is designed to reveal.

Second, we learn that both space and time are patchy in this account, neither contiguously located, nor continuously recorded. Attempting to "fill in the details" of the Creation Week by invoking watery firmaments or changing physical constants is as doomed as reconstructing a new phylum from a single tooth. There are so many more things we do not know than things we do know, and the Creation Week does not provide a framework for reconstructing the full story. If it did, we might hear more about trilobites and dinosaurs and less about lichens and dragonflies. Rather, the story is following a single thread through a very complex tapestry for some purpose other than providing us an exhaustive scientific account of origins.

That is to say, we approach a text with an expectation, a genre, a mental filter that allows only certain concepts through. Because our exegetical tendencies have been shaped in part by Greek philosophy, Western education has always emphasized the importance of communication in language and texts. Greek schooling began with the trivium—Grammar, Logic, and Rhetoric—learning first the rules of language, then the rules of reasoning, and finally the rules of persuasion. But notice all the other functions of language that are ignored: poetry, prayer, music, worship, blessing, cursing, promising, encouraging, yes, even courting.

So it seems with sacred texts. The purpose of Genesis 1 does not appear to replace Cosmology 101, as if it were the communication of facts alone that justifies the opening chapter of the Bible. We vainly imagine that if God had used a GoPro camera, we would not be struggling with obscure Hebrew. But as we have shown, this text has far more functions than video because words are multivalued. They can do things that no movie can capture. The "lesser lightmaker" could only be one object in a video, but in a text it could be dozens of different things, all of which contribute meaning depending on our knowledge and sophistication. Likewise, when translating a text, we must choose which function of the text to translate and to which genre the text belongs. It is nearly impossible for a translation to incorporate all the multivalued meanings of the original text. Once we see how every translation misses something, whether poetry, prayer, music, worship, blessing, cursing, promising, encouraging, or courting, then we will begin to understand what every Jew, every Muslim, every Hindu already knows: If we want to study Scripture, we will have to learn the original language.

Finally, having recognized the importance of the original language, we come to the main purpose of this section on Creation Week, the meaning of *yom*, the matter of "days." Since one purpose of this chapter is to show how Genesis is not only compatible with science but also provides guidance for science, then Creation Week is scientifically more important than Noah's Flood. It affects not just archaeology, but also cosmology, physics, chemistry, and especially, biology.

If I am to defend the six Days as representing 13.7 billion years, I must answer the question, "Is it possible to translate *yom*, "day," in a way that is compatible with science?"

There have been many suggestions: *yom* = 1000 years; an age; an unspecified analogical time; twenty-four miraculous hours; discontinuous days within a longer span; or even a non-chronological framework. Each of these approaches has its supporters and detractors, and in the spirit of *midrash*, we assign them all a measure of truth. But here is another suggestion, one that does not fit the above list: Perhaps the Days are of decreasing duration, following a formula. The advantages of this view are (a) the order of Days remains the same; (b) the Days can be continuous or discontinuous; (c) the Days start out as long ages, transition to millennia, and end up at twenty-four hours; (d) the Days provide a framework but it is cosmological rather than ecological; (e) they capture the analogy, the essence, of a day—its beginning and end, its duration and sequence—without losing the forest for the trees. But the "decreasing days" approach offers one more thing that none of the others can: It can be experimentally determined.

#	Item	Day	Traditional	YrBC	LogY	New Transl	YrBC	LogY
1	universe	1.00	Big Bang	1.38e10	10.14	Big Bang	1.38e10	10.14
2	water/life	1.17	water world	1.37e10	10.14	comets	1.37e10	10.14
3	light	1.33	1st stars	1.34e10	10.13	1st stars	1.36e10	10.13
4	darkness	1.50	1st ionization	1.30e10	10.11	1st ionization	1.35e10	10.13
5	firmament	2.00	solar nebula	6e9	9.78	galaxy	1.2e10	10.08
6	separated	2.25	planet	5e9	9.70	solar nebula	5e9	9.70
7	heaven	2.50	end of L.B.	3.85e9	9.58	late bombard.	3.85e9	9.58
8	dry land	3.00	plate tectonics	3.7e9	9.57	plate tectonics	3e9	9.48
9	vegetation	3.17	moss	4.34e8	8.64	cyanobacteria*	**3.85e9**	**9.58**
10	seed/spore	3.33	grass	2.8e8	8.44	lichen*	**5e8**	**8.69**
11	fruit tree	3.50	fruit tree	1.3e8	8.11	vascular plant*	**3.2e8**	**8.50**
12	stars	4.00	1st star	1.1e10	10.04	nearby stars	5e9	9.70
13	greater light	4.25	sun	5e9	9.7	sun	5e9	9.70
14	lesser light	4.50	moon	4e9	9.6	aurorae	3.45e9	9.53
15	large sea	5.00	whale	4.5e7	7.65	fish	5e8	8.69
16	*'owph*	5.50	bird	1.5e8	8.17	dragonfly	2.5e8	8.39
17	livestock	6.00	cattle	6e4	4.78	tetrapoda	3.95e8	8.60
18	creeping	6.17	reptile	3.15e8	8.50	reptiles	3.51e8	8.50
19	beast o'earth	6.33	mammal	1.67e8	8.48	mammal	1.67e8	8.48
20	man	6.50	man	6e4	4.78	man	5e4	4.70

*based on oldest Earth fossils, meteorite fossils may be older

Table 5.10: Genesis creation day and year of earliest fossil lifeforms.

We can construct Table 5.10 by recording the Genesis Day on which an entity was created, assuming that all the items were evenly distributed during the first half of the day (the second half being night), giving them a fractional day value. For example, if there were three items created, the first gets Day.00, the second Day.25, and the third Day.50. We then attempted to find the "Smithsonian" years-before-Christ (yBC) for the first appearance of this object,[63] using generic biology categories wherever we could, e.g., Order Odonata instead of "Dragonfly." We put the traditional definitions (old

63. Smithsonian. "Human Evolution Timeline Interactive."

earth creation, e.g., Hugh Ross) in columns 4–6, and the new translations in columns 7–10. Since yBC varies from 13,000,000,000 to 50,000, we converted it to a logarithm. The numbers in the table use "FORTRAN" compressed formatting where 3e8 yBC represents 3×10^8, or 300,000,000 years BC, and the logarithm (base 10) is then $8 + \log(3) = 8.477$, listed in columns 6 and 10. We fit the data using a spreadsheet "linear least squares" fitting algorithm, where the "% deviation" is minimized. That is equivalent to plotting the data on lin-log paper and finding the best fit line. This algorithm gives an estimate of the goodness of fit, R^2, called the "correlation coefficient" where a perfect correlation would be 1.0, perfectly backwards would be -1.0 and no correlation at all would be 0. A correlation below 0.5 is not significant, whereas 0.7 is promising, and above 0.9 is quite significant.

Figure 5.2 shows the results of our fitting procedure, with the left panel showing the traditional definitions and the right panel showing the new definitions. In the left panel, we show the straight-line fit with Day 4 (dark line) and without Day 4 (light line), because some argue for a non-chronological creation of the Sun/Moon. In the right panel, the dark fit includes Day 3 and the light excludes Day 3 because the creation of cyanobacteria, as seen in comet fossils, may possibly predate the Sun. But because we do not have a fossil date, we plot with and without this data point, which hardly changes the slope of the line. The R^2=0.85 correlation for the final, new translation without Day 3 is truly remarkable, suggesting that the Days of Genesis are simply logarithms of the years preceding Moses.

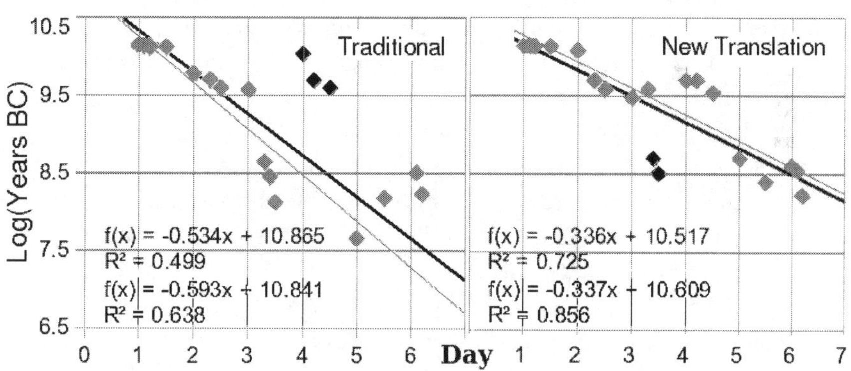

Figure 5.2: Decimal Genesis day versus log(Scientific year).

What does this mean?

At a minimum, it means that Genesis shows some mathematical sophistication that no one suspected.

Do decimal logarithms or some other logarithm match the Genesis numbering scheme best? We have the fit log(yBC) = -0.337*GenesisDay + 10.609. If we get rid of the logarithm by raising to the power 10, we have:

$$yBC = 10^{10:609} 10^{0:337\ GenesisDay} = 40.644\ (1/2.1727)^{GenesisDay}\ Gya$$

The 10.609 number is just the logarithmic way of writing the x-intercept or "birthday" of the universe set by the zero of our choice of calendar. If we make "Day 1" into a mathematician's "Day 0" by adding an arbitrary offset of about -1.4 days then this origin will be the expected 13.7 Gya. More significant than this manual adjustment of the x-intercept is the unadjusted 0.337 slope of the fit, which is equivalent to a logarithmic base for a Genesis day of 1/2.1727. It is also reminiscent of Euler's number, e = 2.7182818, discovered in the seventeenth century as the unique logarithmic base whose derivative (slope) looks exactly like the original function, hence a "natural" logarithm.

Why are we using "years BC"? Does our choice not put the calendar zero at Jesus's birth? Why should the writer of Genesis know where future medieval monks would later put the zero birth date?

Logarithms are not possible for negative numbers or zero. So we need to either move the zero date to the far left of the time line, or move it to the far right and "flip" the time line to turn negative dates into positive numbers. Then there are two obvious spots where the time line might be mapped to the calendar zero: either at the Big Bang on Day 1 on the far left or at the present/future with a flipped time line on the far right. Because logarithms expand the time line around zero while compressing the time line far from zero, the best way to represent the slow progression of life on Earth would be to put the zero on the right and flip the time line backwards. Then the calendar origin (Day 7+) could be placed at 6000 BC or 0 BC with no effect on the Genesis Day numbers because the few thousand years' difference is minuscule when compared to the 13.7 billion years elapsed.

Well, if the Days of Genesis really were logarithmic, how long exactly were they? Plugging in the formula for each Day and normalizing Day 1.00 = 13.7 billion years, we subtract the yBC to find the length of a Genesis Day. Because it is logarithmic, it gets shorter and shorter as the Creation Week progresses, so about 7.4 Gy elapse the first Day, 3.4 Gy the second Day, 332 My on the fifth Day (and finally 24 hours on the fortieth Day). According to this formula, Day 6 should last 152 My which starts at 283 MyBC and finishes at 130 MyBC. This time span is nowhere near the creation of Man, which is how Genesis ends Day 6.

So Day 6 of Genesis 1 is a bit problematic. The special creation of man does not plot on this graph at all! Australopithecines like "Lucy" at 3 million years (Log yBC=6.48), Neanderthals at 250,000 years (5.4), Cro-Magnons at 40,000 years (4.7), and Modern Man at 10,000 years (4.0) all fall off the bottom of this chart. There seems no way to fit the creation of Man into this chart with a straight line or even with a curved line.

Does that mean that our fit line is useless?

No, we should rather take it to mean that Man is special, as the remainder of Genesis 1 goes on to explain. Whether we look at this creation from the standpoint of Genesis or science, Man remains an exception. In an implicit way, Creation Week demonstrates that the creation of Man is not like the creation of any other thing. That is the danger of using the chronology of Creation Week to extrapolate the time of Man's creation.

This is an important exegetical point. Science reveals discontinuities that the text does not. As a result, we can err greatly when we infer a chronological or scientific continuity from a syntactic (but not semantic) continuity. Science is visual and text is linguistic; therefore, science is dumb and texts are blind (Ps 19:1–3). Textual exegesis and scientific research are not interchangeable. Rather, they are complementary and codependent in such a way that neither trumps the other.[64]

In Anselm's words, *Neque enim quaero intelligere ut credam, sed credo ut intelligam*, "I do not seek to understand in order that I may believe, I believe in order that I may understand."[65] Indeed, the text of Genesis 1 gives us far more information about Man than any other creation story. But to understand the significance of the text, we will need to understand some of the scientific characteristics of ancient hominids—Australopithecines, Neanderthals, Cro-Magnons and Moderns—that are all potential candidates for the *Imago Dei* of Gen 1:26.

5.3 The Stone Ages

The previous section on the exegesis of Creation Week in Genesis 1 has so intertwined Hebrew and science that it almost seems that a new chapter is needed for the remaining three or four verses regarding Man. But I include it here because I will mainly exegete scientific data. And exegesis really is the right word because so many interpretations of the data fill the bookshelves already. But having the arc of Genesis 1 behind us and the glory of Eden awaiting us, we finally understand what no scientist can see—the purpose of the Stone Ages. In this section, we show how the Stone Ages can be understood as a fulfillment of all the promises of Genesis 1 and the necessary preparation for Eden.

64. Hodge, *Systematic Theology*.

65. St Anselm. *Proslogion*; St Augustine. *Tract. Ev. Jo.*

5.3.1 The Paleolithic

The reason we call these ancient periods of human existence, "stone ages," is that stone was the principal tool, and certainly the best preserved. It was not the only tool. For example, we think early humans used deer antlers to flake off the little chips of flint to make blades, but the antlers did not survive the tens of thousands of years that the stones did. Some of the earliest stone tools date back to 1.7 million years, and whenever a different type of stone tool arrives, the archaeologist announces a new culture. Based on the tools, there were something like four or five periods of human stone-tool culture: Lower Paleolithic (1700–300 kyBC), Middle Paleolithic (300–40 kyBC), Upper Paleolithic (40–10 kyBC), Mesolithic (10–6 kyBC), and Neolithic (8–4 kyBC). As the data get better, the divisions get finer, and different locations may exhibit diverse time lines.

The Lower Paleolithic (1700–300 kyBC) is the reign of Australopithecines, *homo erectus* and/or *homo heidelbergensis*. The field offers more theories and proposed evolutionary trees than there are bones, which is usually the case with a data-starved science. The recent discovery of five highly diverse skeletons in a single cave suggested that many proposed "species" are just natural variations in body type within a single population.[66] Genome research might cut the Gordian knot but the DNA is poorly preserved in these oldest bones.

The Middle Paleolithic (300–40 kyBC) is dominated by the Mousterian stone-making culture and the bones of *homo neanderthalensis*, popularly called Neanderthal.[67] The data is far more abundant for this time period. We even know what they wore and recently, the mitochondrial DNA and the full somatic DNA genome has been transcribed for several individuals.[68] The DNA is highly fragmented as well as contaminated with bacterial DNA, so we should view the data as provisional and any conclusions as tentative. Recent genome transcription argues that Neanderthals split off from the modern human lineage some 500 kyBC, or 250 kyBC before they arrived in Europe. That is to say, they are not ancestors of modern man at all,[69] despite the (popular culture) claim that "Europeans are 6 percent Neanderthal," which is about as true as the claim that "Humans are 97 percent chimpanzee." A little consideration of the discrepancy between these two

66. Margvelashvili et al. "Tooth wear" 17278–17283.

67. Arsuaga et al. "Neandertal roots" 1358–1363.

68. Noonan et al. "Sequencing and Analysis of Neanderthal Genomic DNA" 1113–1118.

69. Rieux, "Improved calibration of the human mitochondrial clock."

claims reveals that "% similarity" is both an undefined measure and a poor proxy of ancestry.

The term Upper Paleolithic (45–10 kyBC) refers to a family of different stone-tool cultures, each based in a particular locality. The people who made the tools were quite different from the Neanderthals, who had mysteriously vanished a few millennia earlier. They were taller, with distinct chins and broad foreheads. From the differences between tools, we may conclude that cultures were diversifying, perhaps because they were growing and becoming less nomadic. Or perhaps they were increasing in creativity and intelligence, so that local innovations created diversity. It also suggests that language skills, which would otherwise diffuse knowledge, were minimal or nonexistent. This is also the time period when caves were painted, venus statues carved, bows and arrows employed, and fishhooks invented. The DNA of the entire genome of these populations has been transcribed multiple times. Unlike Neanderthal DNA, it is indistinguishable from that of modern man, though it derived from multiple sources.[70] Because the oldest of these settlements were found in the Levant, current theories inexplicably claim an African origin followed by migration through the Levant. While "Cro-Magnon" is no longer a technical term for the Aurignacian or the Gravettian culture, I will here affectionately call all these diverse Upper Paleolithic people groups "Cro-Magnons."

The term Mesolithic (10–6 kyBC) has not been universally accepted because there are many competing criteria for establishing a distinct break from Upper Paleolithic. Yet it is not Neolithic either, so the literature sometimes refers to the period as Pre-Pottery Neolithic A and B, (PPNA/B). The clue that unlocks this subtle flint-knapping transition, is the rapid spread of this culture away from Levant but without a corresponding gene flow. It also spread faster than the Cro-Magnon cultures preceding it, though not as dramatically as the Neolithic culture that followed it. I attribute this rapid transport of culture to the acquisition of language, a hypothesis strengthened by recent publications in historical linguistics that connect language origin to this time and place.[71] The absence of gene flow indicates that this spread of language in the Mesolithic is either social (e.g., hunting clubs) or epigenetic (e.g., folic acid supplements). But given the 2000 year time lag of the onset, which is too slow to be consistent with a social spread, I argue that it was epigenetic.

The Neolithic (8–4 kyBC) period saw the rapid spread of farming technology out of the Levant accompanied by gene flow and the Indo-European

70. Caramelli, "A 28,000 Years Old."

71. Pagel et al. "Ultraconserved words" 8471–8476.

language group. That was so radical a change that it has been christened the Neolithic Revolution (NR). The cultural migration was about the same speed as that of the Mesolithic—three kilometers per year, or roughly a snail's pace—but because it was accompanied by gene flow, I see it as a replacement population. Part of the difficulty in describing the Mesolithic lies precisely in its similarity to the Neolithic, which followed closely on its heels. The early work on NR with blood-types has been redone with much higher precision, with recent publications showing the three people groups that make up modern Europe: the West European red-headed hunter-gatherers, the Middle Eastern brown-eyed dark-haired farmers coming up from the Levant, and a few millennia later, the Uralic (Finnish) blue-eyed platinum blonds migrating down from Scandinavia.[72] Not only are these genetic migrations reflected in the languages of Europe, but they are also reflected in the technologies and cultures of these groups.

This is a rough overview of Anthropology 101 with uncontroversial conclusions for the purpose of integrating the MT of Genesis into a schematic timeline. Since Day 6 ends some 200 Mya, even were we to pick the emergence of the earliest hominid—the Australopithecines at 3 Mya—as the creation of man, it still would not fit on the Genesis 1 logarithmic time line. But other features of the Biblical account exclude both Australopithecines and Neanderthals as candidates for "first man." Indeed, the list of human attributes given in Gen 1:26–27 only makes sense if we know what it excludes.

5.3.2 Male and Female

Now the section of Genesis 1 concerning man has been a theological gold mine, so there is a natural reluctance to reinterpret the Hebrew text. I reiterate that *midrash* does not invalidate previous interpretations, it merely multiplies them. The only interpretations it invalidates are those that argue for exclusivity, that argue for the absence of alternatives, which are the weakest sort of argument in any case. To address the heavy theology burden laid upon these last verses of Genesis 1, this section needs to be theological and philosophical. But we are not abandoning our exegetical principles for the heady droughts of reason. Rather, we use them as a foil to show why the exegetical minutiae are important. I will not avoid all the pitfalls and land mines, but in the words of Job 13:8, I do not want to show partiality to God; Scripture can defend itself and needs no special pleading. When we meet Genesis 1, it is evaluating us even as we interpret it, for it is the

72. Lazaridis et al. "Ancient human genomes" 409–413.

entrance exam to the rest of Scripture, the gate to the riches of heaven. And, after coming all this way, we do not want to be found lacking the means to purchase the pearl of great price, which is why we must make use of every resource available.

1:26a *Let us make man in our image, according to our likeness;*

This is possibly the verse in the Bible most often quoted by theologians because it provides the basis for all attempts to find the divine in man or the human in God. It has been used to baptize all manner of human characteristics with divinity, including art, music, math, emotion, reason, or language. In the past I have thought exactly that, finding in language the divine spark that makes us special. But while all of these things are indeed divine gifts, they are probably not what this verse is talking about. In Gen 1:26, the divine characteristic is visual, it is an image.

What is so special about an image?

Visual information is quite distinct from textual information. It is processed in different parts of the brain with different properties. Logician Bertrand Russell wanted to eliminate metaphysics (and religion!) by defining language as communication, with every word a concrete reference to something in the external world, but he was stymied by recursive references. Philosopher Ludwig Wittgenstein, as a positivist and student of Russell, tried to reduce language to a mental "picture," but discovered it was impossible and recanted his youthful naïvete in his "*Brown and Blue*" books.[73] His colleague J. L. Austin, though no follower of Wittgenstein, demonstrated in *How To Do Things With Words* that language does far more than simply communicate static knowledge like a picture. It remains active and dynamic, with non-visual, "creative" functions such as covenants and wedding vows.[74] Applying those insights to Gen 1:26, the term "image" is as significant for what it excludes as for what it includes: It excludes language and song; it excludes music and math; it excludes reason and emotion. Because all those things are intangible, immaterial, and invisible, they are "language properties" while Gen 1:26 specifically refers to "image" and "likeness."

One reason for thinking that the Imago excludes these auditory, immaterial things is that the immaterial word phrase "God said," precedes the Imago some ten times. John the Evangelist begins his Gospel by expanding on this same passage when he writes (John 1:1) "*In the beginning was the Word.*" He shows that the ideas of Creation are present as linguistic text prior to the visual image of Gen 1:26, so that the immaterial implies the

73. Wittgenstein. *Blue and Brown Books.*

74. Austin. "How to do Things with Words"

material and not vice versa. Therefore, the audio-visual distinction in Genesis is actual and not just implied. Theologian Norman Shepherd makes the same point—arguing that this Imago passage is about visual material substances, not textual immaterial information.[75]

Taking the matter one step further, the force of a logical implication is not easily reversible: All that is the Image of God implies man, but all that is man does not necessarily imply the Image of God. Rather, what is not in man is also not in the image of God, or written ID→M, then !M→!ID whereas !ID→!M is incorrect because it means M→ID (where "!" represents "not"). In contrast to the teachings of other religions, Genesis tells us that man is in the Image of God, not God in the image of man.

What is this Image of God in which man was formed?

The image, the picture, the video reveals bilateral symmetry—two arms, two legs, two eyes, two ears—as well as blood, sweat, tears, and plasma. Everything that the biologist tells us about man is visual information, is static knowledge, and therefore potentially is also the Image of God. Since the DNA is the blueprint for all that the biologist sees, then it would seem the Imago also involves DNA.

Therefore if Neanderthals, Denisovans, and Australopithecines do not share our DNA, they are not made in the Image of God. And conversely, if Cro-Magnons do share our DNA, then they too are made in the Image of God. Since Genesis 1 is a chapter about beginnings, about origins, then it would appear that Gen 1:26 puts the origin of man with the Cro-Magnons, approximately 50 kyBC. This is the bodily creation, the DNA creation, but not the Adamic creation of Gen 2:7, which I date to the preparation of Eden about 12 kyBC as discussed in the previous chapter. Then it appears that Gen 1:26 and Gen 2:7 are separated by about 40,000 years, though the text gives no indication of the gap.

How can we be sure that Gen 1:26 refers to the Cro-Magnons and not to Adamic man?

Because the next few verses describe the differences between the Aurignacian and the Mousterian culture, between Cro-Magnons and Neanderthals.

> Gen 1:26b "*. . . and let them rule over the fish of the sea and over the birds of the sky and over the cattle and over all the earth, and over every creeping thing that creeps on the earth.*"

When God gives dominion to man, the implication is that nothing previously created, which includes Australopithecines and Neanderthals,

75. Shepherd. "Man in the Image of God."

had been given this dominion. For despite 250 ky of recorded culture, the Neanderthals (and the preceding Australopithecines) had never learned to make fishhooks or, from the preserved contents of their middens (garbage pits), to eat fish. Nor had they invented the net to catch birds. Not only that, but Neanderthals lack the rotator cuff that allows the shoulder joint to throw rocks or nock an arrow. Their principle hunting tool was a stout stone-tipped lance. Their diet was almost exclusively mega-fauna, such as mammoth and giant elk, which could be hunted with a lance. That perhaps explains why we only find Neanderthal remains in the Northern (boreal) forests where the mega-fauna lived.[76] By contrast, Cro-Magnons hunted with arrows, fished with fishhooks, and spread over the entire globe. So even if we did not have DNA evidence, Gen 1:26 would exclude all varieties of hominin before Cro-Magnon.

How do I know that the image and likeness begins with Cro-Magnon at 50 kyBC and not Adam at 12 kyBC?

There is a subtle difference between Cro-Magnons and Adam, which I have argued was Adam's ability to speak. The next few verses tell us that this creation was a non-speaking and therefore non-Adamic man.

> Gen 1:27 *God created man in His own image, in the image of God He created him; male and female He created them.*

Ver.	Text
MT	(1) וַיִּבְרָא אֱלֹהִים אֶת־הָאָדָם בְּצַלְמוֹ
KJV	So God created man in his own image,
LXX	καὶ ἐποίησεν ὁ θεὸς τὸν ἄνθρωπον
MT	(2) בְּצֶלֶם אֱלֹהִים בָּרָא אֹתוֹ
KJV	in the image of God created he him;
LXX	κατ᾽ εἰκόνα θεοῦ ἐποίησεν αὐτόν
MT	(3) זָכָר וּנְקֵבָה בָּרָא אֹתָם׃
KJV	male and female created he them.
LXX	ἄρσεν καὶ θῆλυ ἐποίησεν αὐτούς

Table 5.11: The צֶלֶם אֱלֹהִים (*Imago Dei*) of Gen 1:27 in translation.

76. Geist. "The Neanderthal Paradigm"; Adler et al. "Ahead of the Game."

We are told the same thing three times. That is rather odd for a compressed story, so we can infer that the information must be important. The differences among the three clauses are in the ordering of the parts of the clause using a verb with valency of almost three (as discussed in Chapter 2), which permits several arrangements. In Table 5.11 we give the MT and two translations: KJV and LXX.

In the first clause, the verb *bara* is in the first, emphatic slot but it is also in the *qal-wayyiqtol* or continuous dialogue mode to provide continuity with the previous sentence. That mode diminishes its importance, transferring the emphasis to the next (underlined) word, the subject Elohim. The LXX (Greek) lacks the type of emphasis created by word order that we find in Hebrew and English so it indicates the emphasis by inserting a definite article "ὁ." The receiver of the action (the direct object) is "man," modified by the (oblique) prepositional phrase "in his image." The emphasis is on the subject, Elohim, and only secondarily on the thing accomplished, "man." But if that were all that we had, we could not really be sure whether "his image" means the image of God or of man. Nor could we be sure that the creation was finished or still in progress.

To lessen the ambiguity, the second clause puts "the image of God" in the emphatic slot. To further emphasize "the image of God," the subject has been absorbed into the conjugation of the verb, and the direct object has been reduced to a pronoun.

In addition, the verb is now in the perfect tense, to emphasize a completed act. When combined with the *wayyiqtol* of the first clause, it suggests an action beginning in the past and continuing up until a recently completed act. So the MT vaguely suggests that the creation of man took some time, consistent with our 40,000 year gap between Genesis 1 and 2. Some ambiguity remains because Elohim is a plural masculine noun and "man" is a singular masculine noun. It would seem that the image matches the gender but not the number.

The last clause resolves the ambiguity by expanding the direct object to "male and female," putting these words in the emphatic slot, where again the *qal*-perfect indicates a completed action as well as a complete parallel with the second clause. The existence of both sexes is clearly the emphasis here, which implies that the multiplicity of both genders was the nature of the image of Elohim. It seems paradoxical but, as we discussed earlier, the cryptic nature of the X-chromosome is hiding in the Y-dominant male XY genome. That might be the explanation lost by the LXX but retained by the ever-conservative KJV.

Why is it important to tell us that man had two sexes? That is a mere detail in the earlier creation of animals, even when we are given verbs such as "waters teem," which defined a reproductive limitation. Why is sexuality significant now?

Gen 1:28 gives an immediate reason, but it does not mention marriage. It is only much later in Gen 2:22 that the creation of Eve, following the creation of Adam, is accompanied by many restrictions that we might characterize as vows. There are no restrictions listed here in Gen 1:27, suggesting that something changed between the two chapters, something that makes a huge difference in male-female relationships. Because the marriage vows in Chapter 2 absolutely require language, what is missing in Chapter 1 is most probably language. That is, contrary to Karl Barth, I do not think that Gen 1:27 establishes marriage,[77] rather it establishes the divinely ordered division of the sexes. Not until Genesis 2 do I find textual evidence for the institution of marriage. Therefore, when Jesus defended marriage against divorce (Matt 19:4–5), he quoted both Genesis 1 and 2, covering both the physical and the spiritual-linguistic aspects. That is, both the Gnostic denial of sex and the Modernist denial of marriage are forbidden by Jesus.

> Gen 1:28 *God blessed them; and God said to them, "Be fruitful and multiply, and fill the earth, and subdue it; and rule over the fish of the sea and over the birds of the sky and over every living thing that moves on the earth."*

If we missed the reference to Neanderthals in Gen 1:26, Gen 1:28 repeats the many ways that Cro-Magnons are blessed with greater gifts than Neanderthals. The "male and female" of Gen 1:27 are now given a purpose by the first blessing, "be fruitful." Despite surviving 250 millennia, Neanderthals had surprisingly small populations, estimates lie between 7,000 and 50,000 persons at any given time.[78] When the Cro-Magnons arrived, the population density climbed tenfold. Combining the increased density with the increased range of the Cro-Magnons, God's blessing included a 100-fold, if not 1000-fold, increase in population. Simultaneous with the spread of Cro-Magnons was the extinction of Neanderthals, which some take to be causal and others coincidental.

No matter the reason, God's blessing was on the race that could in principle fill the earth, as well as subdue it. It was Cro-Magnons that filled every continent with hunting tools such as bows, stone arrowheads, and knapped stone blades. It was Cro-Magnons who migrated to India, along the coast, and down into Australia. It was Cro-Magnons who crossed the Bering land bridge into North America. Only after Cro-Magnons had

77. Barth. *Church Dogmatics III/ 1.*

78. Bocquet-Appel and Degioanni. "Neanderthal Demographic Estimates."

completed the task assigned to them, only after the Earth was filled from East to West and from North to South, only after the last Clovis migration from Alaska had arrived in Patagonia around 13,000 BC, does Gen 2:5 give us the next development in the story.

> Gen 1:29 *Behold, I have given you every plant yielding seed that is on the surface of all the earth, and every tree which has fruit yielding seed; it shall be food for you;*
>
> Gen 1:30 *and to every beast of the earth and to every bird of the sky and to every thing that moves on the earth which has life [I have given] every green plant for food; and it was so.*

Some exegetes have taken Gen 1:29 to suggest that man was created vegetarian, but from the burnt bones and middens of archaeology, I see no evidence for that conclusion. Rather, it would appear that Gen 1:29 references an expanding diet. For Cro-Magnons excelled over Neanderthals in more ways than just hunting; they could also use fruits and cereals in ways that Neanderthals apparently did not. Carbon isotope analysis reveals that Neanderthals ate almost no plants, whereas at the miraculously preserved Upper Paleolithic site discovered under the Dead Sea at Ohalo II, there is no doubt that Cro-Magnon ate seeds, and not just uncultivated grass seeds but tree seeds. They also ate mollusks.[79]

Notice that Gen 1:29 does not mention cereal grains, nor anything associated with cultivation. The plants yielding seed or green plants are given for food, but there is no discussion of heads of grain, sowing, reaping, threshing, or winnowing. It appears that a hunter-gatherer culture is being described. Therefore God's blessing is the novel ability of the Cro-Magnon to process grains and plant food. That takes both skill and patience, especially because gathering wild nuts or grains does not produce as many calories as hunting but it is less sporadic and dangerous. Unlike nomadic hunters who had to follow the large game when it migrated, gatherers can supplement an intermittent meat supply, as well as store grain and thus travel less frequently. These benefits likely account for the fact that the Cro-Magnon population density was ten times that of the Neanderthals. All these abilities are yet another indication of the superior learning abilities of the Cro-Magnon mind.

Why is this verse so often translated as if man originally had a vegetarian diet?

79. Richards et al. "Neanderthal diet" 7663–7666; Weiss et al. "The broad spectrum revisited" 9551–9555.

The bracketed words in Gen 1:30 are where the NAS/KJV/ESV add a subject and a verb to Gen 1:30, on the supposition that there is an ellipsis with Gen 1:29, one which converts animals from edible objects to herbivorous subjects. But "beast of the earth" and "bird of the heavens" are both singular, which as I have argued earlier, indicates that they are dominated by man. If this verse gives them freedom to eat green plants, then they are dominating creation and the word should have been given in the plural. Clearly, inserting this verb does not work.

If we look for a verb where Man is the subject, we will find it at the end of Gen 1:29, "to you it shall be for food." If we note that there is a direct object marker on "every green herb," we have the skeleton of the sentence: "*to you it shall be for food . . . every green herb*." But then we do not know where to put the prepositional phrases: "to every beast . . . bird . . . reptile." The *lamedh* preposition used here, can have seven meanings, as discussed earlier: 1) in regard to; 2) locality at; 3) object of an intransitive verb; 4) a transition; 5) on account of; 6) concurrence during; and, 7) purpose when used with an infinitive. Eliminating 4), 5), 6) and 7), and noting that the quantifier "every" seems to also rule out 2), I am left with 1) and 3) as options. The verse now reads: "*to you with respect to (1) edibility there shall be (3) every beast, (3) bird, (3) reptile, even every green herb for food*." Clumsy, but at least it handles the direct object correctly and keeps the animals domestic.

> Gen 1:31 *God saw all that He had made, and behold, it was very good. And there was evening and there was morning, the sixth day.*

This verse ends the chapter with a sense of completion, for we are told "all . . .was very good." So far, I have demonstrated that Genesis 1 is completely consistent with the departure of Neanderthals and the arrival of Cro-Magnons. I have reconciled these mysterious cavemen with Genesis, explained the 40,000-year gap, and prepared the canvas for the remarkable developments of Genesis 2 and the discovery of Eden. What I was not prepared for, however, was the discovery of the Cro-Magnon schools.

5.3.3 The Mesolithic Revolution

Historically, the Mesolithic has been associated with big stones, with megaliths and monuments. The iconic Mesolithic monument is Stonehenge, with its enormous pillars of rock arranged in a circle (Figure 5.3). While impressive, Stonehenge is not unique, hundreds of these *menhir*, these giant stones, litter Europe. What initially attracted attention was the size of the rocks. Many cultures have associated them with giants and men of impossible strength. Less noticed was the fact, that over the 3000 miles from the Orkneys to Egypt, many of these stones are in circular monuments.[80]

Figure 5.3: Blue stones at Stonehenge and computer rendering of original. (Wiki Commons)

With advances in computer software, it became possible to visualize the celestial bodies of ancient skies, so that the positions of the stars and planets could be ascertained for spring nights in prehistoric Britain. Many of these Mesolithic monuments were discovered to have astronomical properties—the sun rose on the vernal equinox over one particular stone, for example, and the summer solstice was marked by a line on another stone.[81]

Yet why did structures like Stonehenge need so many additional rocks not used to mark changes in the night sky?

I believe that the astronomical uses of these "henges" may have been a later development and that the circular construction originally served a more immediate need. It is also my claim that the elaborate quarrying and creation of these monuments occurred nearly simultaneously, during the rise and fall of a forgotten empire. I doubt that the stone quarrying skills displayed in Britain, in Egypt, and in Turkey arose independently three separate times; they point rather to a class of "stone carvers" with interregional mobility. For example, the radius of the Stonehenge bluestones is related to the length of an Egyptian calendar measure.[82] But the claim of a single stonecutters union is harder to defend: The conventional dating of the Turkish Göbekli Tepe is 9700 BC, Stonehenge about 3500 BC, and the Pyramids roughly 2500 BC. Because the fall of this empire corresponds to

80. NASA. "Egyptian Stonehenge."
81. Ruggles. "Astronomy Before History" 6.
82. deSalvo. "Stonehenge and the Great Pyramid."

the time of Noah's Flood, 8500 BC or possibly 7500 BC is the latest period for the complete loss of stone-quarrying technology to occur as a result. But that does not seem compatible with the later time periods for these monuments. However, these later monuments show continuous reworking, so that the dates normally associated with them may reflect the last "active" use of the site. It may be that the golden shovel broke the first ground much earlier; thus it is possible that they were all begun at roughly the same time. Recognizing that I may have overlooked a crucial piece of data that precludes an earlier date, I will nonetheless argue that all these monuments were built at the same time and for the same purpose—to bring about the Mesolithic Revolution.

This transitional Mesolithic culture has only been recognized very recently, and it still carries ambiguous names like "Pre-Pottery Neolithic A" which implicitly witness the difficulty archaeologists have in separating the period from the later, Neolithic era. In Volume 2, I will argue that the Neolithic era can be recognized as a distinct transition from the Upper Paleolithic in three different fields—archaeology, linguistics, and genetics—which I summarize briefly. Archaeology looks at the tools and the technologies employed, such as the Neolithic use of polished stone tools, animal husbandry, and cereal grain cultivation. Linguistics looks at language development, such as the Neolithic Proto-Indo-European (PIE) split from Proto-Uralic and at even older language splits such as Proto-Kartvelian or even the much abused Nostratic. Genetics shows how the Neolithic peoples carried a unique set of genes or alleles throughout Europe, with five-foot, brown-haired and brown-eyed PIE Sardinians moving north into Europe, displacing the six-foot, red-haired, Cro-Magnon Basques and later mixing with the blond-haired Asian/blue-eyed Proto-Uralic Scandinavians.

The Mesolithic Revolution, in contrast, shows almost none of these features. The microliths and flint knapping technology is more advanced than that of the Cro-Magnons, but not markedly so. The farming technology may have included domesticated geese and more grains, but it can hardly be compared to the intense agricultural practices of the Neolithic. Summarizing the detailed discussion in Volume 3, the linguistics are shadowy, almost completely erased by the PIE migration that arrived 1000 years later. But they might possibly be spotted in isolated groups such as the Basque, Elamite and Sumerian. We will also see in Volume 3 that the genetics can only be observed by subtraction, by removing the effects of the Neolithic, the Uralic, the Botai, and the Greek migrations. What remains is a shadowy group, a triangular spread of European alleles that includes the Basque in one corner, the Asian Uralics in another, and something Middle Eastern in the third. Or if I use the global genetics plot of either Lazaridis or Seguin-Orlando, then that triangle's corners are the Basque, the Han Chinese, and all of Africa.[83] All this is evidence for a Mesolithic Revolution with very different properties from the NR that arrived one or two millennia later.

Why insist that there was a coherent, unified Mesolithic transition between the Upper Paleolithic and Neolithic eras, as opposed to a random diffusion of changes in the period verging on the Neolithic, changes that are not correlated either in space or time?

The reason is that all across Europe and down into Egypt, we discover the simultaneous construction of large stone monuments during that period, often with the same layout.

5.3.4 Middle Stone Mega-Stone Monuments

5.3.4.1 Turkish Megaliths: Göbekli Tepe

Göbekli Tepe ("belly-button hill")[84] is a location in south-central Turkey that features peculiar circular stone-walled constructions with poured concrete floors, pillars all around the outside, and two T-shaped carved "head stones" set in sockets in the middle (Figure 5.4).[85] Shapes of animals are exquisitely carved on the outer pillars of the buildings but they have apparently been razed and rebuilt about every decade for almost 2000 years, starting around 9600 BC. Each rebuilding replaces the pillars with a new set, inside the circumference of the previous set, and each rebuilding is less skilled than the previous one (Figure 5.5).[86] There are no signs that these were habitations and there is no water source nearby—a requirement for permanent habitation in this climate. However, there are pits full of arrowheads and flint tools, as well as food remains, suggesting both temporary residence and some sort of ritual, which would make this the oldest known "temple" site.

83. Lazaridis, "Ancient human genomes"; Seguin-Orlando et al. "Genomic structure in Europeans."

84. Curry. "Göbekli Tepe: the world's first temple?"

85. Teomancimit. "Göbekli Tepe Şanlıurfa."

86. Wang. "Göbekli Tepe site."

Figure 5.4: Göbekli Tepe, "belly button hill," Sanliurfa, Turkey. (Wiki Commons)

The "cultural evolution" model of humans gaining sophistication and religious rituals by accretion and progressive evolution does not account for Göbekli Tepe. Rather, it seems to display the exact opposite characteristic—the degradation and devolution of technical skills. Stonehenge, by comparison, is not a puzzle. Human strength is limited but the Pyramids of Egypt and the Easter Island statues show, along with Stonehenge, that sufficient labor will suffice. It was the transportation and arrangement of Stonehenge stones that shows anachronistic design. While no one disputes that stone-carving tools were available to quarry both Stonehenge and the Pyramids, Göbekli Tepe was built 6000 years earlier at a time when the Cro-Magnons had only flint implements. Without the right tools no amount of human labor can sculpt stone. Klaus Schmidt, the archaeologist who has spent more than fifteen years excavating the site, says it is like "finding that someone had built a [Boeing] 747 in a basement with an X-Acto knife."[87]

So the puzzles of Göbekli Tepe are many and deep. The T-shaped stone pillars, 20-feet high, do not look like architectural supports so much as stylized human shapes. They are carved very skillfully by unknown persons, presumably with flint tools (Figure 5.5b). The T-stones fit snugly in poured concrete sockets, some 8000 years before the Greeks invented cement. The site was constructed neither for habitation nor ritual, and the buildings were repeatedly demolished and replaced with inferior quality simulacra. And all

87. Mann. "The Birth of Religion."

this was accomplished when Cro-Magnons were, so far as we know, living in caves with a population density of three per square kilometer!

Figure 5.5: T-pillars at Göbekli Tepe and carved animal detail (Wiki Commons)

The key that unlocks this mystery is the chronology; Göbekli Tepe was contemporary with the rise of the Natufian culture, the Levantine precursor to the Neolithic. If we do not assume an evolutionary rise of culture but rather a vigorous origin followed by decline—as happened with the Roman, Byzantine, Inca, and other Empires—we can discern a consistent history. Let us call this hypothetical advanced culture "the Empire." Then Göbekli Tepe is a surviving outpost of an empire whose influence also created the Natufian culture. If most of an empire is annihilated, we may have no direct evidence for it, which can make the surviving indirect evidence appear mysterious. This explanation can also be inverted; separate archaeological mysteries may fit the same model. The Sphinx, Stonehenge, and the Bosporus channel can all provide evidence of the same vanished Empire.

If this explanation is correct, the Empire must have vanished at the same time at all of its outposts. Göbekli Tepe began its decline about 8400 BC. The Sphinx, surprisingly, is not dated by archaeology but by a textual (historical) reference that attributes it to Pharaoh Khafre. Geological or astronomical dating methods yield a much older date, around 10,500 BC for the carving of the Sphinx. Likewise, recent excavations at Stonehenge have found post-holes and a wooden palisade that date from 8000–7000 BC, as well as evidence of several later stages of remodeling where stones were moved and other circles were created and destroyed. Because the dating was done with C-14, which means that newer material obscures older material, the C-14 date would only reveal the younger "reworked" date. That does not preclude an older date for the original construction. In other words, the 8000 BC dating may not be an outlier but evidence for the creation of the site. Weathered carvings on some of the stones also show many similarities to the Göbekli Tepe site. While the dating methods are too crude to show simultaneity, it seems that several large stone-carving projects were all undertaken in the time period corresponding to the Cro-Magnon/Natufian (PPNA) transition about 9000 BC in the Levant.[88] And, as with the Göbekli site, the remarkable technologies used to construct all of these wonders degenerated and then vanished, surely the defining characteristic of a fallen empire.

Supposing that Göbekli Tepe was an outpost of a vanished empire, what would its function have been? Was it really used as a temple?

I am by no means an expert at reconstructing temple rituals, but if the cargo cult of the Pacific is any guide, then the temple function only came into practice after the Empire had vanished.[89] During World War II, isolated atolls of the Pacific became important staging areas for the US Navy but they were later abandoned. This inspired the islanders to make wooden radar antennae and mock hangars in an attempt to bring back the vanished cargoes. Likewise, the original function of the Paleolithic sites could have been pragmatic but they might later become temples as the remaining inhabitants attempted to maintain the fiction that the Empire still existed. Particularly telling are the decorated T-shaped stones erected in the center of the rings at the Göbekli Tepe site, as well as at the Nevali Çori site some 50 km north-northwest which is 500 years more recent. While the oldest T-stones were seven meters high, the later T-stones and the Nevali T-stones were only three meters high. Some of them have carvings suggestive of human features. The stones were placed in carved sockets, but after ten or so years, they were removed and buried, seemingly according to a timetable. One buries people, not rocks, which suggests that these T-stones represented people, even with the carved animal decorations. There are two oversized T-stones in the middle of each circle, surrounded by smaller and more numerous T-stones on the perimeter.

What mythological event involves two special people surrounded by many lesser ones?

Several stories come to mind, but nearly all of them are creation myths, where the primal pair are the first inhabitants: Adam and Eve. Now this interpretation should strike us as peculiar, for the simple reason that dualistic worship centers are extremely rare. Even in Zoroastrian dualism, the two deities are not presented as two actors in an arena. Rather, religions tend to either celebrate individual deities—a temple to Zeus, a temple to Diana—or all important deities, as in the Pantheon. Using human emotions as a guide

88. Bar-Josef and Valla, "The Natufian Culture."

89. Worsley. *The Trumpet Shall Sound.*

to ritual can help us understand this tendency: The competing divine attributes are jealousy and generosity; either the god is powerful, selfish, and monotheistic, or the gods are weak, inclusive, and polytheistic.

How does one explain the apparent fact that the most ancient supposed temples on Earth have two and only two deities, represented by identically sized and centrally placed T-stones?

I think the answer must be that these structures did not start out as temples, and the T-stones did not start out as representations of deity. Rather, the building and the stones acquired these characteristics long after their original design and use had been "cast in stone," as it were. If the Flood is reliably dated to 9590 BC, then the first T-stones were constructed before the Flood and erected during the existence of the Edenic Empire. This solution removes the paradox of how Paleolithic peoples carved the stones with flint tools. They were in fact carved by Adamic stone-cutters, using the same advanced technology seen in Egypt. It also means that the T-pillars probably lacked any cultic significance, unless the Empire was encouraging emperor-worship. Given modern examples like Stalinist Russia, that is always possible. But, more likely, the cultic significance came after the fall of the Edenic Empire, as we saw happen with the cargo cults. This explanation would account for their advanced technology, their peculiar construction, and even the particulars of the rite that saw this site gradually fall into decay over the next 1500 years.

If Göbekli Tepe was a relic of the vanished Edenic Empire, built by an advanced Adamic race, then why would they have come to this distant hill in Turkey, far from Eden, rivers, or local attractions?

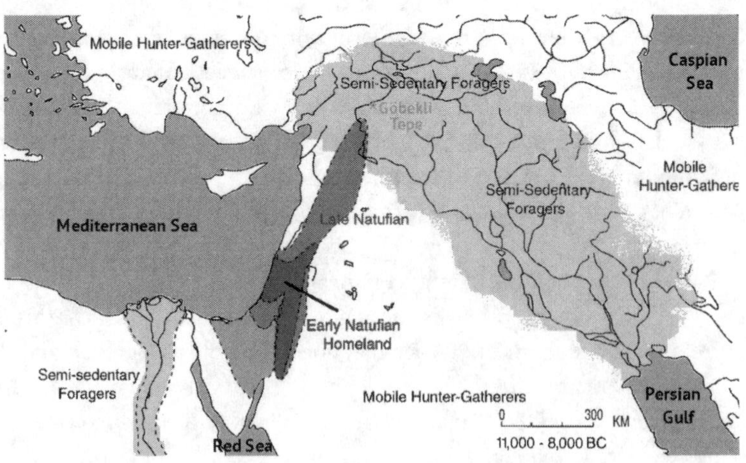

Figure 5.6: The spread of Mesolithic Natufian civilization (after Bar-Josef)

Now that we have asked the right question, we can begin a search for answers from archaeology, genetics, and linguistics. The first clue comes from several recent papers published on the Mesolithic era.[90] The earliest remains characterized as Natufian Mesolithic show that this transition occurred first in the deepest valley on Earth—the valley of the Dead Sea. Over the next few hundred years, the Mesolithic settlements followed the rift valley up the Jordan river into Lebanon and then west toward the Euphrates and north into the mountains of Turkey (Figure 5.6).

Why this dispersal route?

Because Eden was 3000 meters below sea level, it must have been a hardship for Adamites to function at sea level, much as if our jobs took us to the Tibetan plateau. For them, the valley of the probably empty Dead Sea would have been the only place outside Eden where the air pressure was comfortable. As I remarked before, the adiabatic lapse rate for dry air is 10C per kilometer, or 15C/27F warmer in the Dead Sea valley than at sea level. One of the marked differences between modern humans and apes is our hairless skin and our abundance of sweat glands.[91] So not only were Adamites adapted to high pressure, they were adapted to the high temperatures as well, assuming they could get enough water to drink. Using these three criteria—high pressure, warm temperatures, and available water supplies—I can begin to map the regions adjacent to Eden that would have been most easily visited by Adamites, and that map nicely overlays the Mesolithic settlement sites.

If the Mesolithic peoples were Adamites, one might ask why did their genes not show the same changes that were observed in the Neolithic settlements?

No, I do not think they were Adamites, but because the Neolithics followed on the heels of the Mesolithics, it is difficult to see the gene changes through the translucent screen of history. Hopefully, some of the bones from Mesolithic man will have their DNA transcribed and we will discover more about these peoples. But the Mesolithics looked like, and possessed DNA identical with, the Upper Paleolithic cultures they replaced. There was no gene flow, as observed in the later NR, but there was cultural "meme" flow, there was information flow. Thus it is my argument that the Mesolithic Revolution was the education of the Cro-Magnons by the Adamic races, an education that made a lasting, trans-generational imprint on the people. As I discussed earlier, an inherited environmental adaption is an "epigenetic" change. And that is why I think the Mesolithic Revolution was an Epigenetic Revolution, where the Cro-Magnons learned to talk, and the "talking virus"

90. Bar-Yosef. "The natufian culture" 159–177; Munro. "Small game, the younger dryas" 47–71.

91. Jablonski. "The Naked Truth: why humans have no fur" 42–49.

spread throughout the world at about the same speed as, one thousand years later, the NR spread the "middle eastern farmer" genes.

Why would epigenetics spread at all, much less spread at the same rate as genes?

We know that the brain is "plastic" and wires up functions as they are used. If babies are not exposed to language in the first two years of their lives, they do not learn how to talk, and their brains are wired without the faculty. We also know that languages learned before puberty are independently "stored" in memory, whereas after puberty the brain stores "dictionaries" that convert to and from the mother tongue.[92] So if Eve were to pick up Cro-Magnon babies and sing to them, they would grow up speaking, and if they sung to their children, the epigenetic changes would pass down the generations. And because rewiring primarily affects pre-pubescent children, it could only spread at a speed slightly faster than the birth rate, or not much faster than the Neolithic Revolution that followed it.

The investment of time for such an education in language would be several years, though it might take several generations to produce highly efficient speakers, much the way that IQ scores show a 10 point "generational" increase, the Flynn Effect, throughout the twentieth century.[93] The more children or pregnant mothers that were exposed to language, the faster this process could become self-sustaining. So, if promoting speech were a goal of the Adamites, one would expect to find "talking schools" where many children and mothers could be accommodated within earshot, as, for example, in a Greek amphitheater. Small children who need this exposure the most, however, are also least likely to patiently endure it. Likewise, the Greek amphitheater architecture would be too dangerous for toddlers.

What then would a "talking school" look like?

I would expect that these talking-schools were structured like playpens or pediatrician's waiting rooms: smooth flat floors, high walls, no doors accessible to children, lots of benches for weary mothers, and air-conditioning. As in a waiting room, provision would have to be made for the mothers, who, though they might never learn to talk, had to be entertained, or better yet, educated too. Mobile medical clinics in remote third-world countries often have wordless "picture books," describing hygiene and other educational resources, for the mothers who are waiting for treatment. I argue that this is the original function of the decorated T-pillars, which would describe nutritional sources to the Cro-Magnon mothers, for example, domesticated geese, or warn against the dangers of poor hygiene, as represented by

92. Johnson and Newport. "Critical period effects" 60–99.

93. Flynn. "IQ Gains over Time" 25–66.

vultures and crocodiles. The two large pillars in the center, like the smaller ones around the sides, probably held a wood-lattice or wood plank roof to would have provide shade for the teacher/speaker in the center. The shape of the pillars would not handle much lateral stress, so the roof must have been made of a light material, perhaps it was a pergola lattice with a climbing vine that provided natural air conditioning.

The persistence of these buildings shows that the schools became self-sustaining, even after the Adamites had left or been destroyed in the Flood. The decay of the buildings is to be expected because the upkeep fell to the Cro-Magnons. The final desertion of the site reflects the change that occurred with the Neolithic Revolution: Talking schools were no longer necessary due to improved epi/genetics. This is a key point. The schools persisted even after the Edenic Empire vanished, which suggests that the Cro-Magnons themselves valued and even needed constant reinforcement of language skills. It did not come naturally to them as it did to the Neolithic peoples, a point I will discuss later.

If building is valuable, why would the pillars be removed from their sockets, laid flat, and buried every decade or century for a millennia and a half?

That schedule may represent the frequency with which Adamites arrived. Perhaps every 10 years Eve would make a visit and redo the "picture book" T-pillars with the latest hygiene message. That could become a cargo cult ritual outlasting the Edenic Empire. Perhaps some hoped that if they replicated the deed, Eve would reappear. There are probably better answers waiting to be found but this one should not be discounted because many such "cargo-cult" rituals are derived from useful functions.[94]

Why do I think Eve would be teaching Cro-Magnons to talk?

Because in Gen 2:19 Adam is told to name the animals, which given the controlling power of naming, I take to mean that he was also to teach the Cro-Magnons to talk. In Gen 2:18, God decides Adam needs a helper. The adjacency of these verses suggests that teaching was Eve's first task. We saw earlier that Cain and Abel took over the first two farming tasks given to Adam; here we see Eve taking over the third, non-farming task given to Adam, "naming." Thus, we see how the first family was distributing its tasks, and how Adam indeed was obtaining help from them.

And now we also know the answer to the anthropologist's favorite question, "What is the world's oldest profession?"

Schoolmarm.

94. Worsley, *The Trumpet Shall Sound.*

5.3.4.2 Egyptian monuments: Sphinx, Pyramids

The advantage of discussing Göbekli Tepe first is that it is so recent a discovery that there is hardly any literature at all on it. By contrast, every conceivable theory already has been proposed for the Sphinx and other Egyptian monuments. Nevertheless, it is intriguing that the Sphinx seems older than the Pyramids (possibly as a reworked Lion statue) and that the three oldest pyramids are aligned with the stars in Orion's belt.[95] The astronomical significance of these monuments, which I first heard of from astronomer Virginia Trimble, along with their mysterious 200-ton megalithic block construction, is reminiscent of Stonehenge, and the T-pillars of Göbekli Tepe.[96] Unlike both Stonehenge and Göbekli Tepe, however, the largest Egyptian monuments are not placed in circles, so they do not seem to have the same function. However, 100 km west of Abu Simbel in the desert there is a circular stone "henge" (Fig 5.7).[97] And the starting era of their construction is possibly in the same ninth or tenth millennium BC, which may mean that they were planned during the Edenic Empire. In that case, even before the Flood, the Giza plateau location chosen was seventy-four meters above current sea level, a level even above the Holocene maximum sea level. In other words, the Empire seemingly knew of the possibility of a Flood and planned this construction to outlast even the worst possible disaster.

Figure 5.7: Stone circles 3000 miles apart in Orkneys and Egypt (Wiki, NASA)

What would this Empire use such megalithic monuments for?

Assuming that the monuments were intended to survive any potential Flood suggests that they were meant to be a library or a memorial. Various theories have suggested that hidden rooms within the Pyramids are

95. Bauval and Gilbert. *The Orion Mystery;* Hancock and Bauval. *The Message of the Sphinx.*

96. Trimble. "Astronomical Investigations" 183–187.

97. NASA. "Egyptian Stonehenge"; Keiretsu. "Ring of Brodgar."

storage rooms for manuscripts, and certainly the walls are both painted and inscribed with hieroglyphics. Many expeditions have been financed on the promise of finding another hidden room, perhaps even one containing the fabled Book of the Records. I think that all such searches for hidden rooms will prove fruitless, not because such rooms do not exist but because the messages they might contain have already been read and circulated. It is very probable that Moses read these ancient messages when he wrote Genesis, finding the names of the buried rivers of the Pishon and the Phrat (in Volume 2). Somebody had named them before the Flood and somewhere those names had been preserved. The fact that Moses, who wrote Genesis, was an Egyptian-educated prince, reflects a written history stored in Egypt.

If the purpose of these monuments is didactic, why would they feature astronomical alignments?

Perhaps they were also astronomical observatories for Noah's generation. But even more simply, it was aesthetically satisfying. Aesthetics gives evidence of design, design indicates purpose, and purpose holds a goal. These monuments had a goal that careful analysis should be able to extract. They were time capsules waiting for a generation that asked all the right questions. It seems likely that, should ancient manuscripts or inscriptions be recovered from chambers below the Sphinx or the Queen's Burial Chamber in the Great Pyramid, C-14 tests will date them to about the tenth millennium BC. They will be remnants of the Edenic Empire and will contain substantially the same information as Genesis 1–11.

5.3.4.3 *British Monuments: Stonehenge, Seahenge*

Stonehenge is but one of an entire class of "henges" that feature circular construction. Many of the henges have audio amplification properties, so that a speaker at one location can be heard better within the circle of stones.[98] Likewise, "Seahenge" off the coast of England was a wooden construction with similar acoustic reflection properties, built around 2200–2100 BC.[99] There could not be too many people who fit inside a henge, nor is it clear why a solid wall of stones would not have better acoustic properties, but in any event, acoustics are a noted property of these circular constructions. It is also worth noting that the standing stones in Stonehenge's inner circle are more massive than those in the outer circle; that is much the same way as the Göbekli Tepe T-stones are constructed. The bluestones in the middle were

98. Fazenda and Drumm. "Recreating the sound of Stonehenge"; Fazenda. "The Acoustics of Stonehenge" 32–37.

99. Watson. *Seahenge: An Archaeological Conundrum*.

apparently quarried some 320 kilometers (200 miles) distant and moved to the site. Some have claimed that this extra labor is due to their "lithophone" or ringing qualities when struck, not unlike the echoes in a cathedral.

So these far northern Mesolithic monuments have intermediate properties between Göbekli Tepe and the Sphinx. Like Göbekli, they seem to involve a small group of people who can stand inside the circle and listen to messages. Like the Sphinx, Stonehenge features monumental stones that are intended to advertise design and intention over many millennia. While the construction period of Göbekli falls during the Edenic Empire, the construction of the Sphinx arguably comes right afterward. But Stonehenge was constructed well after the Empire— even allowing for the 8275 BC C-14 dated post-holes that broke ground for the original construction.[100]

Therefore, I suggest that, as the Mesolithic Revolution traveled north, it also embodied aspects of a Mesolithic Retreat, a retreat from a more advanced people group. For the northward spread of speaking-schools and rituals surrounding them enabled both the survival of the Cro-Magnons and their principal resistance to the Neolithics, the descendants of Noah. The latter arrived with their superior epigenes, language, and technology, out-reproducing the hunter-gatherer Mesolithics. In that case, perhaps the monumental construction was the Mesolithic way of establishing permanence even on land that would soon be lost to Neolithic farming. That is, the twin Cro-Magnon projects of the Edenic Empire—schools and monuments—were combined into a single Mesolithic monument "cargo" culture that was under continuous encroachment from a more successful farming culture.

Similarly the Sioux Indians used the newly-introduced European horse to eke out a culture on the sliver of land between the advancing Europeans and the retreating hunter-gatherer Amerindians.[101] It was a dynamic equilibrium, moving inexorably toward European settlement and farming. But for a century or two in the Americas, or a millennium or two in Europe, this semi-nomadic lifestyle provided a way of life for the soon-to-be-expelled people group.

In this dynamic equilibrium, the Mesolithic Revolution and Retreat is at the same time ephemeral and essential for the next step in human revolutions. It is not that the epigenetic must always precede the genetic. These same Upper Paleolithic Cro-Magnons had covered the globe over the preceding 40 millennia, genetically replacing the preceding Neanderthals. Rather, every genetic revolution goes through a maturation process,

100. Lawson. *Chalkland: An Archaeology of Stonehenge and its Region.*

101. Hämäläinen. "The Rise and Fall of Plains Indian Horse Culture" 833–862.

where the next step after genetic replacement is epigenetic enhancement or adaption.

It was often thought that people groups spread mostly by conquest. But strangely, there is little sign of warfare in this clash of cultures, perhaps because it is expressly forbidden to Noah and his sons in Gen 9:2–6. So as Noah and his descendants spread the NR northward, they did not conquer but rather settled the European continent. The example of the wounded Neolithic, Ötzi the Iceman, is instructive because it is the first evidence to date of warfare. But the era was after the NR at 5000 BC and the victim was a Neolithic, killed by a Neolithic weapon.[102] We have no evidence of Neolithics killing Cro-Magnons or Mesolithics, and from the snail's pace of the NR northward, we can safely infer that they refrained from doing so. If so, understanding this transition is critical to understanding the rest of Genesis, and by extrapolation, the *midrash* letters of John the Evangelist, the beginning and the end. The Mesolithic Revolution was an Epigenetic Revolution, and we tease out its properties by comparing and contrasting it to the genetic revolution that came before and the cultural revolution that came after it.

5.3.5 Epigenetic Revolutions

5.3.5.1 Adaption is Epigenetic

We should not let the new terminology confuse us, as if we have never observed an epigenetic change before the twenty-first century. The biological terminology used in previous centuries is "adaption," such as the ability to move from Boston to Alabama and get used to the summer heat; or the ability to take a job at a Chilean telescope in the Atacama plateau and become acclimated to the altitude. Physiologically, the human body adapts to heat by increasing sweat production, reducing heat-generating "brown fat," and increasing the blood volume to handle the heat load.[103] Similarly, the body adapts to high altitude by producing more red blood cells through elevating the erythropoietin hormone, which is better known to the public from its use as an illegal sports "doping" drug.[104] Altitude sickness is the condition where the body cannot find a stable equilibrium and death is certain unless the sufferer can return to lower altitude. Less severe symptoms can sometimes be overcome by making a slower ascent to higher altitudes, allowing

102. Keller et al. "New insights into the Tyrolean Iceman's origin"

103. Anouk et al. "Cold acclimation" 3395–3403.

104. Berglund. "High-altitude training" 289–303.

the body to adjust gradually. For my argument, the significance of these environmentally driven physiological changes is that they can be inherited by the next generation. For example, it was almost always Colombians from the Andes who dominated the mountain stage of the Tour de France, so every cycling club has their Andean "mountain climbers" to provide the team support for their heralded "yellow shirt" cyclist.

Why is this adaption not a genetic change?

The genes remain the same before and after the environmental stress but they are expressed differently. It is as if the human body comes with a tool kit in the trunk. When the journey takes us into the mountains, it gets out the chains and straps them onto the wheels. The tool kit was always there, just not brought out until needed. And as the human genome project has shown, over 90 percent of the genetic material in humans is not currently "expressed" as proteins.

If epigenetics is not genetics, how can it be inherited by the next generation?

The fertilized egg cell carries more than just half the genes from its mother and father; it carries a large amount of cytoplasm, RNA, and proteins that tell the nucleus which genes need to be expressed. Thus the baby inherits many gene "switches" from the mother and, surprisingly, even more from the father, despite the much smaller volume of the sperm than the egg. This is epigenetic inheritance, and it is indistinguishable from inheritable adaption.

5.3.5.2 *Epigenetic is Evolution*

When Darwin saw the variations between finch beaks on each of the islands in the Galapagos chain, he was not seeing evolution of genes, he was seeing adaption.[105] When, in industrialized England, some peppered moths turn black and some white, we are not seeing evolution, we are seeing adaption.[106] When some islands have pygmy elephants and some islands have giant eagles, we are, once again, not seeing evolution but adaption.[107] One way that we know, is that, for example, the Galapagos finch beaks change their shape every ten years, as climate shifts affect the rainfall on the islands. Similarly, the peppered moths' proportions of dark and light pigments change according to the level of industrial pollution. When Darwin watched pigeon

105. Grant and Grant. "Evolution of Character Displacement in Darwins' Finches" 224–226.

106. Wells, *Icons of Evolution.*

107. Keogh et al. "Rapid and repeated origin of insular gigantism" 226–233.

breeders producing fantails with large showy tails, he was seeing adaption. Such flourishes vanish when pigeons are allowed to "go wild." Because much of the textbook literature has resolutely confused these two concepts, epigenetic changes are often called a type of evolution. While it is incapable of producing new species, it does produce a great deal of the variation that is often mistaken for speciation.

Applying this insight to Cro-Magnons, we can say that they adapted as they spread over the globe, producing much of the variation observed today among the races. Skin color is one of the more obvious adaptions, with extra melanin protecting tropical inhabitants from damaging UV radiation. Depleted melanin in northern inhabitants enhances the UV penetration and produces essential vitamin D. All these adaptions are reversible. And because they can be inherited, they are epigenetic.

None of this should be controversial but for the Academy. The academic consensus after World War II was that the Nazis were not dangerous for being materialist Darwinists (or else Communists would be equally sinister), but because they were racists. Therefore, it was believed, we can prevent another Holocaust simply by denying that race exists. This modernist attitude provoked G. K. Chesterton's comment,[108]

> " If it be true (as it certainly is) that a man can feel exquisite happiness in skinning a cat, then the religious philosopher can only draw one of two deductions. He must either deny the existence of God, as all atheists do; or he must deny the present union between God and man, as all Christians do. The new theologians seem to think it a highly rationalistic solution to deny the cat."

Much of Luigi Luca Cavalli-Sforza's promising work in the 1980's on the epigenetics of race was denied and suppressed for thirty years to defend that consensus position, e.g., by Richard Lewontin.[109] Fortunately, the genome mapping tools made available in the twenty-first century have fully vindicated Cavalli-Sforza, and we are once again seeing books published on the epigenetics of race, and the importance of environmental effects, e.g., Nicholas Wade.[110]

108. Chesterton, *Orthodoxy.*

109. Frost. "L.L. Cavalli-Sforza: A Bird in a Gilded Cage."

110. Wade. *A Troublesome Inheritance.*

5.3.5.3 *Evolution is Environment*

If adaptation is merely a re-expression, or fine-tuning of the genes, why do I make a distinction between epigenetic and genetic revolutions? Do they not both involve genes?

The difference between these two revolutions is profound. A genetic revolution is about information in the genes, whereas an epigenetic revolution is about information in the environment. When the environment drives the epigenetic expression of genes, we have a coupling, a flow of information from outside to inside. But as the organism responds to its environment, it also changes the environment to make it more livable. According to the Gaia theory of Margulis and Lovelock, global environmental change can result, such as the oxygen atmosphere created by cyanobacterial photosynthesis.[111] The Cro-Magnons who covered the globe may not have changed the atmosphere but they certainly changed their environment. The Plains Indians routinely burnt the prairie grass, a measure which destroyed the invasive trees and left a layer of fertilizing ash that helped next year's annuals to flourish. In turn, the vast grasslands became ideal habitats for the bison, who provided the sustenance for the Plains Indians, transforming their language, their religion, and their quality of life. Therefore before Columbus, the entire American Midwest was a managed beef-raising habitat created by man. In this way, information in the human mind was transferred to the ecosystem.[112]

Likewise, every epigenetic adaptation also reflects an environmental change, an information flow from inside to outside the organism, an ecological enrichment. Thus the epigenetic gene expression keeps changing along with the new environment until they are in equilibrium, an information-rich equilibrium. At that point, everything would appear to be in stasis. But that is precisely the point at which new organisms, new DNA that could not have survived in the past, can now rapidly spread through this information-rich ecosystem.

One example would be the European-style farming of the four-meter-thick black topsoil of the millenially burned Iowa prairie. The Plains Indians prepared it for the buffalo, but the Europeans used it more profitably for corn. Another example might be a burned over forest that is first colonized by grass, then by bushes, pines and finally climax oaks. As the forest canopy recovers, the carbon (information) content of the land increases.

111. Lovelock and Margulis. "Atmospheric homeostasis" 2–10.

112. Lentz. *Imperfect balance,* xviii–xix.

There is a constant flow of information with genetic revolutions rapidly expanding the internal information and epigenetic revolutions slowly expanding the external information. The two types of revolution are then in mutual cycle or ratchet, which increases the information content of the ecosystem as a whole. The increase is not a consequence of a law of natural selection, rather a law of mutual collaboration and inherent purposeful adaption. Notice that the information, though it ebbs and flows, has a net direction. It is always begun, both in adaption and in genetic invasion, from the inside, from the tools in the trunk, from the nucleus itself.

Where exactly did those tools in the car trunk come from?

There must be a purpose hiding in this cryptic DNA that suddenly finds a use in a future environment. For both revolutions are expressions of a design, of a plan that has a distinct goal.

5.3.5.4 Environment plus Epigenetic is Cultural

Therefore, if the goal is embedded in the genes, if it is cryptically hidden in the cell, we can begin to find the purpose of the first two chapters of Genesis, a purpose expressed in the genetic and epigenetic revolutions that produced the first talking, thinking, rationalizing modern civilization.

The Cro-Magnon creation in 50 kyBC was the first genetic step in an environment that was friendly to modern genes. This genetic revolution took place in the middle of the last Ice Age and spread across the globe with the help of lowered sea levels during the Last Glacial Maximum.

Then when the Earth warmed up in the Holocene, the land was now ripe for the next epigenetic revolution, one that would modify the world forever. Seemingly it began in the dried up bed of the Mediterranean, where oxygen and carbon dioxide levels were higher than at any previous time or any previous place in the Earth's history. The temperature was moderated by the European glaciation event known as the Younger Dryas, and an inexplicable epigenetic change produced Adam and the talking Cro-Magnons. This change spread over the whole world, first epigenetically by means of talking to babies, then (quasi)genetically by hybridizing with Adam's descendants. (Some epigenetics, such as allele distributions for height or intelligence, move together and behave as pseudo-genes. This is especially true for bottlenecks and "founders effects," hence "quasi-genetic.") These changes led to advances such as prairie management in North America, horse breeding in the Caucasus, and sheep and cereal farming in the Levant. Every advance led to further changes in the environment.

If we now live in a world that is fundamentally changed by *homo sapiens*, in a world where the atmosphere has been fertilized by coal-fired power plants, where the desert is watered by irrigation, and the mountain rivers tamed for hydroelectricity, then we have achieved everything that an epigenetic revolution should accomplish for its environment.

Should we now expect a more advanced genetic life form to rapidly exploit this new environment? Or is there something else designed into our genes, some other tool in the kit in the trunk, another revolution whose information was encoded from the first time a Cro-Magnon picked up a spear?

Yes, for indeed, there is another revolution hiding in Genesis 2 that I have already mentioned. It is the cultural revolution. If the epigenetic revolution is an equilibrium between environment and organism mediated by internal genetic information, then the cultural revolution is an equilibrium between environment and organism mediated by external information, that is, by civilization.

By analogy, many algae growing on rocks can convert water and carbon dioxide into carbohydrates with the help of sunshine and photosynthesis. But they are limited in their growth because they cannot acquire minerals such as magnesium needed for essential enzymes for growth. They also are stressed whenever the rain does not fall, because they have no roots or any other way to store water when their homey little puddle dries out. Fungi, on the other hand, have the hyphae to dissolve rocks and store water, but do not have the chlorophyll to make carbohydrates from sunlight. The two life forms find, however, that they can help each other. As the fungal hyphae interact with the algae chloroplasts, suddenly a new organism is born, a hybrid lichen. A lichen can be teased apart into the two separate organisms (or possibly 1 algae + 2 species of fungi) that make it up, but when recombined, it appears completely different from either fungi or algae alone.

Similarly, a culture that forms when humans communicate via telephones, internet, newspapers, and videos can be teased apart into components. But phone booths plus a populous nation look nothing like modern India's billion inhabitants connected by cell phones. Something unique happens when India goes to the voting booth and acts like a single, unified population, informed about each of the candidates. This cultural transformation began with messenger-boys and news kiosks, but now is more complete with cell phones and the internet. The environment has been incorporated into the individual through the internet, and a new organism has emerged, *homo globalensis*.

We now live in a world where matter-based needs like food, water, and shelter have been met but new non-matter needs like information, fungibility, and electricity have become more valuable. Richard Dawkins calls this a transition from biological genes to cultural memes, or from material to immaterial information bits, with a life of their own.[113] It is a cultural revolution, because it consists of many immaterial exchanges where the immaterial economy exceeds the material economy. When steel and concrete lost their pride of place to software and services, we become a world producing and consuming immaterial goods in a far larger economy than that of merely material goods. And that is why Genesis is telling us about three revolutions: genetic, epigenetic and cultural.

If this is true, then why is the world such a humanitarian disaster of bombed buildings, hungry children, and bulldozed ruins? Has civilization learned anything since Ötzi the Iceman was killed by an arrow 7000 years ago? Can there ever be a victory in the battle against human aggression?

Yes, but perhaps it takes an academic, disinterested approach to see the signal in the noise. Dylan Matthews put together a slide show of twenty-five charts to make the argument that the world is far better off today than it was in 1000, 1880, 1960, and 2000 AD (depending on the extent of the statistics).[114] He does not give a sociological reason for this improvement, but sociologist Rodney Stark argues that the West went through a cultural transformation that produced individual freedom and peace due to Christianity.[115]

What is this "weakness" that has conquered the world?[116]

The race does not go to the swift, nor the battle to the strong (Eccl 9:11), but to those who believe in the value of innocent children. Our current war is not, as Woodrow Wilson once said, "a War to end all Wars." Nor is it even as Winston Churchill said a little later, "the end of the beginning." Rather it is as if we are watching a violent tribe replaced by a peaceable society. We are watching the beginning of the end to Cain's epigenetic curse.

For despite the setbacks created by terrorism, computer viruses, electronic warfare, and cell phone bans, we are becoming a globally connected, cosmopolitan civilization. This is both a blessing and a curse. The Flood was necessary because the third revolution of culture was subverted by the second revolution, by Cain's violent epigenetics. It has been ~13,000 years since Cain's betrayal, but step-by-step, we are drawing closer to the completion of the three tasks assigned to Adam in Eden. The epigenetic changes are drawing near with the ability to subjugate the environment, to prolong life, to edit genomes, to desalinate water, populate deserts, urbanize tundra, and

113. Dawkins, *The Selfish Gene.*

114. Matthews. "26 charts and maps"; Kenny. *Getting Better.*

115. Stark. *The Rise of Christianity*; Stark. *The Victory of Reason.*

116. Huntington. *The Clash of Civilizations.*

even tame near-Earth orbit. Our final frontier is ourselves. Finally, we are once again facing the same temptations, the same *chatta'ath* crouching at the door, the same capabilities as Noah's generation.

Will we use our global reach to eliminate our enemies or to make new friends? Will we use the internet to subvert the young or to educate the poor? Will we exterminate 90 percent of the population to provide breathing space for the lucky 10 percent, or will we exterminate 90 percent of disease and provide help for the irreplaceable ailing 10 percent? How will we use our new-found power of genetic editing—to enable a few wealthy ones to live forever at the expense of most or to increase the population to the discomfort of the elite? Will we cherish life or embrace death? Will we spread peace or foment rebellion?

For the first command given to the Cro-Magnons is also the last command given to Jesus's disciples: "Go into all the Earth"(Matt 28:19).

PART 6

Some time later appalling earthquakes and floods occurred, and in the course of a single, terrible day and night the whole fighting-force of your city sank all at once beneath the earth, and the island of Atlantis likewise sank beneath the sea and vanished. That is why the sea there cannot now be navigated or explored; the mud which the island left behind as it settled lies a little below the surface and gets in the way.

PLATO'S *TIMAEUS* (TRANSL. ROBIN WATERFIELD)

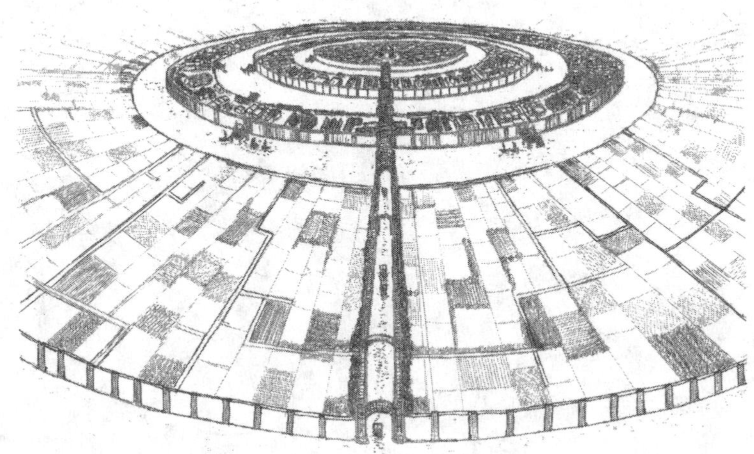

Figure 6.0: Map of Atlantis after Plato. (Courtesy Hannah Sadar)

CHAPTER 6

Interbiblia

THIS HAS BEEN THE first of a three volume series on Genesis 1–11, covering the first four chapters of Genesis. We began by learning how to use the new tools of linguistics and science to perform technical exegesis, which is a method of interpreting technical texts by incorporating artifactual/scientific information in the discovery of meaning. If classical exegesis uses a dictionary, technical exegesis uses a picture book. We used this tool to understand the time and scale of the Flood, moving backwards into Genesis 4, Genesis 2, and Genesis 1. We tacked down the days of Genesis into the time frame of science, finding that they were highly complementary accounts. Because science is mute and text is blind, science can only give us material details of the past, while Genesis can give us immaterial purposes. We discovered that Genesis 1 not only sketches out the Big Bang, but suggests that comets play a very important role in it. Significantly, the discussion of man's origins in Genesis 2 gives us a deep understanding of the tripartite nature of man, explaining how evil crept into the human lineage. Genetics provided the interpretive framework that explained the pernicious nature of this evil and the necessity of the cleansing Flood. This framework operates in parallel to the theological "redemptive history," filling in missing details and suggesting how all races on Earth are related to Eden.

The time frame we discovered suggests that between Noah and Abraham lies the Mesolithic, the era of Stonehenge and Göbekli Tepe. This prehistoric period is now seen to provide the important transition between Noah and Abraham. Therefore the Bible does not stand outside of science as some mythical pastiche that must be peeled off the harsh realities of modern sensibility. Nor does the Bible stand inside science, as some emanation of fevered scribes avoiding the work brigades of Pharaoh. Rather, the Bible stands alongside science, ready to give a hand, ready to take the lead. They are both describing the same actual story; they are both interpreting real historical events. The Bible explains the meaning, while science explains the means.

In the next two volumes, I take up Genesis 5–11, which covers the Flood, the subsequent Neolithic Revolution, and the spread of language. I look closely at the genetic evidence of people migrations, to investigate whether they are consistent with Genesis 10 and 11. The genetic information proves to be invaluable in sorting out the fate of civilization after the greatest calamity mankind ever faced. We take a look at the ways in which forgotten scribes preserved important information over millennia of conquest and disaster. We start with Gilgamesh, travel to Egypt, and end in Greece, where Plato records Egyptian wisdom as only a Greek can. Plato gives us a detailed account of Noah's generation in his description of Atlantis, corroborating the brief account mentioned in Genesis 5 and 6. We find the same themes of Genesis 1–4 repeated by Plato and one other thing: the location of the capital city of Atlantis.

Finally, we look at the Flood in great detail, comparing all the different accounts of this greatest event in the history of mankind. Echoes of the Flood are found as far away as the Amerindian and Inca myths, as well as in the Hindu Vedas. To our lasting astonishment, Norse sagas have the most detailed description of the Flood of any report, which may explain the eerie similarities with Tolkien's Middle Earth. With newly opened eyes, we re-examine Beowulf and find in it post-Flood details that tantalize our imagination. We discover that many historical details have been cleverly hidden in plain texts, which completely transforms our view of myth, wisdom literature and the priesthood. For in some peculiar way, this was accomplished by a purposeful misdirection of the LXX translation in 200 BC, awaiting a time when the true story might be heard.

The reason for this encryption now becomes clear, and our research rapidly draws to a conclusion.

Bibliography

Adler, Daniel S. et al. "Ahead of the Game: Middle and Upper Palaeolithic Hunting Behaviors in the Southern Caucasus". In: *Current Anthropology* 47.1 (Feb. 2006).

Ammerman, Albert and Luigi Luca Cavalli-Sforza. The Neolithic Transition and the Genetics of Populations in Europe. *Princeton U Press*, 1984.

Anouk, A. J., J. van der Lans, et al. "Cold Acclimation Recruits Human Brown Fat and Increases Nonshivering Thermogenesis". In: *J Clin Invest* 123.8 (2013) 3395–3403.

Anselm, St. *Proslogion*. 1100.

Arecchi, Alberto. Atlantide: un mondo scomparso un'ipotesi per ritrovarlo. *Mimesis*, 2001.

Arsuaga, J. L. et al. "Neandertal Roots: Cranial and Chronological Evidence from Sima de los Huesos." In: *Science* 344.6190 (2014) 1358–1363.

ASA, "About" In: *American Scientific Affiliation* (2015). url: network.asa3.org.

Aubrey, Jane "Lance Armstrong Confesses to EPO and Blood Doping" *Cycling News*, Jan 18, 2013. url: www.cyclingnews.com/news/lance-armstrong-confesses-to-epo-and-blood-doping/

Augustine, St. *Confessions*. Grand Rapids: Christian Classics Ethereal Library, 393.

——— *Tract. Ev. Jo.* Vol. 29.6. Grand Rapids: Christian Classics Ethereal Library, 390.

Austin, J. L. *How to do Things with Words: The William James Lectures delivered at Harvard University in 1955*. J. O. Urmson and Marina Sbiso, eds. Oxford: Clarendon, 1962.

Ayala, Francisco J. et al. "Molecular Genetics of Speciation and Human Origins". In: *PNAS* 91 (July 19, 1994) 6787. url: www.ncbi.nlm.nih.gov/pmc/articles.

Bar-Yosef, O. "The Natufian Culture in the Levant, Threshold to the Origins of Agriculture". In: *Evol. Anthropology: Issues, News and Reviews* 6.5 (1998) 159–177. url: www.columbia.edu/itc/anthropology/v1007/baryo.pdf.

Bar-Yosef, O. and F. Valla. "The Natufian Culture and the Origin of the Neolithic in the Levant". In: *Current Anthropology* 31.4 (1990).

Barney, James. *The Genesis Key*. New York: Harper, 2011.

Barth, Karl. *Church Dogmatics III/1*. Edinburgh: T&T Clark, 1958.

Batten, Don. "What is the gap theory?" In: *Christian Ministries International* (2000). url: www.christiananswers.net/q-aig/aig-c003.html.

Bauval, Robert and Adrian Gilbert. *The Orion Mystery: Unlocking the Secrets of the Pyramids*. Broadway, 1995.

Bell, Chris. "Epigenetics: How to Alter your Genes". In: *The Telegraph* (Oct. 16, 2013). url: www.telegraph.co.uk/science/10369861/Epigenetics-How-to-alter-your-genes .html.

Bell, Elizabeth A. et al. "Potentially Biogenic Carbon Preserved in a 4.1 Billion-year-old Zircon". In: *Proc. Nat. Acad. Sci.* (Oct. 2015).

Benetatos, Constantin. "Atlantis History". In: *atlantishistory* (2007). url: web. archive. org/web/20071206010941/"http ://www.atlantishistory.com/".

Benzmüller, Christoph and Bruno Woltzenlogel-Paleo. "Formalization, Mechanization and Automation of Gödel's Proof of God's Existence". In: *arXiv* 1308.4526 (2013).

Berg, Richard and David Stork. *The Physics of Sound 3rd ed.* Addison-Wesley, 2004.

Berglund, B. "High-altitude Training. Aspects of Haematological Adaptation". In: *Sports Med.* 14.5 (Nov. 1992) 289–303. url: www.ncbi.nlm.nih.gov/pubmed/143939.

Best-Commentaries. In: *bestcommentaries* (2015). url: www.bestcommentaries. com.

Bocquet-Appel, J.-P. and A. Degioanni. "Neanderthal Demographic Estimates". In: *Current Anthropology* 54.Supp. 8 (Dec. 2013). url: www.jstor.org/ stable/10.1086/67372.

Boley, A. C., A. P. Granados Contreras, and B. Gladman. "The In Situ Formation of Giant Planets at Short Orbital Periods". In: *ArXiv* (2015).

Bonhoeffer, Dietrich. *Gemeinsames Leben*. München: Chr. Kaiser, 1939.

———. "*Sanctorum Communio: eine Dogmatische Untersuchung zur Soziologie der Kirche*". PhD thesis. 1930.

Bork, Robert. *A Time to Speak.* Intercollegiate Studies Institute, 2008.

Brandenberger, Robert H. "Introduction to Early Universe Cosmology". In: *ArXiv* (2011).

Bretz, J. Harlen. "The Channeled Scabland of the Columbia Plateau". In: *J. of Geology* 31 (1923) 617–649.

Broecker, W. S. et al. "Putting the Younger Dryas Cold Event into Context". In: *Quaternary Science Rev* 29 (2010) 1078–1081. url: www.realclimate.org/index. php/archives/2010/07/revisiting-the-younger-dryas.

Brown, Francis, Samuel Driver, and Charles Briggs. *A Hebrew and English Lexicon of the Old Testament.* Oxford: Clarendon,1906.

Buck, Pearl S. *The Good Earth.* John Day, 1931.

Calder, Todd. "The Concept of Evil". In: The *Stanford Encyclopedia of Philosophy* (Fall 2015 Edition) (2015). Edward N. Zalta, ed. url: plato.stanford.edu/archives/ fall2015/entries/concept-evil/.

Callaway, Ewen. "Studies Slow the Human DNA Clock". In: *Nature* 489.7416 (Sept. 2012) 343–344. url: www.nature.com/news/studies-slow-the-human-dna-clock-1.11431.

Calvin, John. *Commentary on Genesis.* Vol. 1. 1554. url: www.ccel.org/ccel/calvin/ calcom01.viii.i.htm.

Campbell, Joseph. *The Hero with a Thousand Faces.* New York: Pantheon, 1949.

Caramelli, David et al. "A 28,000 Years Old Cro-Magnon mtDNA Sequence Differs from All Potentially Contaminating Modern Sequences". In: *PloS ONE* 3.7 (July 2008), e2700.

Carey, Nessa. *The Epigenetics Revolution: How Modern Biology Is Rewriting Our Understanding of Genetics, Disease, and Inheritance.* Columbia U. Press, 2013.

Carroll, Lewis. *Through the Looking Glass, and What Alice Found There.* Macmillan, 1871.

Carus, Titus Lucretius. *De Rerum Natura.* 50BC.

Cassuto, Umberto. *Commentary on the Book of Genesis,* Translated by Israel Abrahams. Jerusalem: Magnes, 1961.

Cathcart, Richard B. "Gibraltar Strait Dam Macroprojects". In: *Encyclopedia of Science* (2015). url: www.daviddarling.info/encyclopedia/G/Gibraltar_Strait_Dam_Macro projects_Cathcart.html.

Cavalli-Sforza, Luigi Lucas and W. F. Bodmer. *The Genetics of Human Populations.* San Francisco: W. H. Freeman, 1971.

Chapelle, Albert de la. "Analytic Review: Nature and Origin of Males with XX Sex Chromosomes". In: *Am. J. Hum. Genet.* 24.1 (1972), 71–105.

Chesterton, Gilbert K. *Ballad of the White Horse.* London: Methuen & Co., 1911.

———. *Orthodoxy.* New York: Dodd, Mead & Co., 1908.

Childress, David H. *Lost Cities of Atlantis, Ancient Europe & the Mediterranean.* Adventures Unlimited, 1996.

Chisolm, Hugh. "Johnstown Flood". In: *Encylopedia Brittanica*: Cambridge U. Press, p. 475, 1911. url: britannica.com/event/Johnstown-flood.

Cita, Maria Bianca. "The Messinian Salinity Crisis in the Mediterranean: A Review". In: *AGU Geodynamics.* 7th ser. (1972), pp. 113–140. url: agu.org/books/gd/v007/ GD007p0113/GD007p0113.pdf.

Collins, C. John. *Did Adam and Eve really exist?* Wheaton: Crossway, 2011.

———. "Discourse Analysis and the Interpretation of Gen 2:4–7". In: *WTJ* 61 (1999), pp. 269–276.

Collins, Francis et al. "The Human Genome Project: Lessons from Large-Scale Biology". In: *Science* 300.5617 (Apr. 11, 2003) 286–290. url: www.sciencemag.org/ content/300/5617/286.abstract.

CRISPR. "CRISPR Editing of Human Embryos Approved in the UK". In: *GEN* (Feb. 1, 2016). url: www.genengnews.com/gen-news-highlights/crispr-editing-of-human-embryos-approved-in-the-u-k/81252308/.

Cui, Yanou. "A Review of WIMP baryogenesis Mechanism". In: *ArXiv* (Oct. 2015).

Curry, Andrew. "Göbekli Tepe: the World's First Temple?" In: *Smithsonian Magazine* (Nov. 2008). url: www.smithsonianmag.com/history/Göbekli-tepe-the-worlds-first-temple-83613665.

Danninger, Matthias and Carsten Rott. "Solar WIMPs Unravelled: Experiments, Astrophysical Uncertainties, and Interactive Tools". In: *Physics of the Dark Universe* (Dec. 2014).

Darwin, Charles. *On the Origin of Species by Means of Natural Selection.* London: John Murray, 1859.

———. *The Descent of Man, and Selection in Relation to Sex.* John Murray, 1871.

Davis, Tamara M. "Cosmological Constraints on Dark Energy". In: *Gen. Rel. and Gravitation* 46 (June 2014) p.1731.

Dawkins, Richard. *The Selfish Gene.* Oxford U. Press, 1976.

Dekalb. "Dekalb hybrids". In: *aganytime.com* (2015). url: www.dekalb.ca/eastern/en/ corn.

deSalvo, John. "Stonehenge and the Great Pyramid". In: *Great Pyramid of Giza Research Association* (2013). url: www.gizapyramid.com/stonehenge.htm.

Diaz-Montexano, Georgeos. *ATLÁNTIDA Historia y Ciencia: Las fuentes primarias greco-latinas, cartaginesas, tartésicas, árabes y egipcias de la historia de la civilización* Vol 8. CreateSpace Independent, 2015.

Dimond, P. F. "What Junk DNA? It's an Operating System". In: *Genetic Engineering & Biotechnology News* (Aug. 8, 2013). url: www.genengnews.com/insight-and-intelligence/what-junk-dna-it-s-an-operating-system.

Dumont, H. J. "The Nile: Origin, Environments, Limnology and Human Use". In: *Monographiae Biologicae*. 89. Berlin: Springer, 2009.

Einstein, Albert. ""Die Feldgleichungen der Gravitation"". In: *Sitzungsberichte der Preussischen Akademie der Wissenschaften zu Berlin* (1915) 844–847.

———. "On the Electrodynamics of Moving Bodies". In: *The Principle of Relativity*. Translated by George Barker Jeffery and Wilfrid Perrett. London: Methuen and Company, Ltd., 1923.

———. "Science and Religion". In: *Science, Philosophy and Religion: a Symposium*. New York: Conference on Science, Philosophy and Religion in Their Relation to the Democratic Way of Life, Inc, 1941.

———. "Zur Elektrodynamik bewegter Körper". In: *Annalen der Physik* 17.10 (1905), 891–921.

Ellul, Joseph S. *Malta's Prediluvian Culture at the Stone Age Temples*. Malta: Joseph Ellul, 1988.

ENCODE-Consortium. "ENCODE". In: *Nature* 489 (Sept. 6, 2012). url: www. genome. gov/1100694.

Encyclopedia-Britannica. "Wellhausen". In: *Encyclopedia Brittanica*. 2015. url: www. britannica.com/EBchecked/topic/639379/Julius-Wellhausen.

Epigenetics-Society. "What is it? A Simplified Description of DNA Methylation". In: *es.landesbioscience.com* (2015).

Etkind, Alexander. "Beyond Eugenics: The Forgotten Scandal of Hybridizing Humans and Apes". In: *Studies in History and Philosophy of Biological and Biomedical Sciences* 39.2 (June 2008) 205–210.

Evans, Donald D. *The Logic of Self Involvement. A Philosophical Study of Everyday Language with Special Reference to the Christian Use of Language about God as Creator*. London: SCM, 1963.

Fazenda, B. "The Acoustics of Stonehenge". In: *Acoustics Bulletin* 38.1 (Jan. 2013), pp. 32–37.

Fazenda, B. and I. Drumm. "Recreating the Sound of Stonehenge". In: *The Acoustics of Ancient Theatres Conf. Patras* (Sept. 2011).

Finkel, Irving. *The Ark Before Noah: Decoding the Story of the Flood*. Nan A. Talese, 2014.

Firestone, R. B. et al. "Evidence for an Extraterrestrial Impact 12,900 Years Ago that Contributed to the Megafaunal Extinctions and the Younger Dryas Cooling". In: *PNAS* 104 (2007) 16016–16021.

Fish, Stanley. *Is There a Text in This Class? The Authority of Interpretive Communities*. Harvard U. Press, 1982.

Flynn, James. "IQ Gains over Time: Toward Finding the Causes". In: *The Rising Curve: Long-Term Gains in IQ and Related Measures*. Ed. by Ulric Neisser. Washington DC: American Psychological Association, (1998) 25–66.

Foundation, Biologos. "BioLogos". In: *BioLogos Org* (2016). url: www.biologos. org/about-us/our-team.

Frazer, James. *The Golden Bough*. London: Macmillan, 1890.

Friedman, William E. "The meaning of Darwin's "Abominable Mystery"". In: *Am. J. Botany* 96.1 (2009) 1–18.

Frost, Peter. "L.L. Cavalli-Sforza: A Bird in a Gilded Cage". In: *openpsych* (2014). url: openpsych.net/OBG/wp-content/uploads/2014/03/L.L.-Cavalli-Sforza.-A-bird-in-a-gilded-cage-final-version.pdf.

Galilei, Galileo. *Dialogue Concerning the Two Chief World Systems* Translated by Stillman Drake. 1632.

Gall, Alexander. "Atlantropa: A Technological Vision of a United Europe". In: *Networking Europe: Transnational Infrastructures and the Shaping of Europe, 1850–2000*. Erik van der Vleutena and Arne Kaijser, eds. Sagamore Beach: Science History, (2006) 99–128.

Gauger, Ann. *Science and Human Origins*. Seattle: Discovery Institute, 2012.

Geist, Valerius. "The Neanderthal Paradigm". In: *cogweb* (2000). url: cogweb.ucla.edu/ep/NeanderthalParadigm.html.

George, Andrew. *The Epic of Gilgamesh: The Babylonian Epic Poem and Other Texts in Akkadian and Sumerian*. Penguin, 2002.

Gesenius, Wilhelm. *Hebräische Grammatik* (1813) Translated by Arthur Cowley. Oxford: Oxford U. Press, 1910.

Gillespie, John H. *Population Genetics: A Concise Guide*. JHU Press, 2004.

Glass, J. B., F. Wolfe-Simon, and A. D. Anbar. "Coevolution of Metal Availability and Nitrogen Assimilation in Cyanobacteria and Algae". In: *Geobiology* 7.2 (Mar. 2009) 100–123.

Gledhill, R. "Catholic Church No Longer Swears by the Truth of the Bible". In: *The Times* (Oct. 5, 2005).

Glertz, Seth H. and Jacob Feldman. "Economic Costs of Policy Uncertainty". In: *Mercatus Center* (Nov. 27, 2012). url: mercatus.org/publication/economic-costs-tax-policy-uncertainty-implications-fundamental-tax-reform.

Goldman, David P. "The God of the Mathematicians: The Religious Beliefs that Guided Kurt Gödel's Revolutionary Ideas". In: *First Things* (Aug. 2010). url: www.firstthings.com/article/2010/08/the-god-of-the-mathematicians.

Gomes, R. et al. "Origin of the Cataclysmic Late Heavy Bombardment Period of the Terrestrial Planets". In: *Nature* 435 (May 2005) 466–469.

Gonzalez, Guillermo and Jay Richards. *The Privileged Planet: How our Place in the Cosmos is Designed for Discovery*. Washington, D.C.: Regnery, 2004.

Gråe Jørgensen, U. et al. "The Earth-Moon System During the Late Heavy Bombardment Period–Geochemical Support for Impacts Dominated by Comets". In: *Icarus* 204 (Dec. 2009) 368–380.

Graham, Loren and Jean-Michel Kantor. *Naming Infinity: A True Story of Religious Mysticism and Mathematical Creativity*. Belknap, 2009.

Grant, P. and R. Grant. "Evolution of Character Displacement in Darwins' Finches". In: *Science* 313 (2006) 224–226.

Green, R. E. et al. "A Complete Neandertal Mitochondrial Genome Sequence Determined by High-throughput Sequencing". In: *Cell* 134 (2008) 416–426.

———. "A Draft Sequence of the Neandertal Genome". In: *Science* 328 (2010) 710–722. url: www.eva.mpg.de/neandertal/press/presskit- neandertal/pdf/Science_Green.pdf.

Haak, Wolfgang et al. "Ancient DNA from the First European Farmers in 7500-Year-Old Neolithic Sites". In: *Science* 310.5750 (2005) 1016–1018.

Ham, Ken. *The New Answers Book Vol. 2: Over 30 Questions on Evolution/Creation and the Bible*. Master, 2008.

Ham, Ken et al. *The Global Flood: A Biblical and Scientific Look at the Catastrophe that Changed the Earth*. 2009.

Hämäläinen, Pekka. "The Rise and Fall of Plains Indian Horse Culture". In: *J. Am. History* 90 (Dec. 2003) 833–862.

Hancock, Graham. *Underworld—The Mysterious Origins of Civilization*. Three Rivers, 2003.

Hancock, Graham and Robert Bauval. *The Message of the Sphinx*. Broadway, 1997.

Harris, R. L., G. L. Archer Jr., and B. K. Waltke. *Theological Wordbook of the Old Testament*. Moody, 2003.

Hawking, S. W. *A Brief History of Time. From the Big Bang to Black Holes*. New York: Bantam, 1988.

Hawking, Stephen and Leonard Mlodinow. *The Grand Design*. New York: Bantam, 2012.

Heller, M. "Lemaître, Big Bang and the Quantum Universe". In: *Pachart History of Astronomy*. 10. Tucson: Pachart Publishing House, 1996.

Hemfelt, Robert, Frank Minirth, and Paul Meier. *Love is a Choice*. Nashville: Thomas Nelson, 1989.

Henry, Matthew. *Commentary on the Whole Bible*. Grand Rapids: Christian Classics Ethereal Library, 1706.

Herriot, James. *All Creatures Great and Small*. New York: Bantam, 1972.

Hill, Carol. "The Noachian Flood: Universal or Local?" In: *JASA*. 54.3 (2002) 170–183.

Hirsch, Eric David. *Validity in Interpretation*. Yale U. Press, 1967.

Hodge, Charles. *Systematic Theology*. Grand Rapids: Christian Classics Ethereal Library, 1871.

Holland, Heinrich D. "The Oxygenation of the Atmosphere and Oceans". In: *Phil. Trans. Soc. B* 361 (May 2006) 903–915.

Hoover, Richard B. "Fossils of Cyanobacteria in CI1 Carbonaceous Meteorites". In: *J. of Cosmology* 13.3 (2011).

———. "Private communication". 2015.

Hoth, Iva. *The Picture Bible*. Wheaton: David C. Cook, 1973.

Hoy, David Couzens. *The Critical Circle: Literature, History and Philosophical Hermeneutics*. U. California Press, 1982.

Huebner, W. F., ed. *Physics and Chemistry of Comets*. New York: Springer Verlag, 1990.

Huntington, Samuel P. *The Clash of Civilizations: and the Remaking of the World Order*. New York: Simon & Schuster, 1996.

Iliff, David. "Greylag Goose". In: *Wikipedia Commons* (2006). url: commons. wikimedia. org/w/index.php?curid=1385555.

Jablonski, N. "The Naked Truth: Why Humans Have No Fur". In: *Sci. Am.* 302 (2010) 42–49. url: www.scientificamerican.com/article/the-naked-truth-why-humans-have-no-fur.

Jastrow, R. *God and the Astronomers*. New York: Norton, 1978.

Jewish-Encyclopedia. "Hapax Legomena". In: *Jewish Encyclopedia* (1906). url:jewishencyclopedia.com/articles/7236-hapax-legomena.

———. "Middot: The Seven, of Hillel". In: *Jewish Encyclopedia* (1906). url: jewishencyclopedia.com/articles/10801-middot-the-seven-of-hillel.

Johnson, J. S. and E. L. Newport. "Critical Period Effects in Second Language Learning: The Influence of Maturational State on the Acquisition of English as a Second

Language". In: *Cogn. Psychol.* 21.1 (Jan. 1989) 60–99. url: www.ncbi.nlm.nih.gov/pubmed/292053.

Johnson, R. G. "Climate Control Requires a Dam at the Strait of Gibraltar". In: *EOS, Trans. AGU* 78.277 (July 8, 1997).

Johnson, Robert. *Secrets of the Ice Ages: The Role of the Mediterranean Sea in Climate Change*. Glenjay, 2002.

Jurvetson, Steve. "Richard Dawkins". In: *Wikipedia Commons* (2006). url: commons.wikimedia.org/w/index.php?curid=2239932.

Keiretsu, Steve. "Ring of Brodgar". In: *Wikipedia Commons* (2014). url: commons.wikimedia.org/w/index.php?curid=35375808.

Keller, A. et al. "New Insights into the Tyrolean Iceman's Origin and Phenotype as Inferred by Whole-genome Sequencing". In: *Nature Communications* 3.698 (2012).

Kenny, Charles. *Getting Better: Why Global Development Is Succeeding–And How We Can Improve the World Even More.* New York: Basic, 2011.

Keogh, J. S., I.A. Scott, and C. Hayes. "Rapid and Repeated Origin of Insular Gigantism and Dwarfism in Australian Tiger Snakes". In: *Evolution* 59.1 (Jan. 2005) 226–233. url: www.ncbi.nlm.nih.gov/pubmed/1579224.

Kepler, S. O., Detlev Koester, and Gustavo Ourique. "A White Dwarf with an Oxygen Atmosphere". In: *Science* 352.6281 (2016) 67–69.

Kermode, Frank. *The Genesis of Secrecy.* Harvard: Harvard U. Press, 1980.

Kidner, Derek. *Genesis: An Introduction and Commentary.* Northwells: InterVarsity, 1967.

Kirk, Donald E. *Optimal Control Theory: An Introduction.* Dover, Electrical Engineering, 2004.

Kline, Meredith G. *Kingdom Prologue: Genesis Foundations for a Covenantal Worldview.* Eugene: Wipf & Stock, 2006.

Kobashi, T., J. P. Severinghaus, and J.-M. Barnola. "4±1.5°C Abrupt Warming 11,270 yr Ago Identified from Trapped Air in Greenland Ice". In: *EPSL* 268 (2008), pp. 397–407.

Koehler, L. and W. Baumgartner. *Hebrew and Aramaic Lexicon of the Old Testament.* Brill, 2002.

Koestler, Arthur. *The Sleepwalkers: A History of Man's Changing Vision of the Universe.* London: Hutchinson, 1959.

Laidlaw, John. *The Bible Doctrine of Man.* Edinburgh: T&T Clark, 1879. url: books.google.com/books?id=Tc4UAAAAYAAJ.

Lander, Eric et al. "Initial Sequencing and Analysis of the Human Genome". In: *Nature* 409 (Feb. 15, 2001) 860–921. url: www.nature.com/nature/journal/v409/n6822/full/409860a0.html.

Larson, G. et al. "Ancient DNA, Pig Domestication, and the Spread of the Neolithic into Europe". In: *PNAS* 104.39 (Sept. 2007) 15276–15281.

Laskar, J., F. Joutel, and P. Robutel. "Stabilization of the Earth's Obliquity by the Moon". In: *Nature* 361.6413 (Feb. 1993) 615–617.

Lawrence, Jerome and Robert E. Lee. *Inherit the Wind.* Stanley Kramer Productions, 1960.

Lawson, Andrew. *Chalkland: An Archaeology of Stonehenge and its Region.* Hobnob, 2007.

Lazaridis, Ioannis et al. "Ancient Human Genomes Suggest Three Ancestral Populations for Present-day Europeans". In: *Nature* 513 (Sept. 18, 2014) 409– 413. url: www. nature.com/nature/journal/v513/n7518/full/nature13673.html.

Leadbetter, Ron. "Cronus". In: *Encyclopedia Mythica* (Feb. 2004). url: www. pantheon. org/articles/c/cronus.html.

Lennox, J. "Aristotle's Biology". In: *Stanford Encyclopedia of Philosophy* (2011). url: plato.stanford.edu/entries/aristotle-biology.

Lentz, David L. ed. *Imperfect Balance: Landscape Transformations in the Precolumbian Americas.* New York: Columbia U. Press (2000) xviii–xix.

Leslie, Alan M. "The Perception of Causality in Infants". In: *Perception* 11 (1982) 173–186.

Lewis, Charlton T. and Charles Short. *A Latin Dictionary.* Oxford U. Press, 1879.

Lewis, Clive Staples. *The Horse and His Boy.* Geoffrey Bles, 1954.

Liang, Puping et al. "CRISPR/Cas9-mediated Gene Editing in Human Tripronuclear Zygotes". In: *Protein & Cell* 6.5 (May 2015), pp. 363–372.

Liddell, Henry George, Robert Scott, and Henry Stuart Jones. *A Greek-English Lexicon.* Oxford U. Press, 1843.

Lossky, Vladimir. *The Image and Likeness of God.* Crestwood: St Vladimir's, 1985.

Lovelock, J.E. and L. Margulis. "Atmospheric Homeostasis by and for the Biosphere: The Gaia hypothesis". In: *Tellus. Series A* 26.1–2 (1974) 2–10.

Lowery, Kirk. "Review of 'Emdros: The Database Engine for Analyzed or Annotated Text'". In: *Language Documentation & Conservation* 2.2 (Dec. 2008) 332–339. url: hdl.handle.net/10125/4346.

MacDonald, George. *The Light Princess.* London: Hurst & Blackett, 1864.

Madsen, Ole. "The Gap Theory Page: Who did Believe?" In: *Creationdays* (2006). url: www.creationdays.dk/myown/1.php.

MagicEye. In: *Magic Eye.com* (2015). url: www.magiceye.com.

Magno, Albino Pereira. *Mitilogia.* Lisboa: J. Rodrigues, 1900.

Mann, Charles C. "The Birth of Religion". In: *National Geographic Magazine* (2011). url: ngm.nationalgeographic.com/print/2011/06/Göbekli-tepe/mann-text.

Margvelashvili, A. et al. "Tooth Wear and Dentoalveolar Remodeling are Key Factors of Morphological Variation in the Dmanisi Mandibles". In: *PNAS* 110.43 (2013) 17278–17283. url: www. theguardian.com/science/2013/oct/17/skull-homo-erectus-human-evolution.

Marx, Karl and Freidrich Engels. *Ludwig Feuerbach und der Ausgang der klassisches deutschen Philosophie.* Stuttgart: J. H. W. Dietz, 1888.

Matthews, Dylan. "26 Charts and Maps that Show the World is Getting Much, Much Better". In: *Vox* 1.4 (Mar. 20, 2015). url: www.vox.com/2014/11/24/7272929/charts-thankful.

McLuhan, Marshall. *Understanding Media: The Extensions of Man.* New York: Mentor, 1964.

Mendel, Johann Gregor. "Versuche über Pflanzenhybriden". In: *Verhandlungen des naturforschenden Vereines in Brünn* 4 (1866). English translation, see: Druery, C.T.; Bateson, William (1901). "Experiments in Plant Hybridization". *J. Royal Horticultural Society* 26: 1–32, 3–47.

Meyer, Stephen C. *Darwin's Doubt: The Explosive Origin of Animal Life and the Case for Intelligent Design.* New York: HarperCollins, 2013.

Miller, Stanley L. "Production of Amino Acids Under Possible Primitive Earth Conditions". In: *Science* 117.3046 (May 1953) 528–529.

Milton, John. *Paradise Lost.* London: Samuel Simmons, 1667.

Monod, Jacques. "Jacques Monod–Nobel Lecture: From Enzymatic Adaption to Allosteric Transitions". In: *Nobel Lectures, Physiology or Medicine 1963– 1970.* Amsterdam: Elsevier, 1972. url: www.nobelprize.org/nobel_prizes/medicine/laureates/1965/index.html.

Morton, Glenn R. *Foundation, Fall and Flood: A Harmonization of Genesis and Science.* Dallas: DMD, 1994.

Munro, N. D. "Small Game, the Younger Dryas, and the Transition to Agriculture in the Southern Levant". In: *Meitteilungen der Gesellschaft fur Urgeschichte* 12 (2003), pp. 47–71.

Nandy, Kousik. "Egyptian Vulture". In: *Wikipedia Commons* (2005). url: commons.wikimedia.org/w/index.php?curid=559134.

NASA. "Egyptian Stonehenge". In: NASA Sun Earth Day (2005). url: sunearthday. nasa.gov/2005/locations/egypt_stone.htm.

National-Geographic. "Africa's Skeleton Coast". In: *National Geographic* 181.1 (1992) 54–85.

Neusner, Jacob. *Genesis Rabbah: The Judaic Commentary to the Book of Genesis.* Brown U. Press, 1985.

Newton, Isaac. *Opticks, or, a Treatise of the Reflections, Refractions, Inflections, and Colours of Light.* London: William Innys, 1730.

Nietzsche, Friedrich Wilhelm. "Also sprach Zarathustra: Ein Buch fur Alle und Keinen". In: *Nietzsches's Werke, Erste Abtheilung, Band VI.* Leipzig: C.G. Naumann, 1895.

NOAA. "GISP". In: *NCDC.NOAA.gov* (2015). url: www.ncdc.noaa.gov/paleo/icecore/greenland/summit/document/gispinfo.htm.

Noonan, James P. et al. "Sequencing and Analysis of Neanderthal Genomic DNA". In: *Science* 314.5802 (Nov. 17, 2006) 1113–1118.

Nutman, Allen P. et al. "Rapid Emergence of Life Shown by Discovery of 3,700-million-year-old Microbial Structures". In: *Nature* 537 (Sept. 22, 2016) 535– 538.

O'Connell, Tony. "Atlantipedia". In: *Atlantipedia* (2016). url: www.atlantipedia. com.

O'Connor, Jim E. and John E. Costa. *The World's Largest Floods, Past and Present: Their Causes and Magnitudes, Circular 1254.* Wash. DC: US Dept. of Interior, US Geological Survey, 2004.

Pagel, M. et al. "Ultraconserved Words Point to Deep Language Ancestry Across Eurasia". In: *PNAS* 110.21 (2013) 8471–8476. url: www.pnas.org/content/110/21/847.

Palmer, Michael. "Sheep in Long Grass". In: *Wikipedia Commons* (2014). url: commons.wikimedia.org/w/index.php?curid=37118697.

Pascal, Blaise. *Pensee 28.* 1662.

Pembrey, M. E. et al. "Sex-specific, Male-line Transgenerational Responses in Humans". In: *European J. Human Genetics* 14 (2006),159–166. url: www.nature.com/ejhg/journal/v14/n2/full/5201538a.html.

Perry, John. "Courtly Combatant". In: *World Magazine* (Dec. 2013). url: www.worldmag.com/issue/2003/12/13/.

Petaev, M. et al. "Large Pt Anomaly in the Greenland Ice Core Points to a Cataclysm at the Onset of Younger Dryas". In: *PNAS* 110.32 (2013) 12917– 12920.

Petersen, Melody. "California Stem Cell Agency May Fund Tests to Edit Genes in Human Embryos". In: *LA Times* (Feb. 12, 2016). url: www.latimes.com/business/la-fi-human-gene-editing-20160212-story.html.

Petersen, Ulrik. "Emdros — a Text Database Engine for Analyzed or Annotated Text". In: *COLING Geneva 2004: 20th International Conference on Computational Linguistics, Vol. II.* Genève: Association for Computational Linguistics. (2004) 1190–1193. url: emdros.org/petersen- emdros- COLING-2004.pdf.

Petley, David. "Landslide Information: The Vajont Landslide. 2001". In: *landman.net* (2008). url: landman.net/vajont/vajont.html.

Plato. *Timaeus-Critias.* (350BC) Translated by B. Jowett, 1871. url:www.gutenberg.org/ebooks/1571.

———. *Timaeus and Critias.* Translated by Robin Waterfield. Oxford World's Classics, 2008.

Pliny, Elder. *Historia Naturalis* (77) Translated by John Bostock. London: Taylor and Francis 1855. url: www.perseus.tufts.edu/hopper/text ? doc = Perseus:text:1999.02.0137.

Pollan, Michael. "The Intelligent Plant". In: *NewYorker* (Dec. 2013). url: www.newyorker.com/magazine/2013/12/23/the-intelligent-plant.

Pope Pius XII. "The Proofs for the Existence of God in the Light of Modern Natural Science". In: *Papal Encycl.* (Nov. 22, 1951). www.papalencyclicals.net/Pius12/P12EXIST.HTM.

Powell, A. "Harvard Researchers Push Human Cereal Use Back 10,000 Years". In: *Harvard Gazette* (July 22, 2004). url: news.harvard.edu/gazette/2004/07.22/07-grain.html.

Poythress, Vern. *Christian Interpretations of Genesis 1.* Phillipsburg: P&R, 2013. url: frame-poythress.org/ebooks/.

———. *Did Adam Exist?* Phillipsburg: P&R, 2014. url: frame- poythress.org/ebooks/.

———. *In the beginning Was the Word.* Wheaton: Crossway, 2000. url: frame-poythress.org/ebooks/.

———. *Redeeming Science: a God centered approach.* Wheaton: Crossway, 2006. url: frame-poythress.org/ebooks/.

———. *Science and Hermeneutics.* Grand Rapids: Zondervan, 1988. url: frame-poythress.org/ebooks/science-and-hermeneutics/.

Praetorius, S. and A. C. Mix. "Synchronization of North Pacific and Greenland Climates Preceded Abrupt Deglacial Warming". In: *Science* 345.444 (2014).

Pringle, H. "Neolithic Agriculture: Reading the Signs of Ancient Animal Domestication". In: *Science* 282.5393 (Nov. 20, 1998) 1448.

Prufer, Kay et al. "The Complete Genome Sequence of a Neanderthal from the Altai Mountains". In: *Nature* 505 (Jan. 2, 2014) 43–49. url: www.nature.com/nature/journal/v505/n7481/full/nature12886.html.

Qin, Siying et al. "A Magnetic Protein Biocompass". In: *Nature Materials* 15 (2016) 217–226. url: www.nature.com/nmat/journal/v15/n2/full/nmat4484.html.

Rafinesque, Constantine Samuel. *The American Nations, Vol. I.* Philadelphia: Rafinesque, 1836. url: www.gutenberg.org.

Ramm, Bernard. *Christian View of Science and Scripture.* Grand Rapids: William B. Eerdmans, 1954.

Richards, M. et al. "Neanderthal Diet at Vindija and Neanderthal Predation: The evidence from stable isotopes". In: *PNAS* 97.13 (2000) 7663–7666. url: www.pnas.org/content/97/13/7663.full.

Rieux, A. et al. "Improved Calibration of the Human Mitochondrial Clock Using Ancient Genomes". In: *Mol. Biol. Evol* 31.10 (Aug. 2014) 2780–2792.

Robertson, Brant E. et al. "Early Star-forming Galaxies and the Reionization of the Universe". In: *Nature* 468.7320 (Nov. 2010) 49–55.

Rodriguez, Angel. "Genesis and Creation in the Wisdom Literature". In: *The Genesis Creation Account and Its Reverberations in the Old Testament*. G. A. Klingbeil, ed. Andrews U. Press, 2015.

Rohl, David M. *Pharaohs and Kings: A Biblical Quest*. Three Rivers, 1997.

Ross, Hugh. *More Than a Theory: Revealing a Testable Model for Creation*. Grand Rapids, MI: Baker Books, 2009.

———. *The Creator and the Cosmos: How the Greatest Scientific Discoveries of the century Reveal God*. Grand Rapids: Baker Books, 1995.

Ruggles, Clive. "Astronomy Before History". In: *The Cambridge Concise History of Astronomy*. Michael Hoskin, ed. Cambridge U. Press, (1999) 6.

Sanz, Paulino Zamarro. *De Gibraltar a la Atlantida*. Alcorcon: Paulino Zamarro Sanz, 2012.

Sarmast, Robert. *Discovery of Atlantis: the Startling Case for the Island of Cyprus*. First Source, 2006.

Saussure, Ferdinand de. *Cours de linguistique generale*. 1916.

Seguin-Orlando, Andain et al. "Genomic Structure in Europeans Dating Back at Least 36,200 Years". In: *Science Express* (Nov. 6, 2014).

Sheldon, Robert B. "A Scientific Survey of the Imago Dei in Genesis 1–2 and Surprising Support for Trichotomy: Body, Soul and Spiritual being". In: *rbsp.info* (2008). url: rbsp.info/WTS/ST761-ii.pdf.

———. "Comets, Water, and Big Bang Nucleosynthesis". In: rbsp.info, 2017. url: rbsp.info/rbs/PDF/HUBE.pdf

——— ."The Cometary Biosphere and the Origin of Life". In: *Instruments, Methods, and Missions for Astrobiology XIV*. R. B. Hoover, G. V. Levin, and A. Y. Rozanov, eds Vol. 8152. Proc of SPIE, (Sept. 2011) 8152–42. url: rbsp.info/rbs/PDF/spie11.pdf.

———. "The Wet Comet Model: Rosetta Redux". In: *Instruments, Methods, and Missions for Astrobiology XVII*. R. B. Hoover et al., eds. Vol. 9606. Proc. of SPIE, (2015) 9606–2?

Sheldon, Robert B. and Richard B. Hoover. "Cosmological Evolution: Spatial Relativity and the Speed of Life". In: *Instruments, Methods, and Missions for Astrobiology XI*. R. B. Hoover, G. V. Levin, and A. Y. Rozanov, eds. Vol. 7097. Proc. of SPIE, (Aug. 2008) 7097–41. url: rbsp.info/rbs/PDF/spie08.pdf.

———. "Evidence for Liquid Water on Comets". In: *Instruments, Methods, and Missions for Astrobiology VII*. R. B. Hoover et al., eds. Vol. 5906. (Sept. 2005) 127–145.

———. "Implications of Cometary Water: Deep Impact, Stardust and Hayabusa". In: *Instruments, Methods, and Missions for Astrobiology IX*. R. B. Hoover, G. V. Levin, and A. Y. Rozanov, eds. Vol. 6309. Proc. of SPIE, (2006) 6309–0L.

———. "The Cometary Biosphere". In: *Instruments, Methods, and Missions for Astrobiology X*. R. B. Hoover, G. V. Levin, and A. Y. Rozanov, eds. Vol. 6694. Proc. of SPIE, (Oct. 2007) 6694–0H. url: rbsp.info/rbs/PDF/spie07.pdf.

Shepherd, Norman. *"Man in the Image of God, ThM Thesis"*. Philadelphia: Westminster Seminary, 1959. url: rbsp.info/WTS/Fall09/NS.pdf.

Shepherd, Schuyler. "Lioness Hunting". In: *Wikipedia Commons* (2006). url: commons.wikimedia.org/w/index.php?curid=520622.

Silk, Joseph. "Will We Ever Know What Dark Matter is?" In: *Nautilus* 045.1 (Feb. 2017).

Smithsonian. "Human Evolution Timeline Interactive". In: *Smithsonian Institution* (2016). url: humanorigins.si.edu/evidence/human- evolution-timeline-interactive.

Spetner, Lee. *Not By Chance: The Fall of Neo-Darwinian Theory*. Judaica, 1996.

Spradley, Joseph L. "Ten Lunar Legacies: Importance of the Moon for Life on Earth". In: *Perspectives on Science and Christian Faith* 62.4 (Dec. 2010) 267–275.

Stackert, Jeffrey, Barbara N. Porter, and David P. Wright, eds. *Heaven and Earth: Asexual Monad and Bisexual Dyad*. Bethesda, MD: CDL, 2010, 293– 326.

Stark, Rodney. *America's Blessings: How Religion Benefits Everyone, Including Atheists*. Templeton, 2013.

———. *The Rise of Christianity: A Sociologist Reconsiders History*. Princeton U. Press, 1996.

———. *The Victory of Reason*. Random, 2005.

Stower, Hannah. "Evolution: Explosive Human Genetic Variation". In: *Nature Reviews Genetics* 14.5 (Jan. 2013).

Strong, James. *The Exhaustive Concordance of the Bible*. Cincinnati: Jennings & Graham, 1890.

Targum, *The Targums of Onkelos and Jonathan ben Uzziel on the Pentateuch*. Translated by J. W. Etheridge. Longman &Co., 1865.

Tennyson, Alfred Lord. *In Memoriam A. H. H.* London: Edward Moxon, 1850.

Teomancimit. "Göbekli Tepe Şanlıurfa". In: *Wikipedia Commons* (2011). url: commons.wikimedia.org/w/index.php?curid=17377542.

Tesniere, Lucien. *Elements of Structural Syntax*. Paris: Klincksieck, 1959. url: en.wikipedia.org/wiki/Tesniere.

Theopedia. "JEDP Theory". In: *Theopedia* (2015). url: www.theopedia.com/JEDP_theory.

Thiagarajan, N. et al. "Abrupt Pre-Bølling–Allerød Warming and Circulation Changes in the Deep Ocean". In: *Nature* 511 (July 3, 2014) 75–78.

Tolkien, J. R. R. *The Lord of the Rings*. New York: Ballantine, 1954.

Tomkins, Jeffrey. "Human DNA Variation Linked to Biblical Event Timeline". In: *Institute for Creation Research* (July 23, 2012). url: www.icr.org/articles/view/6927/289/.

Trimble, Virginia. "Astronomical Investigations Concerning the so-called Airshafts of Cheops Pyramid". In: *Mitteilungen der Instituts fur Orientforschung. Vol. 10*. Akademie der Wissenschaften zu Berlin, (1964) 183–187.

Twain, Mark. *Following the Equator: A Journey around the World*. New York: Doubleday & McClure, 1897.

Urquhart, Fred. "Flight of the Butterflies in 3D". In: *Discovery Institute* (2014). url: www.flightofthebutterflies.com/discovery-story/.

Vassoler, F. M. et al. "Epigenetic Inheritance of a Cocaine-resistance Phenotype". In: *Nature Neuroscience* 16 (2013), 42–47.

Vine, W. E. *Vine's Concise Dictionary of Old and New Testament Words*. Thomas Nelson, 1939.

Wade, Nicholas. *A Troublesome Inheritance: Genes, Race and Human History.* Penguin, 2014.

Walton, John H. *The Lost World of Genesis One: Ancient Cosmology and the Origins Debate.* IVP Academic, 2009.

Wang, Alex. "Göbekli Tepe Site". In: *Wikipedia Commons* (2012). url: commons.wikimedia.org/w/index.php?curid=34568404.

Wang, Lan et al. "Modelling Galaxy Clustering in a High-resolution Simulation of Structure Formation". In: *Mon. Notices Royal Astr. Soc.* 371.2 (Sept. 2006) 537–547.

Ward, P. and D. Brownlee. *Rare Earth : Why Complex Life is Uncommon in the Universe.* 2000.

Waterston, E. et al. "Initial Sequence of the Chimpanzee Genome and Comparison with the Human Genome". In: *Nature* 437.69–87 (Sept. 1, 2005). url: www.nature.com/nature/journal/v437/n7055/full/nature04072.html.

Watson, C. *Seahenge: An Archaeological Conundrum.* Swindon: English Heritage, 2005.

Weeks, Noel K. "The ambiguity of Biblical background". In: *WTJ* 72 (2010) 219–236.

———. "The Bible and the "Universal" Ancient World: a Critique of John Walton". In: *WTJ.* 78 (2016) 1–28.

Weikart, Richard. *From Darwin to Hitler: Evolutionary Ethics, Eugenics and Racism in Germany.* Palgrave: Macmillen, 2006.

Weinberg, Steven. *The First Three Minutes: a Modern View of the Origin of the Universe.* NY: Bantam, 1977.

Weiss, E. et al. "The Broad Spectrum Revisited: Evidence from Plant Remains". In: *PNAS* 101.26 (2004) 9551–9555.

Wells, Herbert George. *The Outline of History: Being a Plain History of Life and Mankind.* New York: Macmillan, 1920.

Wells, Jonathan. *Icons of Evolution.* Regnery, 2002.

———. "Membrane Patterns Carry Ontogenetic Information That Is Specified Independently of DNA". In: *BIO-Complexity* 2014.2 (2014) 1–28. url: bio-complexity.org/ojs/index.php/main/article/view/BIO-C.2014.2/BIO-C.2014.2.

———. *The Myth of Junk DNA.* Seattle: Discovery Institute, 2011.

Westal, B. and B.-Z. Zhou. "Did Chickens Go North? New Evidence for Domestication". In: *World's Poultry Science J.* 45 (1989) 205–218.

Westerman, Terry. "Seismic Circles: An Introduction to Earth's Formation". In: *geoledgers.com* (2015). url: geoledgers.com/Europe/Gibraltar/Gibraltar.html.

Whitcomb, John and Henry M. Morris. *The Genesis Flood: The Biblical Record and Its Scientific Implications.* Baker, 1961.

Wikipedia. "August Weismann". In: *Wikipedia* (2015). url:en.wikipedia.org/wiki/August_Weismann.

———. "Dhoku earthquake". In: *Wikipedia* (2015). url:en.wikipedia.org/wiki/2011_Japan_tsunami.

———. "Lamarck". In: *Wikipedia* (2015). url:en.wikipedia.org/wiki/Lamarck.

———. "Lapse rate". In: *Wikipedia* (2015). url:en.wikipedia.org/wiki/Lapse_rate.

———. "Lysenko, Trofim". In: *Wikipedia* (2015). url:en.wikipedia.org/wiki/Trofim_Lysenko.

———. "Weismann barrier". In: *Wikipedia* (2015). url:en.wikipedia.org/wiki/Weismann_barrier.

Willis, George. "The Bite Fight: Tyson, Holyfield and the Night That Changed Boxing Forever". In: *ABCNews* (1997). url: abcnews.go.com/US/lance-armstrong-confesses-doping/.

Wittgenstein, Ludwig. *Blue and Brown Books.* Harper Torchbooks, 1965. url: www.geocities.jp/mickindex/wittgenstein/witt_blue_en.html.

Wittke, James H. et al. "Evidence for Deposition of 10 Million Tonnes of Impact Spherules across Four Continents 12,800 yrs Ago". In: *PNAS* (May 20, 2013), E2088–E2097. doi: 10.1073/pnas.1301760110.

Wolff, G. L. et al. "Maternal Epigenetics and Methyl Supplements Affect Agouti Gene Expression in Avy/a Mice". In: *FASEB Journal* 12.11 (Aug. 1998) 949–957.

Worsley, Peter. *The Trumpet Shall Sound: A Study of "Cargo Cults" in Melanesia*. New York: Schocken, 1957.

Wu, Yingzhe et al. "Origin and Provenance of Spherules and Magnetic Grains at the Younger Dryas Boundary". In: *PNAS* (Sept. 5, 2013), E3557–E3566. doi: 10.1073/pnas.1304059110.

Younker, Randall W. and Richard M. Davidson. "The Myth of The Solid Heavenly Dome: Another Look at The Hebrew". In: *Andrews U. Seminary Studies* 49.1 (2011). url: digitalcommons.andrews.edu/auss/vol49/iss1/7.

Author Index

Subject Index

Biblical Index

Genesis

Genesis *(continued)*

Exodus

Leviticus

Numbers

Deuteronomy

Joshua

2 Samuel

1 Kings

1 Corinthians

Galatians

Ephesians

Hebrews

1 John

Jude

Revelation